Introduction to R Programming

Maxwell Vector

Contents

2

11

Chapter 1

R Syntax and Structure

Fundamental Syntax

R presents a unique synthesis of a high-level programming language with a focus on statistical computation and data analysis. At its core, the language is built upon a formal syntax that governs the arrangement of symbols, keywords, and expressions. Every statement in R is composed of identifiable tokens and delimiters, including parentheses, curly brackets, and commas, which together orchestrate the logical grouping of operations. The language adheres to a grammatical framework in which every expression is evaluated with an intrinsic understanding of operator precedence and associativity, ensuring that arithmetic, logical, and relational operations yield consistent and mathematically sound results.

The syntax, characterized by its precision and structure, permits the construction of complex expressions from simpler components. This modular approach is reflected in the language's ability to treat functions as first-class objects, thereby allowing them to be composed and nested within larger constructs. Formal expressions, such as the assignment operator denoted by ←, are emblematic of the language's rigorous design, where each symbol carries a specific semantic meaning and its correct usage is paramount to the integrity of computations.

Language Conventions and Structural Elements

The conventions in R are meticulously designed to harmonize readability with computational efficiency. The language is case sensitive and places a strong emphasis on consistent naming conventions for variables and functions. This sensitivity mandates that an identifier, for example, `DataFrame` versus `dataframe`, represents wholly distinct entities, thus underscoring the importance of choosing descriptive and unambiguous labels.

Critical to the language are the structural elements that bind logical fragments into executable blocks. Parentheses, used for grouping, and curly braces, which enclose blocks of code, impose a syntactic discipline reminiscent of mathematical notation. Furthermore, R treats spaces and line breaks with deliberate significance. Although newline characters often serve as implicit statement terminators, semicolons can be employed to explicitly separate multiple instructions on a single line. Such rules render the language both flexible and rigorous, ensuring that the organization of code aligns with formal logical constructs.

Operators in R, including the arithmetic symbols $(+, -, *, /)$, the relational operators $(<, >, \leq, \geq)$, and logical operators $(\&, |, !)$, perform in a manner consistent with their mathematical counterparts. Their interoperation within expressions is governed by a fixed hierarchy that eliminates any ambiguity during evaluation. The structure of expressions is supported by precise rules for the use of delimiters and encapsulation, thereby allowing complex mathematical operations to be expressed in a natural and intuitive style.

Script Organization and Structural Constructs

An R script is more than a mere aggregation of statements; it is a carefully arranged document that reflects the logical progression of data transformations and computations. The script architecture is defined by a sequence of discrete elements, each serving a distinct purpose within the overall program. This includes sections dedicated to preliminary settings, variable declarations, and the application of procedural or functional constructs to extend the computational logic.

The declaration of variables assumes a critical role in establishing the computational context. By following stringent assignment conventions—often using the operator ←—the script delineates values that are subsequently used throughout the program. In addition, the structural framework of an R script accommodates the partitioning of code into logically cohesive segments. Such segmentation is achieved through the implicit arrangement of code blocks, demarcated by curly braces, which encapsulate conditional commands, iterative operations, or function definitions.

This disciplined organization offers a clear roadmap from data input to computational execution. Descriptive comments interspersed throughout the script, although not part of the executable code, contribute to a coherent narrative that explains the rationale behind each structural choice. The deliberate use of whitespace enhances the visual separation between sections and reinforces the clarity of the programming logic. R, in its arrangement and syntactical rigor, stands as a paradigm through which computational processes are rendered both explicit and methodical, facilitating the rigorous manipulation of complex data and ensuring that every element operates within a well-defined structure.

R Code Snippet

```r
# This script demonstrates the core concepts of R syntax, structure,
↪   and operator usage.
# It includes examples of variable assignment, operator precedence,
↪   function definition,
# control flow with conditional statements, vectorized operations,
↪   and the use of anonymous functions.

# Example 1: Quadratic Equation Solver using the Quadratic Formula
# The quadratic equation: ax^2 + bx + c = 0, has roots given by:
#     x = (-b ± sqrt(b^2 - 4ac)) / (2a)
quadratic_roots <- function(a, b, c) {
  # Compute the discriminant (b^2 - 4ac)
  discriminant <- b^2 - 4 * a * c    # b^2 - 4ac

  # Check if discriminant is negative: no real roots exist
  if (discriminant < 0) {
    message("No real roots exist for the given coefficients.")
    return(NULL)
  } else {
    # Compute the two roots using proper grouping and operator
    ↪   precedence
    root1 <- (-b + sqrt(discriminant)) / (2 * a)
```

```r
    root2 <- (-b - sqrt(discriminant)) / (2 * a)
    return(c(root1, root2))
  }
}


# Test the quadratic equation solver with coefficients for: x^2 - 5x
↪   + 6 = 0
a <- 1
b <- -5
c <- 6
roots <- quadratic_roots(a, b, c)
print(roots)  # Expected output: 2 and 3

# Example 2: Demonstrating Operator Precedence and Parenthetical
↪   Grouping
# Operator precedence: multiplication (*) is performed before
↪   addition (+).
# Without parentheses:
value1 <- a + b * c        # Evaluated as a + (b * c)
print(value1)
# With parentheses to override default behavior:
value2 <- (a + b) * c      # Evaluated as (a + b) multiplied by c
print(value2)

# Example 3: Vectorized Computation and Vector Recycling
# Creating vectors and utilizing natural recycling of elements in
↪   operations.
vector1 <- c(1, 2, 3, 4, 5)
vector2 <- c(10, 20)
# The shorter vector (vector2) is recycled to match the length of
↪   vector1.
result_vector <- vector1 + vector2
print(result_vector)

# Example 4: Function as a First-Class Object and Use of Anonymous
↪   Functions
# Define a function to compute the difference of squares of two
↪   numbers.
squared_difference <- function(x, y) {
  # Create an anonymous function to calculate the square of a
  ↪   number.
  square <- function(z) z * z
  # Compute and return the difference of squares.
  return(square(x) - square(y))
}

# Test the squared_difference function:
diff_result <- squared_difference(5, 3)
print(diff_result)

# Example 5: Script Organization with Clear Code Blocks
# Grouping code in a structured manner using curly braces for
↪   logical segments.
```

```
{
    # Declare variables using R's assignment operator.
    DataFrame <- data.frame(ID = 1:3, Value = c(10, 20, 30))
    # Note: 'DataFrame' is different from 'dataframe' due to case
    ↪ sensitivity.

    # Modify the data frame by creating a new column using vectorized
    ↪ operations.
    DataFrame$DoubleValue <- DataFrame$Value * 2
    print(DataFrame)
}

# End of R code snippet demonstrating important equations, formulas,
↪ and algorithms.
```

Chapter 2

Comments and Code Organization

The Function and Significance of Comments

Comments constitute an intrinsic component of scholarly code, serving as an embedded narrative that elucidates the rationale behind algorithmic formulations and the subtleties of implementation decisions. In a computational environment where precision and rigor are paramount, comments provide an avenue for embedding meta-information; they delineate the logical phases of data transformation and signal critical decision points that may not be immediately evident from the operational code alone. This auxiliary layer of documentation facilitates the comprehension of complex constructs by detailing assumptions, specifying invariants, and clarifying the expected outcomes of nontrivial operations. The annotations are not mere ornamental text but are integral to understanding the underlying methodology and preserving the intellectual context of the computational procedures.

Principles Underlying Effective Commenting

The efficacy of comments is measured by a set of criteria that includes clarity, conciseness, and technical precision. Comments that succinctly capture the intent behind a code segment contribute to a more disciplined and coherent representation of the computational logic. The language employed in the annotations is expected to be formal and unambiguous, avoiding colloquialisms in favor of precise terminology consistent with scientific discourse. Consistency in style is imperative, ensuring that every comment adheres to a standardized format capable of conveying methodological intricacies. Variables, operators such as ←, and function parameters are referenced explicitly to maintain a direct connection between the code and its accompanying explanation. Such systematic annotation supports both the maintenance of legacy code and the rigorous validation of algorithmic soundness.

Organizational Strategies for Code Clarity and Maintainability

A meticulously organized codebase exemplifies the confluence of structural coherence and logical segmentation, thereby enhancing the longevity and adaptability of software systems. Code organization is achieved through the methodical partitioning of the program into logically cohesive blocks that reflect distinct phases of the computational process. This hierarchical arrangement is often manifested in the grouping of function definitions, variable declarations, and logical control constructs within dedicated segments demarcated by clearly defined delimiters such as curly braces. The delineation of such segments affords the code a modular character, where discrete functional units are encapsulated, thereby facilitating isolated testing and iterative refinement.

Within a robust organizational framework, comments play a pivotal role by annotating each section with precise descriptions of its purpose and interdependencies. This practice not only preserves the conceptual integrity of the code but also serves as a navigational aid during future modifications and enhancements. An effectively structured codebase emphasizes the interrelation between the computational algorithm and its theoretical foundations; thus, the spatial arrangement of comments relative to the code mirrors the logical progression of thought. The resulting synergy between self-explanatory code blocks and their descriptive annotations lays the groundwork for a software design that is both resilient in the face of evolving requirements and reflective of the highest standards of scholarly computational practice.

R Code Snippet

```
# ================================================================
# This R script demonstrates several key concepts discussed in the
↪    chapter:
#    1. The use of detailed, formal comments to explain algorithmic
↪    choices,
#       variable assignments, and logical control flow.
#    2. A comprehensive implementation of a simple linear regression
↪    model.
#    3. The use of vectorized computations and iterative algorithms.
#
# The linear regression model uses the fundamental formulas:
#    beta1 = sum((x - mean(x)) * (y - mean(y))) / sum((x -
↪    mean(x))^2)
#    beta0 = mean(y) - beta1 * mean(x)
#
# Additionally, an iterative transformation function is provided to
↪    illustrate
# code organization and modular design through a loop construct.
# ================================================================

# Function: simpleLinearRegression
# Purpose: Compute the slope (beta1) and intercept (beta0) of a
↪    simple linear
#          regression model using the least squares method.
# Inputs:
#    x - Numeric vector representing the independent variable.
#    y - Numeric vector representing the dependent variable.
# Output:
#    A named list with components 'intercept' (beta0) and 'slope'
↪    (beta1)
simpleLinearRegression <- function(x, y) {
  # Validate that both inputs are numeric vectors.
  if (!is.numeric(x) || !is.numeric(y)) {
    stop("Error: Both x and y must be numeric vectors.")
  }

  # Ensure the two vectors have identical lengths.
  if (length(x) != length(y)) {
    stop("Error: The vectors x and y must have the same length.")
  }

  # Calculate means of the vectors.
  mean_x <- mean(x)
  mean_y <- mean(y)

  # Compute the numerator and denominator for the slope calculation.
  numerator <- sum((x - mean_x) * (y - mean_y))
  denominator <- sum((x - mean_x)^2)

  # Prevent division by zero.
```

21

```r
  if (denominator == 0) {
    stop("Error: Variance of x is zero; slope cannot be computed.")
  }

  # Calculate the slope (beta1) and intercept (beta0).
  beta1 <- numerator / denominator
  beta0 <- mean_y - beta1 * mean_x

  # Return a named list of estimated coefficients.
  return(list(intercept = beta0, slope = beta1))
}

# Function: predictLinear
# Purpose: Generate predicted values using the linear model:
#          y_pred = beta0 + beta1 * x_new.
# Inputs:
#   beta  - A list containing the regression coefficients
↪   'intercept' and 'slope'.
#   new_x - Numeric vector of new predictor values.
# Output:
#   A numeric vector of predicted responses.
predictLinear <- function(beta, new_x) {
  # Vectorized prediction calculation.
  y_pred <- beta$intercept + beta$slope * new_x
  return(y_pred)
}


# ------------------------------------------------------------
# Demonstration Section: Simple Linear Regression and Prediction
# ------------------------------------------------------------
# Set a seed for reproducibility of random numbers.
set.seed(123)

# Generate sample data:
#   x: Sequence from 1 to 50.
#   y: Linear relationship with some added noise (y = 2.5 + 0.8*x +
↪   noise).
x <- 1:50
y <- 2.5 + 0.8 * x + rnorm(50, mean = 0, sd = 3)

# Compute regression coefficients using the simpleLinearRegression
↪   function.
regression_result <- simpleLinearRegression(x, y)

# Display the computed coefficients.
cat("Estimated Intercept (beta0):", regression_result$intercept,
↪   "\n")
cat("Estimated Slope (beta1):", regression_result$slope, "\n")

# Generate new predictor values for prediction.
new_x <- seq(min(x), max(x), length.out = 20)

# Compute predicted responses using predictLinear.
```

```r
predicted_y <- predictLinear(regression_result, new_x)

# Display predictions in a formatted table.
cat("\nPredicted values for new x:\n")
print(data.frame(new_x = new_x, predicted_y = predicted_y))

# ----------------------------------------------------------------
# Bonus Section: Iterative Transformation Example using a For Loop
# ----------------------------------------------------------------
# Function: iterativeTransformation
# Purpose: Apply an iterative transformation to a numeric vector.
#          In each iteration, each element is multiplied by a
↪   constant factor
#          and then incremented by a fixed additive constant.
# Inputs:
#   data        - Numeric vector to be transformed.
#   iterations  - Number of iterations to apply the transformation
↪   (default = 5).
# Output:
#   A numeric vector representing the transformed data after the
↪   specified iterations.
iterativeTransformation <- function(data, iterations = 5) {
  # Set transformation constants.
  transformation_factor <- 1.1
  additive_constant <- 0.5

  # Initialize the transformed data.
  transformed_data <- data

  # Iterate the transformation process.
  for (i in 1:iterations) {
    # Apply the transformation in a vectorized manner.
    transformed_data <- transformed_data * transformation_factor +
    ↪   additive_constant
    # Debug message (can be uncommented for step-by-step tracing).
    # cat("Iteration", i, ": ", transformed_data, "\n")
  }

  return(transformed_data)
}

# Demonstrate the iterative transformation function.
initial_data <- c(1, 2, 3, 4, 5)
final_data <- iterativeTransformation(initial_data, iterations = 3)

# Print the final transformed data.
cat("\nFinal transformed data after iterations:\n")
print(final_data)

# ================================================================
# End of R script demonstrating organized code, explicit commenting,
↪   and
```

```
# implementation of important equations and algorithms in a
↪  succinct, modular
# format.
# ================================================================
```

Chapter 3

Basic Data Types

Numeric Data Types

Numeric data types constitute a foundational cornerstone within the R programming paradigm, offering a robust framework for representing quantitative values. These data types are primarily instantiated in a double-precision floating-point representation, thereby enabling the encapsulation of both integer and non-integer values with considerable precision. The inherent architecture of numeric types facilitates a comprehensive spectrum of arithmetic operations, numerical approximations, and statistical computations, where each numeric entity is endowed with properties such as magnitude and sign. Furthermore, the syntactic differentiation between explicitly declared integers and their floating-point counterparts, although subtle, underscores a rigorous adherence to the principles of computational accuracy and internal consistency within the language.

Character Data Types

Character data types are dedicated to the manipulation and storage of textual information. Each character element is conceptualized as a sequence of symbols derived from standardized encoding schemes, for example, ASCII or Unicode. The formal structure of character data ensures that textual content is preserved in an immutable fashion, permitting operations such as concatenation, slicing, and pattern matching to be carried out in a methodologically sound manner. These data types are carefully designed to maintain the semantic integrity of text, supporting a plethora of transformation functions that manipulate string sequences while adhering to strict syntactic and cultural encoding rules.

Logical Data Types

Logical data types are integral to the representation of binary states within the R language. Restricted to the canonical values $TRUE$ and $FALSE$, logical entities are fundamental to the evaluation of Boolean expressions and the implementation of control flow constructs. The operational semantics attached to logical types are firmly grounded in the axioms of Boolean algebra, ensuring that logical operations such as conjunction, disjunction, and negation yield results that are both predictable and mathematically consistent. This binary framework provides a mechanism for demarcating conditional pathways, thereby underpinning the logical rigor that is essential for the execution of algorithmically complex procedures.

Other Fundamental Data Types

In addition to the primary classes of numeric, character, and logical data types, the R language incorporates several additional data representations that address specialized computational needs. Among these, complex numbers extend the numeric domain by incorporating an imaginary component, conventionally expressed in the form $a + bi$, where a and b are numeric values and i signifies the imaginary unit. This augmentation permits the modeling of phenomena within the complex plane, thereby broadening the analytical capabilities of the language. Moreover, a dedicated data type exists for raw binary data, enabling the manipulation of byte-level information with precision. The diversity embodied by these supplementary data types underscores a design philosophy centered on versatility and meticulous data representation, providing a comprehensive toolkit for nuanced data processing within a stringent theoretical framework.

R Code Snippet

```r
# Basic Data Types Demonstration in R

# --- Numeric Data Types ---
# Define numeric variables (stored as double-precision by default)
num1 <- 10        # A numeric value (integer-like, but stored as
↪  double)
num2 <- 3.14      # A non-integer numeric value

# Define an explicit integer using the L suffix
int1 <- 5L

# Perform arithmetic operations
add_result <- num1 + num2      # Addition
sub_result <- num1 - num2      # Subtraction
mul_result <- num1 * num2      # Multiplication
div_result <- num1 / num2      # Division

# Exponentiation and modulo operations
exp_result <- num1^2           # Exponentiation: square of num1
mod_result <- num1 %% 3        # Modulo operation

# Print numeric operation results
print(paste("Addition (num1 + num2):", add_result))
print(paste("Subtraction (num1 - num2):", sub_result))
print(paste("Multiplication (num1 * num2):", mul_result))
print(paste("Division (num1 / num2):", div_result))
print(paste("Exponentiation (num1^2):", exp_result))
print(paste("Modulo (num1 %% 3):", mod_result))


# --- Character Data Types ---
# Define character strings
char1 <- "Hello"
char2 <- "World"

# Concatenate strings with a space using paste() and without a space
↪  using paste0()
concatenated <- paste(char1, char2)
concatenated_nospace <- paste0(char1, char2)

# Extract a substring from a longer text
substr_example <- substring("Introduction to R Programming", 1, 12)

# Pattern matching: find strings containing "R" in a vector
pattern_vector <- c(char1, char2, "R is awesome")
pattern_result <- grep("R", pattern_vector, value = TRUE)

# Print character operations results
print(paste("Concatenated with space:", concatenated))
print(paste("Concatenated without space:", concatenated_nospace))
```

```r
print(paste("Substring extraction (first 12 chars):",
↪ substr_example))
print("Pattern matching results (contains 'R'):")
print(pattern_result)


# --- Logical Data Types ---
# Define logical values
bool1 <- TRUE
bool2 <- FALSE

# Logical operations: AND, OR, NOT
and_result <- bool1 && bool2
or_result <- bool1 || bool2
not_result <- !bool1

# Evaluate a numeric condition returning a logical value
numeric_condition <- (num1 > 5)   # Will be TRUE since 10 > 5

# Print logical operation results
print(paste("Logical AND (TRUE && FALSE):", and_result))
print(paste("Logical OR (TRUE || FALSE):", or_result))
print(paste("Logical NOT (!TRUE):", not_result))
print(paste("Numeric condition (num1 > 5):", numeric_condition))


# --- Other Fundamental Data Types ---
# Complex Numbers: Create and extract components
complex_num <- 2 + 3i
real_part <- Re(complex_num)       # Real part extraction
imag_part <- Im(complex_num)       # Imaginary part extraction
abs_value <- Mod(complex_num)      # Magnitude of the complex number
arg_value <- Arg(complex_num)      # Phase (angle in radians)

print(paste("Complex Number (2 + 3i):", complex_num))
print(paste("Real Part:", real_part))
print(paste("Imaginary Part:", imag_part))
print(paste("Magnitude:", abs_value))
print(paste("Phase (radians):", arg_value))

# Raw Binary Data: Convert a character string to its raw byte
↪ representation
raw_data <- charToRaw("Hello, Raw Data!")
print("Raw binary representation:")
print(raw_data)


# --- Data Type Coercion and Conversion ---
# Convert numeric to character
num_to_char <- as.character(num1)
# Convert a character string to numeric
char_to_num <- as.numeric("123.45")
```

```r
# Convert logical TRUE to numeric (TRUE becomes 1 and FALSE becomes
↪   0)
logical_to_num <- as.numeric(bool1)

# Print conversion results
print(paste("Numeric to Character:", num_to_char))
print(paste("Character to Numeric:", char_to_num))
print(paste("Logical (TRUE) to Numeric:", logical_to_num))


# --- Demonstrating Data Structures with Mixed Data Types ---
# Create a list combining various data types
data_list <- list(
  numeric_value   = num1,
  integer_value   = int1,
  character_value = char1,
  logical_value   = bool1,
  complex_value   = complex_num,
  raw_value       = raw_data
)
print("Data List containing various data types:")
print(data_list)


# --- Inspecting Data Types ---
# Use class() and typeof() to check data types of variables
print("Inspecting Data Types:")
print(paste("num1 - Class:", class(num1), "Type:", typeof(num1)))
print(paste("int1 - Class:", class(int1), "Type:", typeof(int1)))
print(paste("char1 - Class:", class(char1), "Type:", typeof(char1)))
print(paste("bool1 - Class:", class(bool1), "Type:", typeof(bool1)))
print(paste("complex_num - Class:", class(complex_num), "Type:",
↪   typeof(complex_num)))
print(paste("raw_data - Class:", class(raw_data), "Type:",
↪   typeof(raw_data)))


# --- Algorithm: Data Type Check Function ---
# Define a function to report the class and type of a variable
check_data_type <- function(var) {
  var_class <- class(var)
  var_type <- typeof(var)
  return(paste("Class:", var_class, "| Type:", var_type))
}

# Apply the function to each element in data_list and print the
↪   result
for(name in names(data_list)) {
  cat("Variable", name, "->", check_data_type(data_list[[name]]),
↪   "\n")
}
```

```r
# End of Comprehensive R Code Snippet Demonstrating Basic Data
↪   Types.
```

Chapter 4

Variables and Assignment

Conceptual Foundations of Variables

Within the R programming paradigm, a variable is understood as a symbolic identifier that is bound to an object residing in an environment. This binding does not denote a container in the conventional imperative sense but rather constitutes a reference in an associative mapping between a symbol and the corresponding data object. In R, the absence of explicit type declarations allows variables to dynamically represent objects of various classes throughout the execution of a session. The association between a variable, such as x, and its corresponding value is maintained by the environment, which serves as a structured repository for all bindings. This semantic framework permits the redefinition or mutation of a binding such that the symbol x may later reference an object of a completely different data type without prior declaration.

Assignment Semantics

The act of assignment in R is executed via specialized operators that not only compute an expression's value but also establish a binding between that computed value and a designated symbol. The predominant operator, denoted by $<-$, evaluates an expression and binds its result to the symbol positioned on its left. An analogous mechanism is provided by the rightward operator $->$, which imposes the binding in the reverse syntactic order. While an alternative operator, =, may also perform assignment in certain contexts, the $< -$ operator retains a distinguished role in conventional R syntax due to its clarity and historical precedence. The assignment operation, expressed conceptually as

$$\text{symbol} \overset{<-}{=} \text{value},$$

embodies the process by which the current environment is updated with a new or modified binding. It is through this mechanism that an evaluated expression becomes accessible via its associated symbol throughout the hierarchical chain of environments.

Assignment Operators and Their Structural Details

The operator $< -$ encapsulates a critical computational operation: it instantiates or updates a binding such that the left-hand symbol references the object produced by the evaluation of the right-hand expression. This process is emblematic of a lazy evaluation strategy in which expressions are evaluated only when necessary and their resulting objects are allocated in memory. The duality of assignment, as seen with both $< -$ and $- >$, offers syntactic flexibility while preserving the underlying semantic equivalence. The utilization of these operators reflects a departure from more rigid assignment schemes found in statically typed languages; in R, the absence of an explicit declaration phase allows for the on-demand creation of variables. Moreover, the operator =, when employed, is syntactically similar to $< -$ within interactive sessions, though its usage is typically reserved for specifying argument names in function calls. This multiplicity of assignment operators underscores the language's emphasis on expressive precision in the establishment of variable bindings.

Variable Naming Conventions and Environmental Context

Identifiers in R obey a set of lexical rules that govern their formation and subsequent use in assignment. An identifier must begin with a letter or a period followed immediately by a letter, with subsequent characters allowed to be letters, digits, or underscores. Such constraints ensure that the symbolic references used in assignment are unambiguous and consistent within the environment. Each binding, once created by an assignment operator, exists within a specific environment which determines the scope and lifetime of the variable. The hierarchical structure of environments—in which a local environment may inherit bindings from a parent—plays a crucial role in variable resolution during the evaluation process. By delineating the scope and accessibility of variables, this mechanism enables a nuanced control over the persistence and visibility of assigned objects. The binding process is intrinsically linked to the environment in which it occurs, rendering the assignment operation both a syntactic and a semantic construct that is indispensable to the structuring of programs in R.

R Code Snippet

```
#--------------------------------------------------------------
# Demonstration of Variables and Assignment in R
#--------------------------------------------------------------

# 1. Basic Assignment using the <- operator
x <- 10   # Assign an integer to x
print(paste("x is initially:", x))

# 2. Reassigning x to a different data type (dynamic typing)
x <- "Hello, R!"   # Reassign x to a character string
print(paste("x has been reassigned to:", x))

# 3. Assignment using the -> operator (rightward assignment)
20 -> y   # Assign 20 to y using the rightward operator
print(paste("y is assigned as:", y))

# 4. Using = for assignment (commonly in function calls)
z = 3.14   # Assign 3.14 to z using the '=' operator
print(paste("z equals:", z))

# 5. Simple Arithmetic and Binding the Result
a <- 5
b <- 6
result <- a + b   # The sum is computed and bound to 'result'
print(paste("The sum of", a, "and", b, "is:", result))

# 6. Function Demonstrating Lazy Evaluation and Iterative Assignment
computeSum <- function(n) {
  sum_total <- 0   # Initialize sum
  for(i in 1:n){
```

```r
    # Each iteration updates the binding of sum_total with a new
    ↪  value
    sum_total <- sum_total + i
  }
  # The final computed value is returned
  return(sum_total)
}
print(paste("Sum of numbers 1 to 10 is:", computeSum(10)))

# 7. Dynamic Reassignment in a Continuous Workflow
variable <- 100
print(paste("Initial variable value:", variable))
variable <- variable / 2  # Reassign variable after computation
print(paste("Variable after division by 2:", variable))

# 8. Environment and Scope Demonstration: Global vs Local Bindings
global_var <- "I am global"
localScopeFunc <- function() {
  local_var <- "I am local"
  # Accessing global_var from within the function
  print(paste("Inside function, global_var:", global_var))
  print(paste("Inside function, local_var:", local_var))
}
localScopeFunc()

# 9. Variable Naming Conventions: Valid Identifiers
.validName1 <- "Starts with a dot followed by a letter"
valid_name_2 <- "Uses lowercase letters with an underscore"
ValidName3 <- "Begins with a capital letter"
print(.validName1)
print(valid_name_2)
print(ValidName3)

# 10. Dynamic Assignment using the assign() function
assign("dynamicVar", 42)
print(paste("dynamicVar (assigned dynamically) equals:",
  ↪  dynamicVar))

# 11. Inspecting the Current Environment: Listing All Bindings
print("List of all variables in the current environment:")
print(ls())
```

Chapter 5

Basic Operators

Arithmetic Operators

Arithmetic operators constitute the foundation for numerical computation within data manipulation frameworks. Standard operators such as $+$, $-$, $\times$, and $\div$ are defined in a manner consistent with elementary arithmetic principles, yet they extend naturally to complex data structures by operating element-wise on vectors and matrices. The operator for exponentiation, typically denoted by $\wedge$, is integral to computations that require the application of non-linear transformations. The implementation of these operators is governed by a hierarchy of precedence and associativity rules which ensure that composite expressions are evaluated in strict conformance with established mathematical conventions. In this context, the abstraction of arithmetic computation allows for dynamic interactions between scalar values and structured arrays, thereby facilitating a highly expressive mode of data manipulation.

Logical Operators

Logical operators underpin the formulation of Boolean expressions and are indispensable in the evaluation of conditions and decision processes. The negation operator, denoted by !, inverts the truth value of a given expression, producing a logical complement. In combination with operators that represent conjunction and disjunction, commonly expressed as and || for scalar comparisons or as and | for element-wise evaluations, these operators enable the systematic aggregation of multiple logical conditions. The formal semantics of logical operations are founded upon Boolean algebra, ensuring that the composition and evaluation of logical statements yield consistent and unambiguous results. Such operators are central to the construction of filter conditions that segment datasets based on specified criteria, thus enhancing the precision of data manipulation tasks.

Relational Operators

Relational operators facilitate the comparison of data elements by establishing binary predicates that yield Boolean outcomes. Operators of this category include the equality operator, $==$; the inequality operator, $!=$; and the order-based operators $<$, $>$, $<=$, and $>=$. Each operator is designed to assess two operands and to produce a truth value that reflects the validity of the imposed relational condition. The usage of relational operators is critical in environments where data validation, sorting, and conditional selection are performed. In data-centric applications, these operators enable the systematic partitioning of datasets by converting quantitative and qualitative relationships into logical indicators. The operational semantics of relational operations ensure that comparisons are executed in a manner that respects the inherent type characteristics of the operands, thereby preserving the integrity and consistency of subsequent data processing routines.

R Code Snippet

```
# Basic Operators in R: Arithmetic, Logical, and Relational Examples

# --------------------
# Arithmetic Operators
# --------------------
# Scalar operations
a <- 5
b <- 8
sum_ab    <- a + b        # Addition
diff_ab   <- a - b        # Subtraction
prod_ab   <- a * b        # Multiplication
quot_ab   <- a / b        # Division
exp_ab    <- a ^ 2        # Exponentiation (5 squared)

# Vectorized arithmetic operations
```

```r
v1 <- c(1, 2, 3, 4)
v2 <- c(10, 20, 30, 40)
sum_vect  <- v1 + v2        # Element-wise addition
prod_vect <- v1 * v2        # Element-wise multiplication

# Demonstrating operator precedence: multiplication has higher
↪  priority than addition
result1 <- a + b * 2        # Evaluated as: a + (b * 2)
result2 <- (a + b) * 2      # Parentheses override default precedence

# --------------------
# Logical Operators
# --------------------
# Create a logical vector for demonstration
logical_vec <- c(TRUE, FALSE, TRUE, FALSE)
logical_neg <- !logical_vec        # Negation: Inverts each Boolean
↪  value

# Element-wise logical operations using & and |
logical_and <- logical_vec & c(FALSE, TRUE, TRUE, FALSE)
logical_or  <- logical_vec | c(FALSE, FALSE, TRUE, TRUE)

# Using scalar logical operators for short-circuit evaluation:
# (Note: && and || evaluate only the first element of each vector)
scalar_and <- TRUE && FALSE
scalar_or  <- TRUE || FALSE

# -----------------------
# Relational Operators
# -----------------------
# Relational comparisons with scalars
is_equal      <- a == 5     # Equality check
is_not_equal  <- b != 5     # Inequality check
is_greater    <- a > b      # Greater than
is_less_equal <- a <= b     # Less than or equal

# Relational operations on vectors (element-wise)
comp_vect <- v1 < v2        # Compare each element of v1 with
↪  corresponding element in v2

# Data filtering example using relational operator
data <- c(5, 10, 15, 20, 25, 30)
filtered_data <- data[data > 15]  # Keep elements greater than 15

# -----------------------
# Conditional Vectorization
# -----------------------
# Using ifelse() to label numeric values as Negative, Zero, or
↪  Positive
x <- -5:5
conditional_result <- ifelse(x < 0, "Negative",
                      ifelse(x == 0, "Zero", "Positive"))
```

```r
# ----------------------------
# Algorithm: Compound Interest
# ----------------------------
# Calculate the future value with compound interest:
# Formula: Future Value = Principal * (1 + Rate)^Years
principal <- 1000
rate <- 0.05        # Annual interest rate (5%)
years <- 10
compound_interest <- principal * (1 + rate)^years


# ----------------------------
# Displaying Results
# ----------------------------
print("Arithmetic Operations:")
print(paste("Sum of", a, "and", b, "=", sum_ab))
print(paste("Difference (a - b) =", diff_ab))
print(paste("Product (a * b) =", prod_ab))
print(paste("Quotient (a / b) =", quot_ab))
print(paste("Exponentiation (a^2) =", exp_ab))
print("Vectorized Addition (v1 + v2):")
print(sum_vect)
print("Operator Precedence:")
print(paste("Without parentheses (a + b * 2) =", result1))
print(paste("With parentheses ((a + b) * 2) =", result2))

print("Logical Operations:")
print("Original Logical Vector:")
print(logical_vec)
print("Negated Vector (!logical_vec):")
print(logical_neg)
print("Element-wise Logical AND:")
print(logical_and)
print("Element-wise Logical OR:")
print(logical_or)
print(paste("Scalar AND (TRUE && FALSE):", scalar_and))
print(paste("Scalar OR (TRUE || FALSE):", scalar_or))

print("Relational Operations:")
print(paste("a equals 5:", is_equal))
print(paste("b not equal to 5:", is_not_equal))
print(paste("a greater than b:", is_greater))
print(paste("a less than or equal to b:", is_less_equal))
print("Element-wise Comparison (v1 < v2):")
print(comp_vect)

print("Data Filtering (Elements > 15):")
print(filtered_data)

print("Conditional Assignment using ifelse():")
print(conditional_result)

print("Compound Interest Calculation:")
```

```
print(paste("Final amount after", years, "years:",
↪    compound_interest))
```

Chapter 6

Vectors in R

Definition and Fundamental Properties

A vector in R is defined as a one-dimensional homogeneous array that stores elements of a single data type. The uniformity of data types within a vector guarantees that operations performed across its elements occur without the need for type reconciliation at the time of execution. The inherent linearity and consecutiveness of memory storage for vectors enable a straightforward correspondence between the mathematical notion of a sequence and its computational representation. Such vectors are fundamental to the language's data structures and serve as the building block for more complex entities.

Creation and Initialization of Vectors

The construction of a vector in R is achieved through mechanisms that assemble individual elements into a contiguous container. Whether generated explicitly through listing a series of elements or derived from functions that yield regular sequences, the process of initialization establishes a vector whose length and mode are determined by the supplied elements. The homogeneity condition imposes that all elements must be interpreted under a common type coercion rule, ensuring consistency throughout the data structure. The established vector thus encodes both the numeric values and metadata that govern subsequent manipulations.

Operations and Manipulation Techniques

The manipulation of vectors relies on an array of operations that are executed in a vectorized fashion. Arithmetic operators such as $+$, $-$, $\times$, and $\div$ act upon each element of a vector independently, without the need for explicit iteration constructs. This element-wise application extends to logical and relational operators, maintaining a strict uniformity of computational behavior across all indices of the vector. Indexing and subsetting operations leverage the positional arrangement inherent in vectors to extract, update, or reassign segments of data. The rigorous rules of recycling are applied in scenarios where operations involve vectors of mismatched lengths, thereby enforcing a predictable and systematic approach to data transformation.

Mathematical Operations and Data Transformation

Mathematical operations performed on vectors are characterized by their adherence to properties such as commutativity and associativity, as observed in scalar arithmetic. The abstraction of these operations facilitates not only simple computational tasks but also more involved data transformations. Operations on one-dimensional arrays are structured to perform calculations sequentially across elements, ensuring that the vector as a single entity is an accurate representation of its constituent data. In addition, conditional operations and selective transformations based on logical predicates enable refined control over the modification of vector elements, supporting complex data manipulation strategies through succinct, element-wise evaluations.

Internal Representation and Memory Considerations

The internal architectural design of vectors in R plays a pivotal role in their operational efficiency. Vectors are implemented as contiguous blocks of memory, which permits rapid access through direct addressing techniques. This contiguous storage pattern not only accelerates arithmetic and logical operations but also facilitates effective memory management. The uniformity of data types within a vector allows the underlying system to apply low-level optimizations that are not feasible in heterogeneous collections. Moreover, the allocation of memory for vectors is directly influenced by the dynamic nature of data processing tasks, where the strategies for resizing and modifying vectors are critical to achieving high-performance computation.

R Code Snippet

```r
# Creation of vectors using explicit listing and sequence generation
vec_explicit  <- c(10, 20, 30, 40, 50)
vec_sequence  <- seq(from = 1, to = 10, by = 2)
vec_repeated  <- rep(5, times = 5)
print("Explicit Vector:")
print(vec_explicit)
print("Sequence Vector:")
print(vec_sequence)
print("Repeated Vector:")
print(vec_repeated)


# Arithmetic and vectorized operations: performing element-wise
↪   calculations
a <- c(1, 2, 3, 4)
b <- c(10, 20, 30, 40)
sum_vec  <- a + b        # Element-wise addition
diff_vec <- b - a        # Element-wise subtraction
prod_vec <- a * b        # Element-wise multiplication
div_vec  <- b / a        # Element-wise division
print("Sum of a and b:")
print(sum_vec)
print("Difference of b and a:")
print(diff_vec)
print("Product of a and b:")
print(prod_vec)
print("Division of b by a:")
print(div_vec)


# Demonstration of vector recycling rules:
# When vectors are of unequal lengths, the shorter one is recycled.
v1 <- c(1, 2, 3, 4, 5)
v2 <- c(10, 20)
sum_recycle <- v1 + v2    # v2 is recycled: (10, 20, 10, 20, 10)
print("Recycling Rule Example (v1 + v2):")
print(sum_recycle)


# Logical and relational operations on vectors:
logical_vec <- a < 3      # Checks each element of 'a'
print("Logical condition (a < 3):")
```

```r
print(logical_vec)

# Conditional operations using vectorized ifelse:
# If the element in 'a' is greater than 2, multiply it by 10;
↪   otherwise, add 5.
result_ifelse <- ifelse(a > 2, a * 10, a + 5)
print("Result of ifelse operation on vector a:")
print(result_ifelse)

# Indexing and subsetting vectors:
# Extract elements from vec_explicit that are greater than 20.
subset_vec <- vec_explicit[vec_explicit > 20]
print("Subset of vec_explicit with elements > 20:")
print(subset_vec)

# Mathematical properties: Commutativity and Associativity in vector
↪   operations.
v1 <- c(1, 2, 3)
v2 <- c(4, 5, 6)
v3 <- c(7, 8, 9)
commutative    <- all(v1 + v2 == v2 + v1)              # Should
↪   return TRUE
associative    <- all((v1 + v2) + v3 == v1 + (v2 + v3))  # Should
↪   return TRUE
print("Commutative Check (v1 + v2 == v2 + v1):")
print(commutative)
print("Associative Check ((v1 + v2) + v3 == v1 + (v2 + v3)):")
print(associative)

# Custom function to calculate the squared difference between two
↪   vectors
squared_diff <- function(x, y) {
  # Compute element-wise difference and square the result
  diff <- x - y
  return(diff^2)
}
# Test the custom function with sample vectors
x <- c(10, 15, 20)
y <- c(2, 5, 8)
squared_diff_result <- squared_diff(x, y)
print("Squared differences between x and y:")
print(squared_diff_result)

# Using lapply to apply a function to each element of a list of
↪   vectors
vec_list <- list(a = a, b = b)
mean_list <- lapply(vec_list, mean)
print("Mean of vectors in the list:")
print(mean_list)
```

Chapter 7

Sequence and Repetition

Mathematical Characterization of Sequences

A sequence in the computational context is rigorously defined as an ordered collection of elements that adhere to a systematic progression. The underlying mathematical model is encapsulated by the expression

$$S = \{a, \, a + d, \, a + 2d, \, \ldots, \, a + (n-1)d\},$$

where a represents the initial value, d denotes the common difference, and n indicates the total number of elements. This formulation is congruent with the concept of an arithmetic progression and forms the foundational basis for sequence generation functions. The abstraction inherent in this representation allows for precise definitions and the careful handling of boundary conditions, such as verifying that the specified step d is non-zero and properly aligned with the prescribed range.

Analysis of Sequence Generation Mechanism

The generation of a numerical sequence adheres to well-defined algorithmic constructs that transform scalar parameters into a contiguous array of values. The mechanism employed leverages parameterization by specifying the starting point, terminal value, and either the step increment or an intended length of the sequence. Such a function computes each successive term by the recurrent application of an additive process, thereby guaranteeing that the resultant sequence maintains a uniform interval between consecutive elements. The underlying implementation is optimized to perform these calculations in linear time relative to the number of elements, ensuring that the computational overhead is kept to a minimum. Furthermore, considerations regarding floating-point precision and rounding errors are systematically managed, as the function must accurately represent both integer and non-integer progressions within the constraints of the digital computational model.

Fundamentals of Element Repetition

Repetition of elements within a data structure is conceptually distinct from the generation of a new sequence, although both operations yield one-dimensional arrays. The repetition process involves the duplication of specified elements, such that a scalar item or a collection of items is reiterated a predetermined number of times. Mathematically, the repetition of an element x can be represented as

$$R(x, k) = \{\underbrace{x, x, \ldots, x}_{k \text{ times}}\},$$

where k specifies the replication count. This operation may be extended to vectors, whereby each individual component is replicated either uniformly or according to a pattern dictated by additional parameters. The computational realization of this functionality is engineered to leverage contiguous memory allocation, thereby ensuring that the replication preserves both the order and the integrity of the original data. The design emphasizes efficiency and scalability, recognizing the frequent need to generate repeated patterns as foundational constructs in experimental design and algorithmic simulation.

Comparative Syntactic Structure and Computational Implications

A systematic comparison of sequence generation and element repetition reveals that both processes constitute fundamental techniques in the assembly of vectorized data structures. The sequence generation function produces arrays through a controlled arithmetic progression, while the repetition function focuses on the duplication of existing elements or patterns. Despite their differing operational objectives, both functions adhere to the principles of vectorization, which facilitate the application of element-wise operations without explicit iterative constructs. This synergy is pivotal in the construction of complex data sets and experimental designs, where indexed sequences may be coupled with replicated values to form matrices or multi-dimensional arrays. The architectural design of these operations underscores the importance of contiguous memory storage and optimized computation, ensuring that the transformation from high-level mathematical specifications to lower-level data representations is both accurate and efficient.

R Code Snippet

```
# Comprehensive R Code Demonstration for Sequence Generation and
↪   Element Repetition

# Function to generate an arithmetic sequence given an initial value
↪   'a', common difference 'd', and length 'n'
generateSequence <- function(a, d, n) {
  # Validate that n is a positive integer
  if (n <= 0 || n != as.integer(n)) {
    stop("Error: 'n' must be a positive integer.")
  }
  # For sequences with more than one element, ensure that 'd' (step)
  ↪   is non-zero
  if (n > 1 && d == 0) {
    stop("Error: For a sequence with more than one element, the step
    ↪   'd' must be non-zero.")
  }

  # Initialize a numeric vector to hold the sequence values
  seq_values <- numeric(n)
  seq_values[1] <- a  # Set the first element

  # Generate the sequence iteratively using the arithmetic
  ↪   progression formula:
```

```r
  # S = {a, a+d, a+2d, ..., a+(n-1)d}
  for (i in 2:n) {
    seq_values[i] <- seq_values[i - 1] + d
  }

  return(seq_values)
}


# Function to replicate an element 'x' exactly 'k' times
generateRepeats <- function(x, k) {
  # Validate that k is a positive integer
  if (k <= 0 || k != as.integer(k)) {
    stop("Error: Replication count 'k' must be a positive integer.")
  }

  # Using R's built-in rep() function to replicate the element
  repeated_vector <- rep(x, times = k)
  return(repeated_vector)
}


#-------------------------------------------------------------#
# Demonstration of the Arithmetic Sequence Generation
#-------------------------------------------------------------#


# Parameters for the arithmetic sequence
a <- 5        # initial value
d <- 3        # common difference
n <- 10       # number of elements

# Generate sequence using our custom function
sequence_custom <- generateSequence(a, d, n)
print("Arithmetic Sequence generated by the custom
↪   generateSequence() function:")
print(sequence_custom)

# Generate sequence using R's built-in seq() function for comparison
sequence_builtin <- seq(from = a, by = d, length.out = n)
print("Arithmetic Sequence generated by R's seq() function:")
print(sequence_builtin)


#-------------------------------------------------------------#
# Demonstration of the Element Repetition Functionality
#-------------------------------------------------------------#


# Parameters for repetition
x <- "R"        # element to be repeated
k <- 8          # replication count

# Generate repetition using our custom function
repeats_custom <- generateRepeats(x, k)
print("Element Repetition generated by the custom generateRepeats()
↪   function:")
print(repeats_custom)
```

47

```r
# Generate repetition using R's built-in rep() function for
↪    verification
repeats_builtin <- rep(x, times = k)
print("Element Repetition generated by R's rep() function:")
print(repeats_builtin)


#-------------------------------------------------------------#
# Additional Demonstration: Vectorized Conditional Assignment
#-------------------------------------------------------------#

# Using ifelse() for classifying elements of the arithmetic sequence
# For example: classify each element as "High" if it is greater than
↪    or equal to the median, otherwise "Low"

median_val <- median(sequence_custom)
classification <- ifelse(sequence_custom >= median_val, "High",
↪    "Low")
print("Classification of sequence elements as 'High' or 'Low' based
↪    on the median:")
print(classification)


#-------------------------------------------------------------#
# Handling Floating-Point Precision in Sequence Generation
#-------------------------------------------------------------#

# Generate a sequence with non-integer parameters to inspect
↪    potential rounding issues
a_fp <- 0.1      # floating-point initial value
d_fp <- 0.1      # floating-point common difference
n_fp <- 15       # number of elements in the sequence

sequence_fp <- seq(from = a_fp, by = d_fp, length.out = n_fp)
print("Arithmetic Sequence with floating-point values (demonstrating
↪    precision handling):")
print(sequence_fp)
```

Chapter 8

Factors for Categorical Data

Representation and Theoretical Foundations

Factors constitute a fundamental data structure for representing categorical information within the R programming environment. Formally, a factor can be conceptualized as an ordered pair

$$F = (C, L),$$

where C represents a vector of underlying integer codes and L denotes the finite set of labels associated with these codes. This formulation encapsulates the dual nature of factors: on one hand, they preserve the compact numerical representation necessary for efficient computation; on the other, they maintain the semantic integrity of the categorical data through explicit labeling. The mathematical abstraction of a factor facilitates rigorous operations on categorical variables, thereby enabling precise statistical and computational analyses that extend naturally into applications such as regression modeling and classification.

In many theoretical frameworks, the factor structure is interpreted as a mapping $f : \mathcal{X} \to \{1, 2, \ldots, k\}$, where $\mathcal{X}$ is a set encompassing the observable categories and k is the number of distinct levels. The implementation strategy adopted by R leverages contiguous memory allocation for the integer vector, while the

49

corresponding mapping to the set L is preserved as an attribute. This design ensures that factors are both memory efficient and amenable to high-performance vectorized operations, a necessity in large-scale data analysis.

Factor Levels: Enumeration and Ordering

A critical aspect of factor design is the explicit enumeration and potential ordering of the categorical levels. Each element $l \in L$ symbolizes an individual category, and the entire set L serves as the spectrum of all possible outcomes that the categorical variable may assume. In cases where the categories possess an inherent rank or order, the factor is designated as an ordered factor. For an ordered factor, if the levels are denoted by

$$L = \{l_1, l_2, \ldots, l_k\},$$

a strict total ordering such that

$$l_1 < l_2 < \cdots < l_k$$

is imposed. This ordered structure is pivotal in statistical methodologies that require the recognition of ordinal relationships, and it ensures that operations such as sorting, ranking, and contrast coding are executed with both numerical efficiency and semantic validity.

The internal representation of factor levels is not merely a passive listing; it is dynamically linked to the computational processes that underpin statistical inferences. This intrinsic association between the integer codes and their descriptive labels permits algebraic manipulations and conditional transformations that are crucial in the analysis of qualitative data. Consequently, rigorous management of factor levels, including explicit definition, reordering, and potential consolidation of levels, is essential for preserving the integrity and interpretability of categorical datasets.

Management and Manipulation of Categorical Data

The management of categorical data via factors in R encompasses a spectrum of operations aimed at ensuring both the robustness and the adaptability of the data representation. The initial conversion of a native vector into a factor entails identifying the set L of unique categories and assigning to each element a corresponding integer code. This transformation is instrumental in reducing redundancy and in standardizing representations across large datasets. Moreover, the maintenance of such categorical data can involve operations such as the renaming of levels, reordering based on domain-specific criteria, and the merging of multiple categories to reflect aggregated groupings.

From a computational perspective, the manipulation of factors is governed by principles of object-oriented design and efficient memory utilization. The operations applied to factors are typically characterized by their adherence to vectorized implementations, thereby eliminating the need for explicit iterative processes. When coupled with additional data transformation protocols, these operations empower the construction of refined data structures that are optimally configured for downstream statistical analyses. For example, the coherent management of factors directly impacts the performance of regression routines, analysis of variance, and clustering algorithms that necessitate categorical delineations.

The procedural management of factors further extends to error detection and anomaly resolution. When an element is encountered that does not correspond to any of the pre-established levels in L, the factor management system is equipped to address such discrepancies through appropriate signaling or the recoding of the data. This systematic approach to error handling underscores the critical role of factors in enforcing data consistency and in underpinning the reliability of the ensuing analytic models.

R Code Snippet

```
# Comprehensive R code snippet illustrating the mathematical
↪   representation,
# ordering, mapping, and manipulation of factors in R, corresponding
↪   to the
# theoretical formulations presented in the chapter.

# Step 1: Create a sample character vector representing categorical
↪   data.
categories <- c("High", "Medium", "Low", "Medium", "High", "Low",
↪   "Medium", "Very High", "Low")
cat("Original Categories:\n")
print(categories)
```

```r
# Step 2: Convert the vector into a basic factor.
factor_categories <- factor(categories)
cat("\nFactor Conversion (F = (C, L)):\n")
print(factor_categories)
cat("\nInternal Integer Codes (C):\n")
print(as.integer(factor_categories))
cat("\nLevels (Label Set L):\n")
print(levels(factor_categories))

# Represent the factor as an ordered pair F = (C, L)
factor_representation <- list(C = as.integer(factor_categories),
                              L = levels(factor_categories))
cat("\nRepresentation of Factor as (C, L):\n")
print(factor_representation)

# Step 3: Create an Ordered Factor with Explicit Ordering.
# Define the explicit order for levels as per the equation:
# L = {l1, l2, ..., lk} with l1 < l2 < ... < lk.
ordered_levels <- c("Low", "Medium", "High", "Very High")
ordered_factor <- factor(categories, levels = ordered_levels,
↪   ordered = TRUE)
cat("\nOrdered Factor with Explicit Levels:\n")
print(ordered_factor)
cat("\nVerification - Levels of Ordered Factor:\n")
print(levels(ordered_factor))
cat("\nIs the factor ordered? ", is.ordered(ordered_factor), "\n")

# Step 4: Mapping the Ordinal Factor.
# Demonstrate how numeric codes map to corresponding levels.
mapping_df <- data.frame(NumericCode = as.integer(ordered_factor),
                         Category    = as.character(ordered_factor))
cat("\nMapping between Integer Codes and Levels:\n")
print(mapping_df)

# Step 5: Algorithm for Merging Levels.
# Consolidate "Medium" and "High" into a new consolidated level
↪   "Normal".
consolidated_categories <- as.character(ordered_factor)
consolidated_categories[consolidated_categories %in% c("Medium",
↪   "High")] <- "Normal"
# Define new ordered levels: "Low" < "Normal" < "Very High"
consolidated_factor <- factor(consolidated_categories,
                              levels = c("Low", "Normal", "Very
                              ↪   High"),
                              ordered = TRUE)
cat("\nConsolidated Factor with 'Medium' and 'High' merged into
↪   'Normal':\n")
print(consolidated_factor)
cat("\nNew Levels after Consolidation:\n")
print(levels(consolidated_factor))

# Step 6: Error Handling in Factor Conversion.
```

```r
# Create a vector with an unexpected category "Unknown" that does
↪   not exist in predefined levels.
new_data <- c("Low", "Medium", "Unknown", "High")
# Convert the vector into an ordered factor specifying only valid
↪   levels.
factor_new_data <- factor(new_data, levels = c("Low", "Medium",
↪   "High"), ordered = TRUE)
cat("\nFactor Conversion with Unknown Category (should yield NA for
↪   'Unknown'):\n")
print(factor_new_data)
cat("\nNA Check for Unknown Values:\n")
print(is.na(factor_new_data))

# Step 7: Vectorized Conditional Assignment using ifelse().
# Assign numerical values to each ordered level based on a defined
↪   ranking.
numeric_codes <- ifelse(ordered_factor == "Low", 1,
                   ifelse(ordered_factor == "Medium", 2,
                   ifelse(ordered_factor == "High", 3,
                   ifelse(ordered_factor == "Very High", 4, NA))))
cat("\nNumeric Codes via ifelse() based on Ordered Factor
↪   Levels:\n")
print(numeric_codes)

# Step 8: Inspect the Structure of the Ordered Factor Object.
cat("\nStructure of the Ordered Factor Object:\n")
str(ordered_factor)

# End of comprehensive R code snippet demonstrating factor
↪   operations,
# mapping as F = (C, L), and vectorized conditional handling,
↪   corresponding
# to the equations and algorithms discussed in the chapter.
```

Chapter 9

Matrices in R

Mathematical Representation and Structural Characteristics

A matrix is rigorously defined as a two-dimensional array $M \in \mathbb{R}^{m \times n}$, where m and n denote the number of rows and columns, respectively. In precise terms, a matrix is expressed as

$$M = \begin{bmatrix} a_{11} & a_{12} & \cdots & a_{1n} \\ a_{21} & a_{22} & \cdots & a_{2n} \\ \vdots & \vdots & \ddots & \vdots \\ a_{m1} & a_{m2} & \cdots & a_{mn} \end{bmatrix},$$

with each element a_{ij} representing the entry in the ith row and jth column. This formalism encapsulates both the geometric arrangement and the algebraic properties inherent to matrices. The representation emphasizes the dual role of matrices as data structures for numerical storage and as entities subject to a wide array of algebraic manipulations.

Matrix Creation and Dimensional Configuration

Matrices in the computational environment are often instantiated through the reshaping of one-dimensional vectors into a two-dimensional layout. The transformation involves the explicit specification of dimensions, ensuring that the length of the original vector v satisfies

$|v| = m \cdot n$, where m and n define the matrix dimensions. The allocation of matrix entries adheres to a systematic order, typically following a column-major sequence, thereby ensuring that the underlying memory organization is both efficient and congruent with the theoretical model. This configuration facilitates rigorous control over the structure and organization of numerical data, establishing a solid foundation for subsequent computations.

Arithmetic Operations and Algebraic Manipulations

The algebraic manipulation of matrices in numerical computations embodies fundamental operations that are defined in accordance with classical linear algebra. Element-wise operations, such as addition and subtraction, require that matrices share identical dimensions, permitting the direct computation

$$(M + N)_{ij} = m_{ij} + n_{ij} \quad \text{and} \quad (M - N)_{ij} = m_{ij} - n_{ij},$$

for matrices $M = [m_{ij}]$ and $N = [n_{ij}]$ of dimensions $m \times n$. In contrast, matrix multiplication is governed by the rule

$$(AB)_{ij} = \sum_{k=1}^{p} a_{ik} b_{kj},$$

where $A \in \mathbb{R}^{m \times p}$ and $B \in \mathbb{R}^{p \times n}$. The implementation of these operations is optimized to take advantage of vectorized computations and low-level linear algebra routines, thereby ensuring that numerical procedures are performed both swiftly and accurately. This mathematical framework also accommodates more elaborate operations such as the computation of determinants, inverses, and eigen-decompositions, all of which are critical in solving systems of linear equations and in various applications of numerical analysis.

Indexing, Slicing, and Submatrix Extraction

The precision of matrix manipulation is further enhanced by sophisticated indexing capabilities that allow for the extraction of substructures. Given a matrix $M \in \mathbb{R}^{m \times n}$, it is possible to isolate a submatrix M' through the selection of specific row and column indices. Mathematically, the extraction is denoted as

$$M' = M[I, J],$$

where $I \subseteq \{1, 2, \ldots, m\}$ and $J \subseteq \{1, 2, \ldots, n\}$. This operation preserves the relational structure inherent in the original matrix while offering a refined lens through which particular segments of the data can be examined. The indexing mechanism is inherently vectorized, thus obviating the need for iterative constructs and ensuring that the extraction process is executed with maximal efficiency.

Advanced Transformations and Data Rearrangement

Beyond the fundamental operations, matrices undergo advanced transformations that are central to many numerical computation methodologies. A quintessential example is the transposition operation, defined by

$$M^T = [a_{ji}],$$

which effectively interchanges the rows and columns of the matrix. Such transformations are indispensable in various algorithmic schemes, including those pertaining to the solution of systems of equations and eigenvalue problems. Additionally, the reordering of rows and columns, as well as the permutation of elements, serves to optimize matrix configurations for specific computational tasks. These operations maintain the internal consistency of the matrix while allowing for dynamic rearrangements that can enhance the performance and accuracy of numerical computations.

R Code Snippet

```
# Matrix Creation and Dimensional Configuration
# Create a vector and reshape it into a 3x4 matrix following
↪   column-major order.
v <- 1:12
M <- matrix(v, nrow = 3, ncol = 4)
cat("Matrix M (3x4):\n")
print(M)

# Create another 3x4 matrix for arithmetic operations.
N <- matrix(12:1, nrow = 3, ncol = 4)
```

```r
cat("\nMatrix N (3x4):\n")
print(N)

# Arithmetic Operations and Algebraic Manipulations
# Element-wise addition and subtraction require matching dimensions.
add_result <- M + N
sub_result <- M - N
cat("\nElement-wise Addition (M + N):\n")
print(add_result)
cat("\nElement-wise Subtraction (M - N):\n")
print(sub_result)

# Matrix Multiplication
# For matrix multiplication, the inner dimensions must match.
# Create matrix A of dimension 2x3 and matrix B of dimension 3x2.
A <- matrix(1:6, nrow = 2, ncol = 3)
B <- matrix(6:1, nrow = 3, ncol = 2)
cat("\nMatrix A (2x3):\n")
print(A)
cat("\nMatrix B (3x2):\n")
print(B)
mult_result <- A %*% B
cat("\nMatrix Multiplication (A %*% B):\n")
print(mult_result)

# Indexing, Slicing, and Submatrix Extraction
# Extract a submatrix from M: selecting rows 2 to 3 and columns 2 to
↪  4.
sub_M <- M[2:3, 2:4]
cat("\nSubmatrix of M (rows 2:3, columns 2:4):\n")
print(sub_M)

# Advanced Transformations and Data Rearrangement
# Transposition: swapping rows and columns of matrix M.
M_transpose <- t(M)
cat("\nTranspose of M:\n")
print(M_transpose)

# Permuting rows of M (e.g., rearranging rows in the order 3, 1, 2).
permuted_M <- M[c(3, 1, 2), ]
cat("\nPermuted M (rows reordered as 3,1,2):\n")
print(permuted_M)

# Additional Algebraic Operations on a Square Matrix
# Create a 2x2 square matrix for determinant, inverse, and eigen
↪  decomposition.
square_M <- matrix(c(4, 7, 2, 6), nrow = 2)
cat("\nSquare Matrix (2x2):\n")
print(square_M)
det_square_M <- det(square_M)
inv_square_M <- solve(square_M)
eig_square_M <- eigen(square_M)
cat("\nDeterminant of square_M:\n")
```

```r
print(det_square_M)
cat("\nInverse of square_M:\n")
print(inv_square_M)
cat("\nEigen Decomposition of square_M:\n")
print(eig_square_M)

# Random Data Generation and Monte Carlo Simulation
# Generate a 4x4 matrix with random normal values.
set.seed(123)
rand_M <- matrix(rnorm(16), nrow = 4)
cat("\nRandom Matrix (4x4) with rnorm:\n")
print(rand_M)

# Monte Carlo Simulation: Estimate Pi using random sampling within a
↪  unit circle.
num_points <- 10000
x <- runif(num_points, min = -1, max = 1)
y <- runif(num_points, min = -1, max = 1)
inside_circle <- (x^2 + y^2) <= 1
pi_estimate <- 4 * sum(inside_circle) / num_points
cat("\nMonte Carlo Estimate of Pi:\n")
print(pi_estimate)
```

Chapter 10

Lists in R

Fundamental Properties and Flexibility

Lists in R constitute a highly versatile data structure capable of encapsulating objects of disparate types. Formally, a list L may be represented as a collection

$$L = \{l_1, l_2, \ldots, l_k\},$$

where each element l_i may be an object of any valid type within the R environment, including atomic vectors, matrices, data frames, functions, or even other lists. This intrinsic heterogeneity distinguishes lists from other data structures that mandate homogeneity, thus providing a robust framework for representing multifaceted data. The flexibility afforded by lists enables a seamless integration of various data forms, thereby supporting the construction and manipulation of complex, hierarchical information without imposing rigid type constraints.

Internal Representation and Memory Considerations

Internally, lists are implemented through a dynamic structure that leverages pointers to R's fundamental S-expression (SEXP) objects. Each element within a list is referenced by an address in a contiguous memory block, facilitating rapid random access and efficient modifications. Given a list $L = \{l_1, l_2, \ldots, l_k\}$, pointers to individual elements are stored in an array-like fashion, with the ith pointer directly referencing the object l_i. This design guarantees that the retrieval of any element operates in constant time $O(1)$, while also accommodating the dynamic allocation of memory as the list grows or shrinks. Moreover, the copy-on-modify behavior inherent to R's memory management ensures that modifications to list elements preserve the integrity of shared data until explicit changes are committed.

Indexing, Manipulation, and Operational Semantics

The operational semantics of lists are characterized by sophisticated indexing capabilities that allow for both positional and associative access to elements. In the positional paradigm, retrieval is performed via the ith element, denoted as $L[i]$ for extracting a sublist or $L[[i]]$ for accessing the element itself in its entirety. When list elements are assigned names, the association can be mathematically represented as a mapping

$$\{n_i \mapsto l_i \mid 1 \leq i \leq k\},$$

where n_i is the name assigned to the element l_i. This dual-access mechanism facilitates both the precise location of data based on its inherent order and the semantic clarity provided by named identifiers. Furthermore, the mutable nature of lists ensures that individual components can be updated or replaced with minimal overhead, a property that is vital in iterative algorithms and dynamic data analyses. The capacity to nest lists within lists further enriches their structure, allowing for recursive constructions that mirror complex relational data.

Applications within Complex Data Aggregation

In advanced computational contexts, lists serve as the backbone for aggregating a variety of data modalities into a single coherent entity. Their heterogeneous nature allows for the simultaneous storage of numerical aggregates, character-based annotations, logical markers, and even higher-level objects such as models or functions.

This multifaceted aggregation is particularly beneficial in scenarios requiring the encapsulation of experimental data, the organization of multidimensional results, or the management of metadata alongside primary data objects. The inherent design of lists, which supports both sequential and associative access, underwrites their utility in constructing composite data types that are both flexible and scalable. As a result, lists emerge as indispensable tools in the formulation of complex data models and algorithmic frameworks where diverse data types must coexist within a uniformly accessible container.

R Code Snippet

```r
# Create a heterogeneous list with various components
myList <- list(
  numbers = 1:10,                              # A numeric vector
  matrixData = matrix(1:12, nrow = 3, ncol = 4),   # A 3x4 matrix
  dataFrame = data.frame(x = rnorm(5), y = runif(5)),   # A simple
  ↪  data frame
  customFunction = function(x) { x * 2 },      # A function to double
  ↪  its input
  nestedList = list(                           # A nested list with
  ↪  named elements
    alpha = letters[1:5],
    beta  = seq(0, 1, length.out = 5)
  )
)

# Print the entire list to check its structure
cat("Initial List Structure:\n")
print(myList)

# -------------------------------------------------
# Demonstration of Fundamental Operations on Lists
# -------------------------------------------------

# 1. Accessing Elements by Position vs. Name

# Access the numeric vector by its position (first element)
cat("\nAccess numeric vector using [[1]]:\n")
print(myList[[1]])

# Access the numeric vector by its name
cat("\nAccess numeric vector using \$numbers:\n")
print(myList$numbers)

# 2. Updating List Elements
```

```r
# Update the first element of the numeric vector to a new value
↪   (e.g., 100)
cat("\nUpdate: Change first element of 'numbers' to 100:\n")
myList$numbers[1] <- 100
print(myList$numbers)

# 3. Accessing and Working with Nested Lists

# Access the nested list element 'alpha'
cat("\nAccess nested list element 'alpha':\n")
print(myList$nestedList$alpha)

# 4. Simulating Constant Time Access (O(1))
# Although R abstracts pointer management, we demonstrate repeated
↪   access to show efficiency.

cat("\nSimulating constant time access for dataFrame\$x over
↪   1,000,000 iterations:\n")
start_time <- proc.time()
for (i in 1:1000000) {
  temp <- myList$dataFrame$x
}
end_time <- proc.time()
compute_time <- end_time - start_time
print(compute_time)

# 5. Using Included Functions from the List

# Calculate using the custom function: doubling the input value 50
cat("\nResult of customFunction(50):\n")
result <- myList$customFunction(50)
print(result)

# 6. Vectorized Conditional Update using ifelse()

# Apply a conditional update to the numeric vector:
# For elements greater than 50, subtract 10; otherwise, add 10.
cat("\nApply ifelse() to update 'numbers':\n")
myList$numbers <- ifelse(myList$numbers > 50, myList$numbers - 10,
↪   myList$numbers + 10)
print(myList$numbers)

# End of R code snippet demonstrating key list operations and
↪   concepts.
```

Chapter 11

Data Frames

Definition and Structural Properties

Data frames represent a two-dimensional, heterogeneous tabular abstraction designed for the effective encapsulation of data in R. A data frame is structured as a collection of column vectors, each of which is internally homogeneous, yet the overall container permits variability in data type across distinct columns. Formally, a data frame may be denoted as

$$D = \langle c_1, c_2, \ldots, c_n \rangle,$$

where every column c_i is a vector satisfying the constraint $|c_i| = m$, with m representing the total number of observations. This consistency in vector length ensures the integrity of row-wise association among variables. The design implicitly aligns with the relational model encountered in database theory, whereby rows correspond to records and columns to distinct attributes, thereby facilitating a systematic approach to data representation and manipulation.

Internal Representation and Memory Organization

Internally, a data frame in R is underpinned by a list-based mechanism that augments primitive vector storage with additional attributes to retain its tabular structure. Each column, implemented as a vector, is stored in contiguous memory segments and is accompanied by metadata such as column names and row identifiers.

The formal representation can be enhanced by associating a set of attributes, for instance,

$$\{\texttt{row.names} = R, \ \texttt{class} = \texttt{"data.frame"}\},$$

which serve to delineate the semantic and structural features of the data frame. The underlying memory model leverages pointer-based references to S-expressions (abbreviated as $SEXP$) to support dynamic allocation and efficient random access. Further, R's copy-on-modify strategy ensures that alterations to a data frame preserve the integrity of shared structures until modifications are explicitly effectuated. This systematic internal organization confers both flexibility and efficiency, characteristics that are essential for handling complex data manipulations in high-performance computing tasks.

Indexing, Subsetting, and Manipulation Techniques

The operational semantics governing data frames are intimately tied to a robust indexing framework that supports both positional and symbolic referencing. For a data frame D, individual elements can be accessed via the notation $D[i, j]$, where the index i signifies the specific row and j corresponds to the column. This bi-dimensional indexing convention ensures precise extraction of submatrices or individual elements, analogous to standard matrix operations. Moreover, symbolic indexing permits referencing a column by its designated label, thereby abstracting the positional dependency in data retrieval. This dual indexing paradigm facilitates a breadth of data manipulation operations including filtering, reordering, and transformation. The coherent alignment of indexing methods with the intrinsic structure of data frames underwrites their efficacy in managing extensive and multifaceted datasets.

Analytical Operations on Tabular Data

The inherent architecture of data frames renders them particularly suitable for the execution of analytical routines on tabular data. Each column c_i, embodying a distinct variable, permits the application of conventional statistical computations such as the arithmetic mean

$$\mu_i = \frac{1}{m} \sum_{j=1}^{m} c_i[j]$$

and the sample variance

$$\sigma_i^2 = \frac{1}{m-1} \sum_{j=1}^{m} (c_i[j] - \mu_i)^2.$$

The uniformity in row length not only maintains consistency across variable measurements but also facilitates the execution of aggregate, descriptive, and inferential statistical methodologies. The tabular configuration further fosters the integration of diverse data transformation operations including merging, joining, and reshaping, thereby establishing data frames as a foundational construct in computational data analysis. Their structural rigor and adaptability enable the consolidation of multi-dimensional data inputs into an analytically tractable form, which is pivotal for systematic quantitative assessments in both theoretical explorations and empirical evaluations.

R Code Snippet

```
# Creating a sample data frame with heterogeneous column types
df <- data.frame(
  id     = 1:5,
  score  = c(85, 90, 78, 92, 88),
  passed = c(TRUE, TRUE, FALSE, TRUE, TRUE)
)

# Display the internal structure and summary of the data frame.
str(df)
print(summary(df))

#-----------------------------------------------
# Calculation of Arithmetic Mean and Sample Variance
#-----------------------------------------------
# Number of observations (m)
m <- nrow(df)
score <- df$score

# Manual computation of the arithmetic mean:
# Formula:  = (1/m) * sum(score)
mu_manual <- sum(score) / m

# Manual computation of the sample variance:
```

```r
# Formula: ² = (1/(m-1)) * sum((score - )²)
sigma2_manual <- sum((score - mu_manual)^2) / (m - 1)

cat("Arithmetic Mean (manual):", mu_manual, "\n")
cat("Sample Variance (manual):", sigma2_manual, "\n")

# Verification using built-in R functions
mu_builtin <- mean(score)
sigma2_builtin <- var(score)

cat("Arithmetic Mean (built-in):", mu_builtin, "\n")
cat("Sample Variance (built-in):", sigma2_builtin, "\n")

#-----------------------------------------------
# Indexing, Subsetting, and Accessing Data
#-----------------------------------------------
# Positional indexing: Access element at 2nd row, 1st column
elem <- df[2, 1]
cat("Element at row 2, column 1:", elem, "\n")

# Bi-dimensional indexing: Extract first 3 rows (all columns)
sub_df <- df[1:3, ]
print(sub_df)

# Using symbolic indexing: Extract the 'score' column by its name
score_col <- df[,"score"]
print(score_col)

# Simplifying expressions using the with() function:
with(df, {
  cat("Mean of scores (with()):", mean(score), "\n")
})

#-----------------------------------------------
# Conditional Vector Assignment and Data Manipulation
#-----------------------------------------------
# Add a new column 'grade_cat' based on a condition (if score >= 90,
↪   mark as "Excellent", otherwise "Good")
df$grade_cat <- ifelse(df$score >= 90, "Excellent", "Good")
print(df)

# Sorting the data frame by the 'score' column
df_sorted <- df[order(df$score), ]
print(df_sorted)

#-----------------------------------------------
# Merging Data Frames
#-----------------------------------------------
# Create another data frame to demonstrate merging operations.
df2 <- data.frame(
  id    = c(3, 4, 5, 6),
  grade = c("C", "B", "A", "B")
)
```

```r
# Merge the two data frames on the 'id' column (outer join)
merged_df <- merge(df, df2, by = "id", all = TRUE)
print(merged_df)

#-----------------------------------------------
# Reshaping Data: Wide to Long Format
#-----------------------------------------------
# Check if package 'reshape2' is installed; if not, install it
↪   first.
if (!require(reshape2)) {
  install.packages("reshape2", dependencies = TRUE)
  library(reshape2)
} else {
  library(reshape2)
}

# Melt the data frame from wide to long format using 'id' as the
↪   identifier
long_df <- melt(df, id.vars = "id")
print(long_df)

#-----------------------------------------------
# Inspecting Internal Structure and Attributes
#-----------------------------------------------
# Display the attributes of the data frame (e.g., row.names, class)
print(attributes(df))

#-----------------------------------------------
# Simulating Copy-on-Modify Behavior
#-----------------------------------------------
# Create a copy of the data frame and modify the 'score' column;
# the original data frame remains unchanged until explicit
↪   modification.
df_copy <- df
df_copy$score <- df_copy$score + 5

cat("Original scores:", df$score, "\n")
cat("Modified scores in copy:", df_copy$score, "\n")
```

67

Chapter 12

Indexing and Subsetting

Indexing Vectors

Consider a one-dimensional homogeneous collection represented as a vector, denoted by

$$v = \langle v_1, v_2, \ldots, v_n \rangle,$$

where $n \in \mathbb{N}$ defines the length of the vector and each v_i $(1 \leq i \leq n)$ corresponds to an individual element. Indexing within this construct is achieved by identifying specific positions within the index set $\{1, 2, \ldots, n\}$. Utilization of positive integer indices retrieves an element directly, as in v_i, while alternative mechanisms, such as negative indexing, exclude particular positions from selection. Logical indexing further refines this process by employing a logical vector

$$\ell = \langle \ell_1, \ell_2, \ldots, \ell_n \rangle \quad \text{with} \quad \ell_i \in \{\text{TRUE}, \text{FALSE}\},$$

to specify the inclusion or exclusion of elements based on conditional criteria. When vectors are augmented with names, symbolic indexing becomes feasible, permitting direct access to elements via their associated labels. These multiple paradigms of indexing are fundamental for precise data manipulation within the vector model.

Indexing Matrices

A matrix is mathematically characterized as a two-dimensional array M of dimensions $m \times n$, where m and n denote the number of rows and columns, respectively. Every element within the matrix is uniquely identified by a pair of indices, employing the notation

$$M[i,j] \quad \text{with} \quad 1 \leq i \leq m \quad \text{and} \quad 1 \leq j \leq n.$$

This framework enables the retrieval of single elements, as well as the extraction of submatrices by selecting subsets of rows and columns. For instance, the specification of a range of indices for the rows and/or columns results in the formation of a submatrix that preserves the ordering and structural properties of the original. The intrinsic layout of matrices, often underpinned by contiguous memory allocation, enhances the efficiency of these indexing operations and supports systematic data manipulation in environments where multidimensional array structures are pervasive.

Indexing Lists

Lists introduce a higher order of abstraction, encapsulating heterogeneous elements within an ordered aggregation denoted by

$$L = (l_1, l_2, \ldots, l_k),$$

where each l_i may itself be an atomic vector, matrix, or an even more complex composite type. Indexing a list necessitates a dual approach: one may extract a component as an isolated element or retrieve a sublist that maintains the overall list structure. The operational distinction between these two forms of extraction lies in the preservation of the original data type. While one form of indexing produces a sublist containing a single element, an alternative mode retrieves the element in its native format. This precise differentiation is critical for ensuring type integrity and for enabling further operations that rely on the inherent structure of the stored elements.

Indexing Data Frames

Data frames extend the matrix paradigm by allowing heterogeneity across columns while enforcing homogeneity within each individual column. A data frame is formally encapsulated as

$$D = \langle c_1, c_2, \ldots, c_p \rangle,$$

where each column c_i is a vector of uniform length m, resulting in a tabular construction of dimensions $m \times p$. Indexing within this structure incorporates a dual modality: positional indexing based on numerical row and column indices, and symbolic indexing that leverages the assignment of names to the constituent columns. The positional scheme employs a two-dimensional reference of the form $D[i, j]$, where i and j specify the row and column indices, respectively, while leaving either index unspecified yields entire rows or columns. Symbolic referencing, by contrast, permits the direct invocation of columns through their designated labels, thereby abstracting the complexity of numerical indexing. This synthesis of approaches facilitates comprehensive subsetting of the data frame, ensuring that both the granularity of individual observations and the collective attributes of the tabular format are maintained for subsequent analytical operations.

R Code Snippet

```
#
↪   ----------------------------------------------------------------------
# R Code Snippet Demonstrating Indexing and Subsetting in R
# This snippet covers vectors, matrices, lists, and data frames.
#
↪   ----------------------------------------------------------------------

# 1. Indexing Vectors

# Create a numeric vector of 10 elements
v <- 1:10
cat("Original vector v:\n")
print(v)

# Positive integer indexing: Access the 4th element
cat("\nAccessing the 4th element using v[4]:\n")
print(v[4])

# Negative indexing: Exclude the first element
cat("\nVector after excluding the 1st element using v[-1]:\n")
print(v[-1])

# Logical indexing: Retrieve elements greater than 5
cat("\nElements greater than 5 using v[v > 5]:\n")
print(v[v > 5])
```

```r
# Named indexing: Assign names and access by name
names(v) <- paste("elem", 1:length(v), sep="_")
cat("\nNamed vector v:\n")
print(v)
cat("\nAccessing element named 'elem_3' using v[\"elem_3\"]:\n")
print(v["elem_3"])

# 2. Indexing Matrices

# Create a 3x4 matrix with values from 1 to 12
M <- matrix(1:12, nrow=3, ncol=4)
cat("\nMatrix M (3x4):\n")
print(M)

# Accessing a single element at row 2, column 3
cat("\nElement at M[2,3]:\n")
print(M[2,3])

# Extracting a submatrix: rows 1 to 2, columns 2 to 4
cat("\nSubmatrix (rows 1-2 and columns 2-4):\n")
print(M[1:2, 2:4])

# 3. Indexing Lists

# Create a list containing a vector, a matrix, and a data frame for
↪   heterogeneous storage
L <- list(
  myVector = c(10, 20, 30, 40),
  myMatrix = matrix(101:108, nrow=2, ncol=4),
  myDataFrame = data.frame(id = 1:3, name = c("Alice", "Bob",
  ↪   "Charlie"))
)
cat("\nList L:\n")
print(L)

# Extract a component as a sublist (preserving the list structure)
cat("\nSublist extraction of 'myVector' using L['myVector']:\n")
print(L["myVector"])

# Extract the element in its native format (vector) using double
↪   bracket indexing
cat("\nNative extraction of 'myVector' using L[['myVector']]:\n")
print(L[["myVector"]])

# 4. Indexing Data Frames

# Create a data frame with heterogeneous column types
D <- data.frame(
  score = c(75, 85, 90, 65),
  grade = c("C", "B", "A", "D"),
  passed = c(TRUE, TRUE, TRUE, FALSE),
  stringsAsFactors = FALSE
```

```
)
cat("\nData frame D:\n")
print(D)

# Positional indexing: Access the element at row 3, column 2 (grade)
cat("\nElement at D[3,2] (grade of the 3rd row):\n")
print(D[3,2])

# Positional indexing: Extract the full first column using D[,1]
cat("\nFirst column of D using D[,1]:\n")
print(D[,1])

# Symbolic indexing: Access the 'grade' column by name
cat("\nAccess column 'grade' using D[['grade']]:\n")
print(D[["grade"]])

# Extract a sub-data frame using logical indexing: Rows where
↪   'score' is greater than 70
cat("\nSub-data frame with rows where score > 70:\n")
print(D[D$score > 70, ])

# Extract a sub-data frame with selected columns using column names
cat("\nSub-data frame with columns 'score' and 'passed':\n")
print(D[, c("score", "passed")])
```

Chapter 13

Logical Indexing

Foundations of Logical Vectors

Logical indexing is predicated on the concept of a logical vector, which is a finite, ordered sequence denoted by

$$\ell = \langle \ell_1, \ell_2, \ldots, \ell_n \rangle,$$

where each component satisfies

$$\ell_i \in \{\text{TRUE}, \text{FALSE}\} \quad \text{for} \quad 1 \leq i \leq n.$$

This formalism serves as a basis for selective extraction within data structures. The logical vector acts as a mask that is intrinsically linked to the outcome of predicate evaluations over an associated data structure. Its binary nature enables the mapping of each element in a data sequence to a decision variable, thereby establishing an unambiguous criterion for inclusion or exclusion during the subsetting process.

Logical Filtering in Data Structures

In the application of logical indexing, a data structure—such as a one-dimensional vector

$$v = \langle v_1, v_2, \ldots, v_n \rangle,$$

is refined by the operation of elementwise selection. The filtering mechanism is mathematically represented by the expression

$$v[\ell] = \langle v_i : \ell_i = \text{TRUE} \rangle,$$

which produces a subsequence comprising solely of those elements whose corresponding logical value is TRUE. This paradigm extends naturally to multidimensional environments, where the selective operation may be applied along individual dimensions (e.g., rows or columns) to extract subarrays that adhere to specified logical conditions. The operational efficiency inherent in this method is due in part to its vectorized implementation, which obviates the need for explicit iterative processing.

Mathematical Formalism of Logical Subsetting

The process of logical subsetting can be rigorously defined through a mapping between an indexed data set and its corresponding logical vector. For any data structure

$$D = \{d_1, d_2, \ldots, d_n\},$$

and an associated logical vector ℓ, the filtered subset D' is obtained via

$$D' = \{d_i \mid \ell_i = \text{TRUE}\}.$$

This expression embodies an indicator function embedded within the indexing operator, which systematically selects only those data elements that satisfy the Boolean condition. The correspondence between index positions and their logical evaluations ensures that the structure of the original data is maintained, while simultaneously enabling the extraction of a refined data set that is both well-defined and semantically meaningful.

Computational Efficiency and Theoretical Implications

The utilization of logical indexing confers significant advantages in terms of computational efficiency, particularly when applied to large-scale data structures. Since the evaluation of the logical vector is inherently vectorized, the associated filtering operation is executed with a time complexity that is linear in the number of elements, i.e., $O(n)$. This efficiency is further enhanced by the fact that each Boolean operation is independently computed, thereby facilitating parallel processing and streamlined memory management. From a theoretical standpoint, logical indexing offers a robust mechanism for data filtering that is both expressive and succinct. The design of logical vectors enables them to serve not only as simple indicators but also as integral components in complex data manipulation routines. Their use encapsulates a high-level abstraction that bridges the mathematical formulation of set selection with practical computational implementations, ensuring that the resultant operations are both precise in execution and optimal in performance.

R Code Snippet

```r
# Set a seed for reproducibility
set.seed(123)

# Example 1: Logical Indexing on a Numeric Vector
# Create a numeric vector v
v <- c(3, 7, 2, 9, 4, 6, 1, 8)

# Create a logical vector based on the condition: value > 5
logical_vector <- v > 5

# Filter the vector using logical indexing
filtered_v <- v[logical_vector]

# Print the results to verify the filtering mechanism
print("Original Vector v:")
print(v)
print("Logical Vector (v > 5):")
print(logical_vector)
print("Filtered Vector (only values where v > 5):")
print(filtered_v)

# ------------------------------------------------------------
# Example 2: Logical Subsetting in a Data Frame
# Create a data frame 'dataset' with an id and a randomly sampled
#    numeric value
dataset <- data.frame(
  id = 1:10,
  value = sample(1:20, 10)
)

# Generate a logical mask to identify even 'value' entries
logical_mask <- dataset$value %% 2 == 0

# Apply logical subsetting to obtain only rows where 'value' is even
filtered_dataset <- dataset[logical_mask, ]
```

```r
# Print the dataset and the results of filtering
print("Original Data Frame:")
print(dataset)
print("Logical Mask (value %% 2 == 0):")
print(logical_mask)
print("Filtered Data Frame (only even 'value'):")
print(filtered_dataset)


# ---------------------------------------------------------------
# Example 3: Logical Indexing in a Matrix
# Create a 4x4 matrix
mat <- matrix(1:16, nrow = 4)
print("Original Matrix:")
print(mat)

# Create a logical matrix that flags elements greater than 10
logical_mat <- mat > 10
print("Logical Matrix (elements > 10):")
print(logical_mat)

# Extract elements from the matrix that satisfy the condition
↪  (greater than 10)
filtered_elements <- mat[logical_mat]
print("Filtered Elements (only those > 10):")
print(filtered_elements)

# ---------------------------------------------------------------
# Example 4: Conditional Vector Assignment using ifelse()
# Create another numeric vector v2
v2 <- c(-3, 0, 5, -1, 8, 2)

# Use ifelse to assign a label to each element based on its sign
sign_labels <- ifelse(v2 > 0, "Positive",
                      ifelse(v2 < 0, "Negative", "Zero"))

# Print the original vector and its corresponding labels
print("Vector v2:")
print(v2)
print("Assigned Sign Labels (using ifelse):")
print(sign_labels)

# ---------------------------------------------------------------
# Example 5: Demonstrating Computational Efficiency of Vectorized
# ↪  Operations
# Create a large numeric vector using random uniform data
v_large <- runif(1e6, min = 0, max = 10)

# Vectorized operation: sum of all elements greater than 5
vec_time <- system.time({
  sum_vec <- sum(v_large[v_large > 5])
})
```

```
# Iterative approach: using a loop to sum elements greater than 5
iter_time <- system.time({
  sum_iter <- 0
  for (i in seq_along(v_large)) {
    if (v_large[i] > 5) {
      sum_iter <- sum_iter + v_large[i]
    }
  }
})

# Print timing results and verify that both methods yield the same
↪   sum
print("Vectorized Sum of elements > 5:")
print(sum_vec)
print("Time taken by vectorized approach:")
print(vec_time)

print("Iterative Sum of elements > 5:")
print(sum_iter)
print("Time taken by iterative loop:")
print(iter_time)
```

Chapter 14

String Manipulation Basics

Character Data and Encoding

In the computational framework of text processing, a string is represented as an ordered sequence of characters, formally described as

$$s = \langle c_1, c_2, \ldots, c_n \rangle,$$

where each element c_i is drawn from a defined alphabet such as the Unicode or ASCII character set. The internal representation of these characters in R is governed by encoding standards that ensure consistency across platforms. This section establishes the theoretical basis for string data by discussing the immutable nature of strings, the impact of multi-byte encoding, and the role of normalization in preserving the semantic equivalence of text despite superficial differences in character composition.

Extraction and Construction of Substrings

By considering a string as a finite sequence, the extraction of subsequences, or substrings, can be rigorously formalized. Given a string $s = \langle c_1, c_2, \ldots, c_n \rangle$, the extraction operation defines a substring $s_{[i:j]}$ as

$$s_{[i:j]} = \langle c_i, c_{i+1}, \ldots, c_j \rangle, \quad 1 \leq i \leq j \leq n.$$

This operation serves as the cornerstone for various text manipulation functions, enabling precise isolation of segments based on positional indices. Furthermore, the construction of new strings through the insertion or deletion of segments involves a concatenation process that builds upon the defined substring extraction, thereby allowing for a systematic exploration of string modification in computational environments.

Concatenation and Formatting

The operation of concatenation is integral to the synthesis of larger strings from constituent fragments. Mathematically, if two strings are defined as

$$s_1 = \langle a_1, a_2, \ldots, a_m \rangle \quad \text{and} \quad s_2 = \langle b_1, b_2, \ldots, b_n \rangle,$$

their concatenation is expressed as

$$s_1 \odot s_2 = \langle a_1, a_2, \ldots, a_m, b_1, b_2, \ldots, b_n \rangle.$$

This binary operation is not merely a matter of joining sequences; it also encapsulates the principles of formatting, where interposing delimiters or embedding structural separators contributes to the clarity and readability of the resulting text. The theoretical underpinnings of concatenation provide a basis for addressing challenges related to variable-length sequences and the dynamic assembly of text within a computational context.

Transformations and Comparisons

Textual data frequently undergoes a variety of transformations aimed at standardizing or reformatting its content. Among the basic operations in this domain are case conversion, whitespace trimming, and the removal of extraneous characters. Such operations can be described as mapping functions that transform a given string $s = \langle c_1, c_2, \ldots, c_n \rangle$ into a new string

$$t = f(s),$$

where the function f applies a deterministic rule to each element or section of the string. In addition to transformation, comparative operations play an essential role in string manipulation. Lexical comparison involves assessing strings via an elementwise examination of character codes, thus establishing a total order over the set of possible strings. This comparison is fundamental to sorting operations and search algorithms, where precise definitions of equality and order are crucial. The interplay between transformation and comparison operations forms the basis for advanced text processing techniques and serves as a bridge between theoretical computer science and practical data handling.

R Code Snippet

```r
# String Manipulation Basics Demonstration in R

# 1. Representing a string as an ordered sequence of characters
#     Mathematical representation: s = < c1, c2, ..., cn >
s <- "Hello, R World!"
# Convert the string to a vector of characters using strsplit
char_seq <- unlist(strsplit(s, split = ""))
cat("Character sequence of s:\n")
print(char_seq)

# 2. Extraction of Substrings
#     Formal definition: s[i:j] = < c_i, c_{i+1}, ..., c_j >
# Using the built-in substring() function to extract a substring:
# For example, extract characters from position 8 to 9
substr_extract <- substring(s, 8, 9)
cat("\nExtracted substring (positions 8 to 9):\n")
print(substr_extract)

# Alternatively, define a custom function to mimic vector indexing
↪     for substring extraction
extract_substring <- function(s, start, end) {
  # Convert the string into a vector of characters
  chars <- unlist(strsplit(s, split = ""))
  # Validate index boundaries
  if (start < 1 || end > length(chars)) {
    stop("Index out of bounds")
  }
  # Extract characters from start to end and concatenate them back
  substring_result <- paste(chars[start:end], collapse = "")
  return(substring_result)
}
# Example usage of custom extraction: extract first 5 characters
custom_substr <- extract_substring(s, 1, 5)
cat("\nCustom function extracted substring (positions 1 to 5):\n")
print(custom_substr)

# 3. Concatenation and Formatting
```

```r
#    Mathematical concatenation: s1   s2 = < a1, a2, ..., a_m, b1,
↪    b2, ..., b_n >
s1 <- "Hello"
s2 <- "R"
# Use paste0 or paste to concatenate; here we add a space delimiter
concatenated <- paste0(s1, " ", s2)
cat("\nConcatenated string (s1  s2):\n")
print(concatenated)


# Constructing a sentence from individual words using concatentation
words <- c("Data", "Science", "with", "R")
sentence <- paste(words, collapse = " ")
cat("\nSentence constructed by concatenating words:\n")
print(sentence)

# 4. Transformations and Comparisons
# Transformation mapping: t = f(s) where f applies a deterministic
↪    rule

s_mixed <- "   R is Amazing!   "
# Case conversion: transform to lowercase and uppercase
s_lower <- tolower(s_mixed)
s_upper <- toupper(s_mixed)
# Trimming whitespace from the beginning and end
s_trim <- trimws(s_mixed)

cat("\nOriginal string with spaces and mixed case:\n")
print(s_mixed)
cat("\nLowercase conversion:\n")
print(s_lower)
cat("\nUppercase conversion:\n")
print(s_upper)
cat("\nTrimmed string:\n")
print(s_trim)


# Removing punctuation using regular expressions (gsub)
# This demonstrates a transformation that maps s to a new string
↪    without punctuation.
s_no_punct <- gsub("[[:punct:]]", "", s)
cat("\nString after removing punctuation:\n")
print(s_no_punct)

# 5. Lexical Comparisons
# Lexical comparison uses elementwise evaluation of character codes
string1 <- "apple"
string2 <- "banana"
# Check for equality and lexicographical order
is_equal <- (string1 == string2)
lex_order <- (string1 < string2)  # TRUE if string1 comes before
↪    string2 lexically

cat("\nLexical Comparison:\n")
cat("Are 'apple' and 'banana' equal? ", is_equal, "\n")
```

81

```
cat("Does 'apple' come before 'banana'? ", lex_order, "\n")
```

Chapter 15

Regular Expressions

Foundational Principles of Regular Expressions

Regular expressions originate in formal language theory and serve as a concise means of describing sets of strings over a finite alphabet Σ. Their definition is inherently recursive. The simplest expressions include the empty string ϵ and individual elements of Σ. More complex expressions are generated by applying fundamental operators such as union, concatenation, and the Kleene star. In this framework, each regular expression corresponds to a well-defined language—a set of strings that satisfy the given expression—thereby forming a mathematical basis for string pattern representation.

Syntactic Constructs and Notational Conventions

The syntax of regular expressions relies on a collection of metacharacters and operators designed for precise pattern specification. Parentheses are employed for grouping and establishing precedence, while square brackets define character classes that encapsulate specific subsets of Σ. The period symbol . is used to represent any single character, and quantifiers such as the asterisk * denote zero or more repetitions of the preceding pattern. Additionally, the plus symbol + indicates one or more occurrences, and the question mark ? signifies optionality. The meticulous use of these operators, coupled with appropriate delimiters, guarantees that even highly intricate pattern specifications can be expressed in a compact and unambiguous form.

Mechanisms of Pattern Matching in Text Processing

In text processing, the execution of pattern matching involves the systematic scanning of a text sequence to identify substrings that conform to a defined regular expression. This process is underpinned by the transformation of regular expressions into abstract automata, which may be either nondeterministic or deterministic in nature. The automata framework facilitates the efficient traversal of text, enabling the rapid detection and extraction of segments that satisfy the pattern. The interaction between the formal properties of regular expressions and the operational principles of finite automata establishes a robust methodology for addressing complex text parsing challenges in R.

Analytical Perspectives on Regular Expression Operators

A detailed examination of regular expression operators reveals a rich algebraic structure that enables the encoding of diverse pattern constraints. Unary operators such as the Kleene star $*$ articulate the iteration of a pattern, while binary operators support the sequential concatenation and alternation (denoted by the vertical bar |) of subpatterns. The precise ordering of these operators, according to well-defined precedence rules, ensures an unambiguous interpretation of composite expressions. Furthermore, the capability to nest expressions within grouped constructs allows for hierarchical pattern specification that effectively mirrors the structural composition of text. This analytical perspective underpins the application of regular expressions to sophisticated text processing tasks, providing a rigorous toolset for the extraction and manipulation of data.

R Code Snippet

```r
# Recursive function to perform simplified regex matching.
# This function supports:
#    - Literal characters.
#    - The dot operator '.' to match any single character.
#    - The Kleene star '*' to match zero or more occurrences of the
#      preceding element.
isMatch <- function(text, pattern) {
  # If the pattern is empty, the text must also be empty for a
  #    complete match.
  if (nchar(pattern) == 0) {
    return(nchar(text) == 0)
  }

  # Check if the first character of the text matches the first
  #    character of the pattern.
  # The match is successful if the text is not empty and either:
  #    - The characters are identical, or
  #    - The pattern contains '.' which matches any character.
  first_match <- (nchar(text) > 0 &&
                  (substr(pattern, 1, 1) == substr(text, 1, 1) ||
                   substr(pattern, 1, 1) == "."))

  # Check if the pattern contains a '*' in the second position.
  if (nchar(pattern) >= 2 && substr(pattern, 2, 2) == "*") {
    # Two scenarios are possible:
    # 1. The '*' signifies 0 occurrences of the preceding element.
    #    Skip these two characters in the pattern.
    # 2. If the first characters match, consume one character from
    #    the text and attempt the match again with the same pattern.
    return(isMatch(text, substr(pattern, 3, nchar(pattern))) ||
           (first_match && isMatch(substr(text, 2, nchar(text)),
              pattern)))
  } else {
    # If there is no '*' operator, proceed to match the next
    #    characters.
    return(first_match && isMatch(substr(text, 2, nchar(text)),
                                  substr(pattern, 2,
                                     nchar(pattern))))
  }
}


# ----------------------------------------------------------------
# Testing the isMatch function with a variety of test cases.
# These tests demonstrate how the recursive matching algorithm
#    processes:
#    - Literal characters.
#    - The Kleene star '*' operator.
#    - The dot '.' wildcard.
test_cases <- list(
```

```r
    list(text = "aa",          pattern = "a",          expected =
    ↪  FALSE),
    list(text = "aa",          pattern = "a*",         expected = TRUE),
    ↪  # 'a*' can match one or more 'a's.
    list(text = "ab",          pattern = ".*",         expected = TRUE),
    ↪  # '.*' matches any sequence of characters.
    list(text = "aab",         pattern = "c*a*b",      expected = TRUE),
    ↪  # Complex pattern with '*' for non-matching prefix.
    list(text = "mississippi",pattern = "mis*is*p*.",expected = FALSE)
)

cat("Testing isMatch function:\n")
for (tc in test_cases) {
  result <- isMatch(tc$text, tc$pattern)
  cat(sprintf("Text: '%s', Pattern: '%s' => Expected: %s, Result:
  ↪  %s\n",
            tc$text, tc$pattern, tc$expected, result))
}


# ----------------------------------------------------------------
# Demonstration of R's built-in regular expression functionality.

# Example 1: Using union (alternation) with the '|' operator.
# The pattern 'apple|banana' matches either "apple" or "banana".
texts <- c("apple", "banana", "cranberry", "date", "elderberry")
pattern_union <- "apple|banana"
matches_union <- grep(pattern_union, texts, value = TRUE)
cat("\nTexts matching the union pattern 'apple|banana':",
    paste(matches_union, collapse = ", "), "\n")

# Example 2: Replacing vowels using a character class.
# The pattern "[aeiou]" matches any vowel; we replace each vowel
↪  with '*'.
pattern_vowels <- "[aeiou]"
texts_replaced <- gsub(pattern_vowels, "*", texts)
cat("Texts after replacing vowels with '*':",
    paste(texts_replaced, collapse = ", "), "\n")

# Example 3: Demonstrating grouping and concatenation.
# Here we insert a dash between a sequence of letters and a sequence
↪  of digits.
text_sample <- "abc123def"
# The pattern "([A-Za-z]+)([0-9]+)" uses grouping to separate
↪  letters and digits.
modified_text <- gsub("([A-Za-z]+)([0-9]+)", "\\1-\\2", text_sample)
cat("\nOriginal text:", text_sample, "\nModified text:",
↪  modified_text, "\n")

# Example 4: Using regexpr to locate a pattern with a wildcard.
# The pattern "a.c" matches 'a' followed by any character and then
↪  'c'.
pattern_dot <- "a.c"
text_ex <- "abc acc adc aec"
```

```r
match_info <- regexpr(pattern_dot, text_ex)
cat("\nSearching for pattern 'a.c' in text:", text_ex, "\n")
cat("Match starts at position:", match_info,
    "with length:", attr(match_info, "match.length"), "\n")

# Example 5: Using gregexpr to find all occurrences of one or more
↪  'a' characters.
# The '+' quantifier specifies one or more occurrences of the
↪  preceding element.
pattern_plus <- "a+"
text_plus <- "caaab  a aaaa aa"
matches_plus <- gregexpr(pattern_plus, text_plus)
all_matches <- regmatches(text_plus, matches_plus)
cat("\nAll matches for pattern 'a+' in text:", text_plus, "\n")
cat("Matches found:", paste(unlist(all_matches), collapse = ", "),
↪  "\n")
```

Chapter 16

Date and Time Classes

Conceptual Framework of Temporal Representations

Temporal data in computational systems often necessitates a rigorous formalism in order to capture the multifaceted representations of dates and times. In the R programming environment, such representations are encapsulated within a small set of built-in classes that provide a robust foundation for handling calendrical and time-of-day values. The inherent complexity of temporal information is addressed by abstracting dates and times into discrete numerical entities, where calendar dates are typically interpreted as counts of days and time instances as counts of seconds relative to a predetermined epoch. This abstraction permits the application of mathematical operations and facilitates the interoperability between various data types within statistical computations.

The *Date* Class and its Internal Encoding

The *Date* class is designed to represent a calendar date independent of any particular time of day, thereby enabling a concentration on the chronology of events without the complications introduced by intra-day variability. Internally, objects of the *Date* class adhere to a scalar representation, often implemented as an integer value that signifies the number of days elapsed since a specified origin. Conventionally, the epoch is established as 1970-01-01, although the internal arithmetic seamlessly accommodates calendar arithmetic and chronological comparisons. The explicit delineation of dates into a singular numerical foundation ensures that operations such as addition, subtraction, and interval determination are executed with both precision and clarity.

The *POSIXct* and *POSIXlt* Classes: Structural and Semantic Nuances

In contrast to the *Date* class, the *POSIXct* and *POSIXlt* classes encapsulate the full granularity of date and time information. The *POSIXct* class typically represents time as a continuous count of seconds since a predefined epoch, thereby offering a simple yet efficient method for temporal representation that is amenable to arithmetic operations. Conversely, the *POSIXlt* class provides a more decomposed view by representing time as a list of distinct components such as seconds, minutes, hours, day, month, and year. This duality between a compact, scalar representation and an expanded, component-based structure facilitates both computational efficiency and human interpretability. The structural design of these classes underpins a broad spectrum of analytical tasks by permitting the conversion between different temporal resolutions and formats within the R ecosystem.

Time Zone Considerations and Localization Mechanisms

Time zones introduce a layer of complexity that is critical when processing temporal data, particularly in applications spanning multiple geographical regions. Within the R environment, temporal objects may incorporate metadata that specifies time zone information, thereby enabling the localization of date and time calculations. The management of time zones is intrinsically linked to the notion of universal coordinated time and local time offsets, aspects that are meticulously handled by the built-in functions associated with temporal classes. The ability to translate between different time zones without loss of precision is achieved through rigorous internal methods that account for factors such as daylight saving transitions and regional time zone variances. Consequently, the treatment of time zones is executed in a manner that ensures both consistency across disparate datasets and the fidelity of temporal computations.

Temporal Arithmetic and Comparative Operations

The manipulation of temporal objects in R is rendered intuitive through the implementation of arithmetic and comparison operations directly on instances of date and time classes. Addition and subtraction operations are defined in such a way that they respect the underlying temporal units—days for the *Date* class and seconds for *POSIXct* objects. Moreover, relational operations such as equality, inequality, and ordering have been rigorously defined to reflect the inherent sequential nature of time. These operations permit the computation of intervals, the derivation of duration differences, and the execution of chronological ordering without necessitating manual conversion procedures. This algebraic treatment of temporal data facilitates complex analytical endeavors, wherein the discrete arithmetic of dates and times is seamlessly interwoven with broader statistical integrations and algorithmic processes.

R Code Snippet

```
# ----------------------------------------------------------------
# Date and Time Classes in R: Comprehensive Code Snippet
# This snippet demonstrates:
# 1. Creation of Date, POSIXct, and POSIXlt objects.
# 2. Internal numerical encoding of dates and times.
# 3. Time zone handling and conversion.
# 4. Temporal arithmetic and comparative operations.
# 5. Vectorized operations and handling of missing values.
# ----------------------------------------------------------------

# 1. Date Class Demonstration
# Create a Date object from a string.
my_date <- as.Date("2023-10-11")
print(my_date)  # Output: "2023-10-11"

# Obtain internal numeric representation: number of days since
↪  "1970-01-01"
days_since_epoch <- as.numeric(my_date)
cat("Days since epoch (1970-01-01):", days_since_epoch, "\n")

# 2. POSIXct Class Demonstration
```

90

```r
# Create a POSIXct object representing a specific date-time in UTC.
my_time_ct <- as.POSIXct("2023-10-11 15:30:00", tz = "UTC")
print(my_time_ct)  # Output will be in UTC

# Convert POSIXct to its numeric representation: seconds since
↪   "1970-01-01 00:00:00 UTC".
seconds_since_epoch <- as.numeric(my_time_ct)
cat("Seconds since epoch:", seconds_since_epoch, "\n")

# 3. POSIXlt Class Demonstration
# Convert the POSIXct object to a POSIXlt object for detailed
↪   component access.
my_time_lt <- as.POSIXlt(my_time_ct)
print(my_time_lt)

# Accessing individual components from POSIXlt (adjusting for R's
↪   indexing)
cat("Year:", my_time_lt$year + 1900, "\n")    # 'year' returns years
↪   since 1900
cat("Month:", my_time_lt$mon + 1, "\n")        # 'mon' is 0-indexed:
↪   0 = January
cat("Day:", my_time_lt$mday, "\n")
cat("Hour:", my_time_lt$hour, "\n")
cat("Minute:", my_time_lt$min, "\n")
cat("Second:", round(my_time_lt$sec, 2), "\n")

# 4. Time Zone Considerations
# Create a POSIXct object in the "America/New_York" timezone.
my_time_est <- as.POSIXct("2023-10-11 15:30:00", tz =
↪   "America/New_York")
print(my_time_est)

# Convert the time from EST to UTC using format() to display the new
↪   time zone.
converted_time <- format(my_time_est, tz = "UTC", usetz = TRUE)
cat("Time in UTC:", converted_time, "\n")

# 5. Temporal Arithmetic and Comparative Operations
# For Date objects, arithmetic operates on days.
new_date <- my_date + 7  # Add 7 days to my_date
cat("New Date after 7 days:", new_date, "\n")

# Calculate difference in days between two Date objects.
date_diff <- as.numeric(new_date - my_date)
cat("Difference in days:", date_diff, "\n")

# For POSIXct objects, arithmetic is performed on seconds.
new_time_ct <- my_time_ct + 3600  # Add 3600 seconds (1 hour) to
↪   my_time_ct
cat("New POSIXct Time after 1 hour:", new_time_ct, "\n")

# Compute the difference in seconds between two POSIXct objects.
time_diff <- as.numeric(new_time_ct - my_time_ct)
```

91

```r
cat("Difference in seconds:", time_diff, "\n")

# 6. Relational Comparisons
# Compare Date objects.
if (my_date < new_date) {
    cat(my_date, "is earlier than", new_date, "\n")
}

# Compare two POSIXct objects.
if (my_time_ct < new_time_ct) {
    cat(my_time_ct, "is earlier than", new_time_ct, "\n")
}

# 7. Vectorized Operations with Dates
# Create a vector of dates.
dates_vector <- as.Date(c("2023-10-10", "2023-10-11", "2023-10-12"))
print(dates_vector)

# Vectorized addition: add different day increments.
dates_vector_plus <- dates_vector + c(1, 2, 3)
print(dates_vector_plus)

# 8. Handling Missing Values with Dates
dates_with_na <- c(as.Date("2023-10-10"), NA, as.Date("2023-10-12"))
print(dates_with_na)
# Calculate differences; note that NA propagates.
dates_diff_na <- diff(dates_with_na)
print(dates_diff_na)

# 9. Converting Strings to Dates with Specified Format
# Given a date string in the format "day-month-year":
date_str <- "11-10-2023"
date_obj <- as.Date(date_str, format = "%d-%m-%Y")
cat("Converted date from string:", date_obj, "\n")
```

Chapter 17

Basic Statistical Functions

Arithmetic Mean

The arithmetic mean is defined for a dataset comprising observations $x_1, x_2, \ldots, x_n$ as

$$\bar{x} = \frac{1}{n} \sum_{i=1}^{n} x_i.$$

This measure encapsulates the central location of the dataset by averaging all values and thereby minimizing the sum of squared deviations from itself. In the context of statistical estimation and error minimization, the arithmetic mean serves as the optimal estimator under the assumption of isotropic error distributions. Its mathematical properties render it fundamental in analyses wherein the dispersion of values is quantified relative to a unique central value.

Median

The median is an order statistic that represents the central element of an ordered dataset. For the ordered sequence $x_{(1)} \leq x_{(2)} \leq \cdots \leq x_{(n)}$, the median is determined by the parity of n. When the number of observations is odd, the median is defined as

$$x_{\left(\frac{n+1}{2}\right)},$$

whereas for an even number of observations the median is computed as the arithmetic mean of the two central values,

$$\frac{x_{\left(\frac{n}{2}\right)} + x_{\left(\frac{n}{2}+1\right)}}{2}.$$

This function is particularly valued in distributional analyses characterized by the presence of outliers or skewed data, as it is not as susceptible to extreme values as the arithmetic mean. The median thereby provides a robust measure of central tendency that complements other statistical indicators.

Standard Deviation

Standard deviation quantifies the spread of a dataset by measuring the average distance of each observation from the arithmetic mean. For a sample consisting of $x_1, x_2, \ldots, x_n$ with arithmetic mean $\bar{x}$, the sample standard deviation is formulated as

$$s = \sqrt{\frac{1}{n-1} \sum_{i=1}^{n} (x_i - \bar{x})^2}.$$

This measure serves as an essential descriptor of variability within the dataset, encapsulating the degree of dispersion through the square root of the average of squared deviations. The sensitivity of the standard deviation to variations in the data makes it a pivotal tool in inferential statistics and error analysis. Its application is central to quantifying uncertainty and assessing the reliability of statistical estimates.

R Code Snippet

```
# Define a sample numeric vector representing a dataset
data <- c(5, 8, 12, 20, 7, 15, 25)

#-------------------------------------------------------------
# 1. Arithmetic Mean
# The arithmetic mean is defined as:
#    mean = (x1 + x2 + ... + xn) / n
# This function computes the arithmetic mean from scratch.
arithmetic_mean <- function(x) {
  n <- length(x)
  total <- sum(x)
```

```
  mean_value <- total / n
  return(mean_value)
}


#---------------------------------------------------------------
# 2. Median
# For an ordered dataset, the median is:
#    - The middle element if the number of observations is odd.
#    - The arithmetic mean of the two middle elements if even.
# This custom function implements the median calculation.
custom_median <- function(x) {
  sorted_x <- sort(x)
  n <- length(sorted_x)
  if(n %% 2 == 1) {
    # Odd number of observations: Return the middle element.
    median_value <- sorted_x[(n + 1) / 2]
  } else {
    # Even number of observations: Return the average of the two
    ↪ central elements.
    median_value <- (sorted_x[n / 2] + sorted_x[(n / 2) + 1]) / 2
  }
  return(median_value)
}


#---------------------------------------------------------------
# 3. Standard Deviation
# The sample standard deviation is defined by:
#    s = sqrt( sum((xi - mean)^2) / (n - 1) )
# This function computes the standard deviation taking into account
# the degrees of freedom (n - 1) for an unbiased estimator.
sample_standard_deviation <- function(x) {
  n <- length(x)
  x_mean <- arithmetic_mean(x)
  squared_diff <- (x - x_mean)^2   # Compute squares of deviations
  variance <- sum(squared_diff) / (n - 1)   # Sample variance
  std_dev <- sqrt(variance)   # Standard deviation
  return(std_dev)
}


#---------------------------------------------------------------
# Using built-in R functions for verification and comparison:
builtin_mean   <- mean(data)
builtin_median <- median(data)
builtin_sd <- sd(data)


#---------------------------------------------------------------
# Print Results: Compare custom implementations with built-in
↪ functions
cat("Data:", data, "\n")
cat("Arithmetic Mean (Custom):", arithmetic_mean(data), "\n")
cat("Arithmetic Mean (Built-in):", builtin_mean, "\n")
cat("Median (Custom):", custom_median(data), "\n")
cat("Median (Built-in):", builtin_median, "\n")
```

```
cat("Standard Deviation (Custom):", sample_standard_deviation(data),
↪  "\n")
cat("Standard Deviation (Built-in):", builtin_sd, "\n")
```

Chapter 18

Summary Functions and Descriptive Statistics

Conceptual Framework for Descriptive Summaries

Descriptive statistics offer a rigorous abstraction that encapsulates the essential characteristics of a dataset. This abstraction is achieved through a series of numerical summaries which capture the central tendency, dispersion, and overall distribution of the data. The summary function exemplifies this abstraction by aggregating multiple statistical measures into a single, coherent output. For a numeric vector x comprising n observations, key metrics such as the minimum value
$min(x)$, the first quartile $Q_1(x)$, the median, the arithmetic mean
$barx =$
$frac1n$
$sum_{i=1}^{n} x_i$, the third quartile $Q_3(x)$, and the maximum value
$max(x)$, are computed and presented together. The resulting compilation provides an immediate numerical portrait of the dataset without necessitating further manipulation of raw values.

Components and Computational Aspects of Summary Functions

The summary function is typically designed to operate polymorphically across different data classes while maintaining computational efficiency and statistical reliability. When the input is a numeric vector, the function orders the data to derive order statistics. Denote the sorted sequence by $x_{(1)}$ $\le x_{(2)}$ $\le$ $\cdots$ $\le x_{(n)}$. From this sequence, the minimum and maximum values are directly available, whereas the quartiles and median are extracted from appropriate positions within the ordered set. In cases where the data are non-numeric, such as factors or character vectors, the summary function adapts by producing frequency counts or other contextually relevant summaries. This multiplicity of output types underscores the function's versatility and its integral role as a bridge between raw data and subsequent analytical procedures.

Statistical and Algorithmic Considerations in Summary Computations

The computation underlying summary functions is anchored both in well-established statistical theory and in efficient algorithmic design. The calculation of order statistics necessitates a sorting procedure, which is executed using optimized algorithms to ensure scalability with respect to dataset size. In determining quantiles, the issue of non-integral index positions often arises; linear interpolation between adjacent order statistics is employed when np is not an integer, ensuring that the quantile estimates remain continuous functions of the probability level p. This methodical approach guarantees that the derived estimates of $Q_1(x)$ and $Q_3(x)$, among others, reflect an accurate representation of the data distribution. Moreover, the algorithms account for data irregularities such as missing or non-finite values, thereby reinforcing the robustness of the summary outputs in the face of real-world complexities.

R Code Snippet

```
#------------------------------------------------------------
# This R code snippet demonstrates the computation of
# key summary statistics for a numeric vector, including:
#    - Minimum and Maximum values
#    - Arithmetic Mean (x), computed as: x = (1/n)*sum(x)
#    - First Quartile Q1, Median, and Third Quartile Q3
#
# The quartiles are computed using a custom linear interpolation
# algorithm when np is not an integer.
#------------------------------------------------------------

# Sample numeric vector (you can change these values to test with
↪    other datasets)
x <- c(12, 7, 3, 15, 20, 8, 10, 5, 18, 25)

# Number of observations
n <- length(x)

# Compute Arithmetic Mean using the formula:
#     x = (1/n) * sum(x_i)
x_mean <- sum(x) / n

# Sorting the vector to get order statistics:
x_sorted <- sort(x)

# Minimum and Maximum values from the sorted vector:
x_min <- x_sorted[1]
x_max <- x_sorted[n]

# Custom function to compute quantiles using linear interpolation.
# For a probability p (e.g., 0.25 for Q1, 0.5 for Median, 0.75 for
↪    Q3):
# 1. Compute the index: idx = n * p.
# 2. If idx is an integer, return the value at that index.
# 3. Otherwise, linearly interpolate between the floor and ceiling
↪    indices.
custom_quantile <- function(vec, p) {
  # Remove NA values and sort the data
  vec <- sort(vec, na.last = NA)
  n <- length(vec)
  if(n == 0) return(NA)
  if(p <= 0) return(vec[1])
  if(p >= 1) return(vec[n])

  # Calculate the index corresponding to the p-th quantile
  idx <- n * p

  # If idx is an integer, no interpolation is needed.
  if(idx == floor(idx)) {
    return(vec[idx])
```

```r
  } else {
    lower <- floor(idx)
    upper <- lower + 1
    weight <- idx - lower
    # Linear interpolation:
    # quantile = x[lower] * (1 - weight) + x[upper] * weight
    return(vec[lower] * (1 - weight) + vec[upper] * weight)
  }
}


# Compute Q1, Median, and Q3 using the custom quantile function
Q1 <- custom_quantile(x, 0.25)
median_custom <- custom_quantile(x, 0.5)
Q3 <- custom_quantile(x, 0.75)

# For comparison, also compute the median using R's built-in
↪ function
median_builtin <- median(x)

# Display the computed summary statistics
cat("Number of observations (n):", n, "\n")
cat("Minimum:", x_min, "\n")
cat("First Quartile (Q1):", Q1, "\n")
cat("Median (Custom):", median_custom, "\n")
cat("Median (Built-in):", median_builtin, "\n")
cat("Arithmetic Mean (x):", x_mean, "\n")
cat("Third Quartile (Q3):", Q3, "\n")
cat("Maximum:", x_max, "\n\n")

# Additionally, show the full summary using the built-in summary()
↪ function
cat("Summary using built-in summary() function:\n")
print(summary(x))
```

Chapter 19

Arithmetic and Vectorized Operations

Foundational Concepts in Vectorized Arithmetic

In many computational environments, arithmetic operations are defined in an element-wise fashion when applied to vector objects. Given two vectors, $x = (x_1, x_2, \ldots, x_n)$ and $y = (y_1, y_2, \ldots, y_n)$, the addition operation is defined as

$$x + y = (x_1 + y_1, x_2 + y_2, \ldots, x_n + y_n).$$

Similarly, subtraction, multiplication, and division are performed element-wise, so that for any scalar a and vector x, the product is given by

$$a \cdot x = (a \cdot x_1, a \cdot x_2, \ldots, a \cdot x_n).$$

This approach negates the need for explicit iteration over vector elements, thereby elevating the abstraction level and enabling concise expression of operations.

Mathematical Formalism of Vectorized Operations

The algebraic properties of these operations mirror those of their scalar counterparts, but with an inherent parallelism. For instance, the distributive property in a vector context is formulated as

$$a \cdot (x + y) = a \cdot x + a \cdot y,$$

where a is a scalar and x, y are vectors of equal length. The associative and commutative properties also persist:

$$x + y = y + x \quad \text{and} \quad (x + y) + z = x + (y + z),$$

where $z = (z_1, z_2, \ldots, z_n)$ is an additional vector. The element-wise operations are underpinned by these fundamental identities, ensuring that the structure of arithmetic remains consistent even when expressed in a high-level vectorized manner.

Operational Efficiency and Computational Mechanisms

The efficiency of vectorized arithmetic operations is a consequence of several factors inherent in optimized computational implementations. Vectorized operations are executed at a lower level by compiled routines that harness the capabilities of modern processor architectures. By applying a single arithmetic operator over an entire vector, the overhead associated with explicit looping constructs is substantially diminished. The internal implementation often takes advantage of low-level memory access patterns and, in cases where the architecture permits, single instruction multiple data (SIMD) techniques. Such optimizations render operations on large data sets both time-efficient and resource-effective.

Computational Implications and Theoretical Considerations

The vectorized paradigm extends beyond mere syntactic convenience; it serves as a bridge between abstract mathematical notation and concrete computational execution. By expressing operations in a vectorized form, mathematical models are represented in a manner that aligns closely with their theoretical formulations. For example, the expression for the Euclidean norm of a vector,

$$\|x\| = \sqrt{x_1^2 + x_2^2 + \cdots + x_n^2},$$

exemplifies how a summation of squared elements can be computed efficiently using vectorized routines. This alignment not only simplifies the translation of mathematical theory into practice but also facilitates parallelization and improved data locality, both of which are critical in large-scale numerical computations.

Numerical Accuracy and Precision in Vectorized Operations

Arithmetic operations performed in a vectorized context are subject to the same concerns regarding numerical precision and rounding errors as encountered in scalar operations. In computations that involve floating-point arithmetic, the accumulation of rounding errors can become significant over large vectors. The inherent strategies for mitigating such issues include algorithmic design choices that prioritize numerical stability. Vectorized environments typically adhere to the IEEE Standard for Floating-Point Arithmetic, thereby ensuring a consistent framework for error analysis and correction when performing extensive arithmetic computations.

R Code Snippet

```
# Comprehensive R code snippet demonstrating vectorized arithmetic
↪   operations

# Define two vectors x and y
x <- c(1, 2, 3, 4, 5)
y <- c(10, 20, 30, 40, 50)

# Element-wise arithmetic operations
addition       <- x + y        # Element-wise addition: (1+10,
↪   2+20, ...)
subtraction    <- y - x        # Element-wise subtraction: (10-1,
↪   20-2, ...)
multiplication <- x * y        # Element-wise multiplication:
↪   (1*10, 2*20, ...)
division       <- y / x        # Element-wise division: (10/1,
↪   20/2, ...)

# Scalar multiplication: multiply every element of x by scalar 'a'
a <- 3
scalar_product <- a * x        # (3*1, 3*2, 3*3, ...)
```

```r
# Demonstrate the distributive property: a * (x + y) == a * x + a *
↪  y
lhs <- a * (x + y)                # Left-hand side of the equation
rhs <- a * x + a * y              # Right-hand side of the equation
distributive_check <- all.equal(lhs, rhs)  # Should return TRUE if
↪  both expressions equal

# Compute the Euclidean norm of vector x: sqrt(sum(x^2))
euclidean_norm <- sqrt(sum(x^2))

# Illustrate potential numerical precision issues with
↪  floating-point arithmetic
# For example, summing 0.1 ten times may not exactly equal 1.0 due
↪  to rounding errors
float_sum <- sum(rep(0.1, 10))
float_sum_rounded <- round(float_sum, 1)

# Print and display all computed results
cat("Vector x:", x, "\n")
cat("Vector y:", y, "\n")
cat("Element-wise Addition (x + y):", addition, "\n")
cat("Element-wise Subtraction (y - x):", subtraction, "\n")
cat("Element-wise Multiplication (x * y):", multiplication, "\n")
cat("Element-wise Division (y / x):", division, "\n")
cat("Scalar Multiplication (", a, " * x):", scalar_product, "\n")
cat("Distributive Property Check (a*(x+y) == a*x + a*y):",
↪  distributive_check, "\n")
cat("Euclidean Norm of x:", euclidean_norm, "\n")
cat("Floating-point Sum of ten 0.1's:", float_sum, " (Rounded:",
↪  float_sum_rounded, ")\n")
```

Chapter 20

Control Flow: If, Else, and Switch

Foundations of Conditional Execution

In modern computing systems, conditional constructs direct the flow of execution by facilitating decision-making processes based on the evaluation of Boolean expressions. Let C denote a condition such that $C \in \{true, false\}$. Upon evaluation, the system selects one of two mutually exclusive paths of execution. This binary decision mechanism is fundamental to algorithmic control, enabling deterministic progression through computational states. Such constructs are pivotal in establishing rigorous execution semantics and form an integral part of formal models in computer science, wherein the behavior of software is characterized through state-transition systems and logical predicates.

The `if` and `else` Constructs: Syntax and Semantics

The conditional construct expressed through the `if` statement constitutes one of the most elemental paradigms for control flow redirection. Consider a condition C and two distinct blocks of instructions, denoted S_1 and S_2. The semantics of the construct are such that if C evaluates to *true*, then the instructions in S_1 are executed; if C evaluates to *false*, the execution continues with the instructions in S_2. Formally, this mechanism can be symbolized as:

$$\text{if } C \text{ then } S_1, \text{ else } S_2.$$

The structure supports further extension through additional conditional tests, resulting in a nested decision hierarchy. The precise formulation of these constructs is essential for the formal analysis of algorithmic correctness and efficiency, as they provide the basis for verifying that the control flow adheres strictly to the intended logical and state-transition models.

The `switch` Statement: An Examination of Multi-Branch Control

An alternative mechanism to manage multiple discrete execution paths is provided by the `switch` statement. In this construction, an expression E is evaluated and compared against a finite set of candidate values, typically denoted as $\{v_1, v_2, \ldots, v_n\}$. For a particular index i satisfying $E = v_i$, the control is transferred to the corresponding block of instructions S_i. This relationship may be abstracted as a mapping function:

$$f : \{v_1, v_2, \ldots, v_n\} \to \{S_1, S_2, \ldots, S_n\},$$

where the evaluation of E triggers the selection of a unique execution branch. The structure of the `switch` statement offers conciseness and clarity in scenarios characterized by a large number of potential discrete cases, thereby alleviating the complexity that otherwise arises from an extensive chain of `if-else` conditions.

Formal Analysis of Conditional Branching Constructs

A rigorous examination of conditional branching mechanisms necessitates an exploration of their underlying formal properties. The semantics of the `if-else` construct adhere to the principles of Boolean algebra, ensuring that operations such as conjunction, disjunction, and negation are faithfully represented within an algorithm's state transitions. In abstract terms, consider the execution of an `if-else` construct as a mapping from an initial state P to a subsequent state P', contingent on the truth value of the condition C. In a similar vein, the `switch` statement may be regarded as a piecewise function defined on a discrete domain; each branch corresponds to a distinct subset of candidate values. This abstraction permits the derivation of metrics regarding average-case and worst-case computational complexities, which are critical for both theoretical analysis and practical optimization. The formal treatment of these conditional structures underpins efforts in proving properties such as termination and correctness, thereby reinforcing the foundational role of conditional execution in the domain of computer science.

R Code Snippet

```
# This R script demonstrates the control flow constructs discussed
↪  in this chapter,
# including the if-else construct and the switch statement to
↪  emulate conditional execution.
#
# Formal Representation:
#   if (C) then S1 else S2
# In our examples, "C" is a Boolean condition based on which a
↪  specific code block is executed.

# Example 1: Demonstration of the if-else construct.
controlFlowDemo <- function(x) {
  # Using if-else clauses to decide between execution blocks
  # S1 and S2 represent two mutually exclusive sets of instructions.
  if (x > 0) {
    message <- "x is positive"
  } else if (x == 0) {
    message <- "x is zero"
  } else {
    message <- "x is negative"
  }
  return(message)
}

# Test the controlFlowDemo function with various inputs
cat("Testing controlFlowDemo:\n")
cat("Input: 7  ->", controlFlowDemo(7), "\n")
cat("Input: 0  ->", controlFlowDemo(0), "\n")
cat("Input: -5 ->", controlFlowDemo(-5), "\n\n")

# Example 2: Demonstration of the switch statement.
# Formal Mapping function:
#   f: {v1, v2, ..., vn} -> {S1, S2, ..., Sn}
```

```r
# Here, based on a given day number (1 for Monday, 2 for Tuesday,
↪   etc.),
# a corresponding activity is selected.
dayOfWeekActivity <- function(day) {
  activity <- switch(as.character(day),
                     "1" = "Go to Gym",          # Monday
                     "2" = "Attend Yoga Class",  # Tuesday
                     "3" = "Team Meeting",        # Wednesday
                     "4" = "Visit the Library",   # Thursday
                     "5" = "Call Friends",        # Friday
                     "6" = "Family Time",         # Saturday
                     "7" = "Rest",                # Sunday
                     "Invalid day")
  return(activity)
}


# Test the dayOfWeekActivity function for each day of the week
cat("Activity Schedule:\n")
for (day in 1:7) {
  cat("Day", day, ":", dayOfWeekActivity(day), "\n")
}
cat("\n")

# Example 3: Simulation combining if-else and switch constructs.
# The function simulateDecision demonstrates:
#    - For values less than 10: using a switch based on the remainder
↪    modulo 3,
#       representing a mapping from an input value to different
↪    outcomes.
#    - For values 10 or above: a nested if-else structure to
↪    distinguish even and odd numbers.
simulateDecision <- function(value) {
  if (value < 10) {
    # Calculate the remainder when value is divided by 3.
    # This resembles the mapping:
    #   f: {0, 1, 2} -> {S0, S1, S2}
    result <- switch(as.character(value %% 3),
                     "0" = paste("Value", value, "is divisible by
                     ↪   3"),
                     "1" = paste("Value", value, "leaves a remainder
                     ↪   1 when divided by 3"),
                     "2" = paste("Value", value, "leaves a remainder
                     ↪   2 when divided by 3")
    )
  } else {
    if (value %% 2 == 0) {
      result <- paste("Value", value, "is even and >= 10")
    } else {
      result <- paste("Value", value, "is odd and >= 10")
    }
  }
  return(result)
}
```

108

```r
# Test the simulateDecision function with a range of values
testValues <- c(2, 3, 8, 10, 15, 21)
cat("Simulation Results:\n")
for (val in testValues) {
  cat(simulateDecision(val), "\n")
}

# End of R Code Snippet demonstrating the key conditional
↪   constructs.
```

Chapter 21

Loop Structures: For, While, Repeat

Fundamentals of Iterative Constructs

Within algorithmic theory and formal models of computation, looping constructs represent a fundamental mechanism for the repeated execution of a designated block of operations. Iteration is modeled as a transformation applied repeatedly over elements of a state space, typically denoted by a function $f : X \to X$, where X symbolizes the space of program states. In the context of loop structures, such transformations are scrutinized for properties such as invariance and convergence. The language semantics assign to each looping construct the ability to induce state transitions in a controlled and predictable manner, guaranteeing that every iteration encapsulates a definite progression towards a termination condition or a prescribed fixed point. This conceptual framework supports rigorous reasoning about the correctness and computational complexity of iterative algorithms.

For Loops: Deterministic Iteration over Finite Domains

The for loop is an imperative construct that iterates over a finite, predetermined set of elements. Typically, a counter variable, denoted by i, is assigned values from a well-defined sequence such as

$\{1, 2, \ldots, n\}$, where $n \in \mathbb{N}$ represents the totality of discrete iterations. Each iteration applies a sequence of operations to the current state, yielding a new state that forms the input for subsequent iterations. The formal semantics of the for loop can be captured by an unrolling mechanism in which the loop is equivalent to the sequential composition of n instances of a statement block S, such that the overall operation is represented by

$$S(1); \ S(2); \ \ldots; \ S(n).$$

This predictable control structure facilitates both explicit performance analysis and the verification of loop invariants, which serve as the backbone for proving algorithmic correctness.

While Loops: Execution Driven by Pre-Test Conditions

Contrasting with the for loop, the while loop is structured around a pre-evaluation of a Boolean condition C. Prior to each iteration, the condition C is assessed, and the loop continues to execute a designated statement block B as long as C evaluates to *true*. Formally, the while loop may be perceived as a recursive process defined by the recurrence relation

$$P_{k+1} = \begin{cases} f(P_k), & \text{if } C(P_k) = \text{true}, \\ P_k, & \text{otherwise}, \end{cases}$$

where P_k represents the program state at the kth iteration and f encapsulates the state transformation corresponding to the execution of B. The termination analysis of while loops centers on determining the existence of a loop invariant I and a well-founded measure that strictly decreases with each iteration. Such formal properties are essential for establishing both termination and the computational efficiency of algorithms integrating while loops.

Repeat Loops: Unbounded Iteration with Explicit Termination Control

The repeat loop employs an unconditional iterative approach, wherein the statement block B is executed indefinitely until an explicit termination mechanism is invoked. Unlike the while loop, the repeat construct does not rely on an implicit condition at the commencement of each cycle. Instead, termination is governed by a deliberate intervention—typically implemented as an internal break operation. This structure may be modeled by the mapping

$$x_0 \mapsto f(x_0) \mapsto f(f(x_0)) \mapsto \cdots \mapsto f^{(k)}(x_0),$$

where $f^{(k)}$ denotes the k-fold composition of f. The existence of an index $k \in \mathbb{N}$ for which the termination condition is satisfied signifies the practical boundedness of such iterations. In theoretical terms, the repeat loop exemplifies an approach to iteration that relies on external state evaluations to initiate cessation, thereby providing a versatile mechanism for operations where the termination criteria depend on dynamically evolving data.

Formal Analysis of Loop Invariants and Termination

A rigorous theoretical examination of loop structures necessitates the formulation and verification of loop invariants. Let I denote a property that holds for the state before the loop commences and is preserved under every iteration; that is, if $I(P_k)$ is true for the state P_k at the start of an iteration, then it must also hold for the state P_{k+1} produced by executing the loop body. Establishing such invariance is critical for the verification of algorithm correctness. Moreover, the notion of termination is intertwined with the existence of a well-founded ordering on the state space. The iterative application of the transformation function f must be shown to lead to a strictly decreasing sequence,

$$\phi(P_0) > \phi(P_1) > \phi(P_2) > \cdots,$$

where $\phi : X \to \mathbb{N}$ maps states to elements of a well-ordered set. The convergence of this sequence guarantees the eventual cessation of the loop. In this formal setting, each looping construct—whether deterministic, condition-driven, or unconditionally repetitive—can be analyzed using the principles of mathematical induction and fixed-point theory, thereby providing a robust framework for understanding and validating iterative algorithms.

R Code Snippet

```r
#
# ----------------------------------------------------------------------
# R Code Demonstration of Loop Structures and Formal Invariants
#
# This script illustrates the use of key loop constructs in R:
#     - For loops: Deterministic iteration over a finite domain.
#     - While loops: Pre-test condition driven iteration.
#     - Repeat loops: Unbounded iteration with explicit termination.
#
# It also incorporates comments reflecting the underlying
#     mathematical
# principles such as:
#     - State transformations f: X -> X (e.g., f(x) = x - 1 or f(x) =
#     x/2 + 1).
#     - Recurrence relations, e.g., P_{k+1} = f(P_k) when condition
#     C(P_k) is true.
#     - Loop invariants and a well-founded measure phi: X -> N with:
#             phi(P_0) > phi(P_1) > phi(P_2) > ...
#
#     ----------------------------------------------------------------------


# ---------------------------
# For Loop Example
# ---------------------------
# In this example we iterate over a finite set {1, 2, ..., n} and
#     compute the
# running sum. The loop invariant here is that at the start of each
#     iteration i,
# the variable sum_total holds the sum of numbers from 1 to i - 1.
n <- 10
sum_total <- 0

for(i in 1:n) {
    # S(i): Operation performed in the i-th iteration.
    sum_total <- sum_total + i

    # Invariant: sum_total == sum(1:(i)) after executing the i-th
    #     iteration.
    cat("For Loop - Iteration:", i, "- Running Sum:", sum_total, "\n")
}

cat("For Loop - Final Sum:", sum_total, "\n\n")

# ---------------------------
# While Loop Example
# ---------------------------
# This example demonstrates a while loop where the condition is
#     checked before each
# iteration. We mimic the recurrence:
#     P_{k+1} = f(P_k)  if C(P_k) is TRUE, where f(x) = x - 1.
```

```r
# The loop invariant is that x remains a positive integer and phi(x)
↪ = x decreases
# strictly in every iteration.
x <- 10  # Initial state P0
while(x > 0) {
  cat("While Loop - Current State x:", x, "\n")

  # Update state: f(x) = x - 1
  x <- x - 1

  # Invariant: At the start of each iteration, we have x > 0 and the
  ↪ sequence of x values
  # satisfies: phi(P_k) > phi(P_{k+1}) with phi(x) = x.
}
cat("While Loop - Loop terminated with x =", x, "\n\n")

# ---------------------------
# Repeat Loop Example
# ---------------------------
# The repeat loop performs an unconditional iteration until an
↪ explicit break is called.
# We simulate a transformation trending towards a fixed point.
# Here, f(result) = result/2 + 1 and the fixed point is the solution
↪ to:
#      x = x/2 + 1  ->  x = 2.
# The invariant is that the sequence converges to the fixed point
↪ as:
#      |new_result - result| becomes very small.
result <- 1        # Initial state
iteration <- 0

repeat {
  iteration <- iteration + 1

  # Transformation: Apply f(result) = result/2 + 1, which models
  ↪ state evolution.
  new_result <- result / 2 + 1
  cat("Repeat Loop - Iteration:", iteration, "- Result:",
  ↪ new_result, "\n")

  # Termination condition: When the change between two consecutive
  ↪ states is negligible.
  if(abs(new_result - result) < 0.001) {
    break
  }

  # Update the state for the next cycle.
  result <- new_result
}
cat("Repeat Loop - Converged Result:", result, "\n")
```

Chapter 22

User-defined Functions

Conceptual Foundations of Function Abstraction

User-defined functions represent a formal mechanism for encapsulating a sequence of operations into a single, reusable abstraction. In mathematical terms, a function is regarded as a mapping $f : A \to B$, where A denotes the domain of valid inputs and B signifies the codomain of potential outputs. When the definition of such a function is provided by the programmer, the mapping is extended beyond built-in operations to include complex, domain-specific processes. This abstraction permits the separation of computational concerns by encapsulating an operation within a definable and callable unit. The intrinsic property of reproducibility and the mathematical rigor of function composition afford both clarity and efficiency in algorithmic implementations.

Encapsulation and Modular Reuse

Encapsulation is achieved by confining a particular computational procedure within a user-defined function; this creates a well-defined interface that separates the internal implementation from its external invocation. The function body comprises a series of statements that operate solely on the provided parameters and local variables, thereby ensuring that the intrinsic logic remains isolated from the global environment. Such modularity not only prevents interference between disparate parts of a program but also enables the independent verification of the function's behavior. In formal terms, given a function f with input parameters $(a_1, a_2, \ldots, a_n)$, the operation executed is equivalent to computing $f(a_1, a_2, \ldots, a_n)$, where the correctness of f is subject to the invariance of the local environment during execution. This design paradigm promotes software reusability and enhances code maintainability.

Interface Specification and Argument Binding

The interface of a user-defined function is rigorously specified via its signature, which declares the number, type, and order of its parameters. This specification is analogous to the formal definition of a mathematical function; that is, for a function f, the relationship between the input tuple $(a_1, a_2, \ldots, a_n)$ and the resulting output b is unambiguously defined. The binding of actual parameters to the formal parameters occurs at the time of function invocation, ensuring that each execution of the function is self-contained. The mathematical expression $f : A_1 \times A_2 \times \cdots \times A_n \to B$ describes the transformation process, wherein each A_i represents an acceptable input domain and B comprises the output range. This rigorous binding mechanism reinforces a contract-based design whereby the operational semantics of the function are preserved consistently.

Scoping, Environments, and Variable Lifetime

The operational context of a user-defined function is characterized by its local environment, within which variables declared in the function have a limited scope. Such confinement prevents unintentional side-effects on variables outside the function, thereby preserving data integrity. A function typically initiates with a fresh environment, within which parameters and locally declared variables coexist. This environment acts as a closure over the function, binding any necessary external variables from its definition context as required by its operational semantics. The clear delineation between local and global scopes adheres to well-established principles in formal language theory, mitigating potential conflicts and promoting systematic reasoning about code behavior.

Higher-Order Abstractions and Functional Composition

In the realm of user-defined functions, the capability to treat functions as first-class objects introduces the concept of higher-order functions. Such functions can accept other functions as arguments or return them as results, thereby enabling the creation of abstract and reusable computational patterns. Formally, a higher-order function H can be represented as $H : (A \to B) \times C \to D$, where a function $f : A \to B$ is integrated into a larger computational scheme. This composition of functions underpins much of advanced algorithm design in the field, as it allows for the construction of new functionality by composing simpler, well-defined operations. The theoretical foundation provided by function composition not only simplifies complex operations but also enhances code modularity, which is a cornerstone of effective software development practices.

R Code Snippet

```
# Comprehensive R Code Demonstrating Key Concepts of User-defined
↪  Functions

# 1. Basic Mathematical Function
# This function represents a simple mathematical mapping:
# f:  ↦  defined by f(x) = (x + 1)^2
f <- function(x) {
  # Encapsulated operation (local computation)
  result <- (x + 1)^2
  return(result)
}

# Test the function f by applying it to a sequence of values
x_values <- seq(-5, 5, by = 1)
f_results <- sapply(x_values, f)
cat("Results of f(x) = (x + 1)^2:\n")
print(f_results)

# 2. Encapsulation and Modular Reuse: Solving a Quadratic Equation
# This function computes the roots of a quadratic equation: ax^2 +
↪  bx + c = 0
# Mathematical specification: f: A1 × A2 × A3 ↦ B, where the output
↪  B is a vector of roots
solve_quadratic <- function(a, b, c) {
  if(a == 0) {
```

```r
    stop("Coefficient 'a' cannot be zero for a quadratic equation.")
  }
  discriminant <- b^2 - 4 * a * c
  if(discriminant < 0) {
    # For simplicity, complex roots are not computed; NA indicates
    ↪  no real roots.
    return(NA)
  }
  root1 <- (-b + sqrt(discriminant)) / (2 * a)
  root2 <- (-b - sqrt(discriminant)) / (2 * a)
  return(c(root1, root2))
}

# Test the quadratic solver function with an example:
# Equation: x^2 - 3x + 2 = 0  should yield roots 1 and 2.
a <- 1; b <- -3; c <- 2
roots <- solve_quadratic(a, b, c)
cat("Roots of the quadratic equation x^2 - 3x + 2 = 0:\n")
print(roots)

# 3. Scoping, Environments, and Variable Lifetime
# Demonstrate that variables declared within a function do not
↪  affect the global environment.
outer_var <- 100  # Global variable

scoped_function <- function(x) {
  # 'outer_var' here is local to the function
  outer_var <- x * 10
  return(outer_var)
}

cat("Global outer_var before calling scoped_function:\n")
print(outer_var)
local_result <- scoped_function(5)
cat("Result from scoped_function(5):\n")
print(local_result)
cat("Global outer_var after calling scoped_function (remains
↪  unchanged):\n")
print(outer_var)

# 4. Higher-Order Functions and Functional Composition
# Define a function to compose two functions: f and g.
# The composition h(x) = g(f(x)) represents the idea of combining
↪  operations.
compose_functions <- function(g, f) {
  h <- function(x) {
    return(g(f(x)))
  }
  return(h)
}

# Define two simple functions:
increment <- function(x) {
```

```r
  return(x + 1)
}

square <- function(x) {
  return(x * x)
}

# Compose the functions so that h(x) = square(increment(x))
h <- compose_functions(square, increment)
test_value <- 4
composed_result <- h(test_value)
cat("Result of the composed function h(x) = square(increment(x)) for
↪   x = 4:\n")
print(composed_result)

# 5. Interface Specification and Argument Binding
# A function with default arguments that transforms a numeric
↪   series.
# The function applies a linear transformation: transformed = scale
↪   * (x + shift)
transform_series <- function(x, scale = 2, shift = 0) {
  return(scale * (x + shift))
}

# Test transform_series using both default parameters and custom
↪   parameters.
series_input <- 1:5
default_transformed <- transform_series(series_input)
custom_transformed <- transform_series(series_input, scale = 3,
↪   shift = 2)
cat("Input series:\n")
print(series_input)
cat("Transformed series with default scale and shift:\n")
print(default_transformed)
cat("Transformed series with scale = 3 and shift = 2:\n")
print(custom_transformed)

# End of comprehensive R code snippet demonstrating:
# - Mathematical function mapping (f:  → )
# - Encapsulation through user-defined functions solving a quadratic
↪   equation
# - Local variable scoping and environment isolation
# - Higher-order functions and function composition
# - Clear interface specification with default argument binding
```

Chapter 23

Function Arguments and Default Values

Formal Parameter Specification

A function is characterized by its signature, which embodies the mapping

$$f : A_1 \times A_2 \times \cdots \times A_n \to B,$$

where each A_i represents the domain corresponding to the ith parameter and B denotes the codomain. The signature delineates not only the quantity and order of the parameters but also implies constraints regarding their types and structural properties. This formalism establishes a clear interface between the internal logic of the function and the external values provided at the moment of invocation, thereby facilitating rigorous reasoning about the function's behavior within a well-defined computational model.

Default Values in Function Signatures

Assigning default values to function parameters introduces a mechanism for optionality that enhances the flexibility of the function's interface. Within a signature where certain parameters are equipped with predetermined values, the function is effectively redefined to accept a reduced input tuple in scenarios where the default assignments suffice. Formally, consider the function

$$g(a_1, a_2, \ldots, a_n),$$

in which a subset of parameters, denoted $\{a_{i_1}, a_{i_2}, \ldots, a_{i_k}\}$ with $1 \leq i_j \leq n$, are associated with default values. In the absence of explicit arguments for these positions during invocation, the function incorporates the preassigned defaults, thereby yielding a mapping that remains well-defined over a broader domain. This embedded default mechanism reduces the cognitive load associated with parameter specification and permits a more succinct description of functions that exhibit variant behavior in response to incomplete input specifications.

Argument Binding and Evaluation Order

The process of associating supplied arguments with their respective formal parameters, known as argument binding, plays a crucial role in ensuring that the function's internal computations operate on well-defined values. The binding mechanism is executed at the moment of the function call and adheres to specific evaluation rules that may be influenced by static or dynamic scoping constraints. In this context, the evaluation strategy dictates the order in which arguments are processed and subsequently assigned, ensuring that side effects and dependency relationships are managed in a controlled manner. Mathematically, this binding can be represented as the instantiation of the mapping

$$\text{binding} : (a_1, a_2, \ldots, a_n) \mapsto (v_1, v_2, \ldots, v_n),$$

where each v_i is derived from either the explicitly provided argument or, in its absence, the corresponding default value. The rigorous application of this substitution model underpins the semantic integrity of function execution and isolates the internal computational environment from external mutations.

Enhancing Flexibility Through Optional Parameters

The inclusion of default values in the definition of function parameters directly contributes to the development of flexible and reusable computational constructs. Optional parameters allow a function to encapsulate a more general behavior that can adapt to a variety of invocation contexts, thereby minimizing the necessity for exhaustive argument specification. This design principle is particularly beneficial in scenarios where certain computational aspects are controlled by ancillary parameters whose values, in many situations, can be standardized. By integrating default assignments into the interface, the functional mapping is effectively extended to accommodate both complete and partial parameterizations without compromising correctness. The resultant abstraction not only simplifies the structural complexity of function calls but also reinforces the modularity and adaptability of the overall design within a robust computational framework.

R Code Snippet

```r
# Comprehensive example function demonstrating formal parameter
↪  specification,
# default values, argument binding, evaluation order, and flexible
↪  interface.

customFunction <- function(
  data,            # A numeric vector (Domain A1)
  method = "mean",  # Statistical method: "mean", "median", "sum",
  ↪  "min", "max" (Default: "mean")
  performLR = FALSE,# Flag for performing linear regression
  ↪  (Default: FALSE)
  predictor = NULL, # Numeric vector for regression predictor
  ↪  (Domain A2; Default: NULL)
  intercept = TRUE  # Logical flag to include intercept in
  ↪  regression (Default: TRUE)
) {
  # Validate the 'data' input ensuring it is numeric.
  if (!is.numeric(data)) {
    stop("Error: 'data' must be a numeric vector.")
  }

  # Step 1: Compute a basic statistic using the chosen method.
  statResult <- switch(method,
                    "mean"   = mean(data),
                    "median" = median(data),
                    "sum"    = sum(data),
                    "min"    = min(data),
                    "max"    = max(data),
                    stop("Unsupported method. Choose 'mean',
                    ↪  'median', 'sum', 'min', or 'max'."))

  # Step 2: Optionally perform linear regression if performLR is
  ↪  TRUE.
  regressionResult <- NULL
  if (performLR) {
```

```r
# Validate the predictor: It must be provided and numeric.
if (is.null(predictor)) {
  stop("Predictor vector must be provided when performLR is
  ↪   TRUE.")
}
if (!is.numeric(predictor)) {
  stop("Error: 'predictor' must be numeric.")
}
if (length(predictor) != length(data)) {
  stop("Error: 'predictor' and 'data' must be of the same
  ↪   length.")
}

# Create a data frame to hold the response and predictor
↪   variables.
modelData <- data.frame(response = data, predictor = predictor)

# Construct the regression formula based on the intercept flag.
regressionFormula <- if (intercept) {
  response ~ predictor
} else {
  response ~ predictor - 1
}

# Perform linear regression using the lm() function.
regressionResult <- lm(regressionFormula, data = modelData)
}

# Step 3: Return a list containing the computed statistic and any
↪   regression result.
return(list(
  statistic = statResult,
  regression = regressionResult
))
}


# Example 1: Basic statistic calculation using default parameter
↪   'method' ("mean").
exampleData <- c(10, 20, 30, 40, 50)
result1 <- customFunction(data = exampleData)
cat("Example 1 - Mean:", result1$statistic, "\n")


# Example 2: Changing the computation method by specifying 'method'
↪   explicitly.
result2 <- customFunction(data = exampleData, method = "sum")
cat("Example 2 - Sum:", result2$statistic, "\n")


# Example 3: Performing linear regression along with basic statistic
↪   computation.
set.seed(42)  # For reproducibility of random numbers.
```

123

```
responseData <- rnorm(100, mean = 100, sd = 15)
predictorData <- rnorm(100, mean = 50, sd = 10)

result3 <- customFunction(
  data = responseData,
  method = "mean",      # Although statistic is mean, regression is
  ↪ computed as well.
  performLR = TRUE,
  predictor = predictorData,
  intercept = FALSE     # Test linear regression without an intercept.
)
cat("Example 3 - Mean:", result3$statistic, "\n")
cat("Example 3 - Regression Summary:\n")
print(summary(result3$regression))
```

Chapter 24

Scope and Environment in Functions

Foundations of Variable Scope

Variable scope is defined as the region within a program where a binding between an identifier and its associated value remains valid and unambiguous. In the context of function execution, scope delineates the confines within which variables are accessible. This demarcation guarantees that an identifier introduced within a function is restricted to the local environment created during the function call, thereby ensuring that bindings in outer environments do not interfere with the internal computations of the function. The rigor of this constraint is essential for maintaining modularity and preventing unintended interactions among disparate parts of a program.

Environments as Structural Mappings

An environment in the computational paradigm can be rigorously modeled as an associative mapping or function, which assigns to every identifier a definite value. Formally, an environment E is a set of ordered pairs $\{(x, v)\}$, where x denotes an identifier and v its corresponding value. In R, each invocation of a function produces a new environment, denoted by E_{local}, that encapsulates all bindings defined within the function. This local environment is linked to a parent environment, E_{parent}, which typically corresponds to the environment in effect at the time of the function's definition. The resulting chain of environments,

$$E_{local} \rightarrow E_{parent} \rightarrow \cdots \rightarrow E_{global},$$

establishes a hierarchical structure that governs variable resolution through recursive lookup procedures.

Lexical Scoping and the Resolution Process

Lexical scoping, the predominant strategy employed within R, stipulates that the binding of an identifier is determined by the physical structure of the program. When a function is defined, its associated environment forms the basis for resolving all variable references within that function. During execution, the current environment $E_{current}$ is examined for the presence of a desired identifier. If the identifier remains unbound within $E_{current}$, the search continues in the parent environment $P(E_{current})$ and progressively ascends the chain until either a binding is located or the global environment is reached. This resolution process is succinctly expressed by the relation

$$x \in E_{local} \quad \text{or} \quad x \in P(E_{local}) \quad \text{or} \quad \ldots \quad \text{or} \quad x \in E_{global},$$

thereby ensuring a deterministic and replicable approach to variable lookup that preserves the integrity of the function's execution context.

Nested Function Contexts and Variable Shadowing

Within the framework of nested functions, each inner function inherits a new environment E_{inner} that is derived from its immediately enclosing environment E_{outer}. This structural arrangement allows for the phenomenon of variable shadowing, wherein a variable declared in E_{inner} with the same identifier as one in E_{outer}

effectively masks the outer binding. Formally, if an identifier x is defined such that

$$(x, v_{inner}) \in E_{inner} \quad \text{and} \quad (x, v_{outer}) \in E_{outer},$$

the binding v_{inner} supersedes v_{outer} within the local context of the inner function. This mechanism isolates modifications to the local environment, ensuring that changes do not inadvertently propagate to the outer or global scopes. The structured separation provided by nested environments is vital for controlled data accessibility and for the avoidance of side effects during function evaluation.

Implications for Data Accessibility in Function Execution

The interplay between variable scope and the environment hierarchy has significant implications for data accessibility during function execution. The formal constructs of environments and lexical scoping collectively establish a paradigm in which the resolution of identifiers is both orderly and predictable. By confining variable bindings to well-defined environments and enforcing a deterministic search sequence through the environment chain, the system mitigates the risks associated with name collisions and unintended data interference. This structural rigor ensures that each function operates within its own encapsulated context, thereby upholding the invariants of the computational model and assuring that data remains accessible only within its intended scope.

R Code Snippet

```
# Global variable definition
x <- 10

# outerFunction demonstrates lexical scoping and variable shadowing.
outerFunction <- function(a) {
  # Local variable in outerFunction shadows the global x.
  x <- a + 5
  cat("Inside outerFunction - local x:", x, "\n")

  # Define an inner function to illustrate nested function
  ↪  environments.
  innerFunction <- function(b) {
```

127

```r
    # Local variable in innerFunction shadows the x from
    ↪  outerFunction.
    x <- b * 2
    cat("Inside innerFunction - local x:", x, "\n")

    # Access the outer x explicitly via the parent environment.
    outer_x <- get("x", envir = parent.env(environment()))
    cat("Accessing outer x from parent environment:", outer_x, "\n")

    # Compute a value combining inner and outer variables
    # This mimics combining values following the environment chain.
    return(x + outer_x)
  }

  # Call the inner function and store its result.
  result_inner <- innerFunction(a)

  # Print the current (local) environment details.
  cat("Environment of outerFunction:\n")
  print(environment())

  # Print the parent environment (typically the global environment
  ↪  or calling context).
  cat("Parent environment of outerFunction:\n")
  print(parent.env(environment()))

  return(result_inner)
}

# Execute outerFunction to verify scoping and variable resolution.
result <- outerFunction(3)
cat("Final result from outerFunction call:", result, "\n")

# Creating a custom environment for dynamic evaluation of
↪  expressions.
customEnv <- new.env()
customEnv$var1 <- 100
customEnv$var2 <- 200

# Parse and evaluate an expression in the context of customEnv.
expr <- parse(text = "var1 + var2")
result_custom <- eval(expr, envir = customEnv)
cat("Result of evaluating 'var1 + var2' in customEnv:",
↪  result_custom, "\n")

# demoFunction illustrates how a nested function inherits variables
↪  from its parent.
demoFunction <- function() {
  y <- 50
  nestedFunction <- function() {
    # y is not redefined in nestedFunction, hence it is taken from
    ↪  demoFunction.
    return(y + 10)
```

```
  }
  return(nestedFunction())
}

# Call demoFunction to observe recursive variable lookup.
result_demo <- demoFunction()
cat("Result of nested function demonstrating lexical scoping:",
↪  result_demo, "\n")
```

Chapter 25

Anonymous Functions and Function Factories

Inline Anonymous Functions

Inline anonymous functions, often interpreted as lambda abstractions in formal functional paradigms, embody the capacity to define behavior on an ad hoc basis without recourse to global naming. In formal terms, such functions correspond to the λ-expressions of the lambda calculus, where an abstraction such as $\lambda x.\, f(x)$ denotes a mapping from an element x in the domain to a value computed by $f(x)$. The transient nature of these constructs enables encapsulation of small, self-contained operations that are instantiated within the local scope of a larger expression. Their ephemeral definition serves to promote modularity, as the transient binding prevents inadvertent interference with identically named entities in broader scopes. This localized expression of behavior facilitates dense compositional paradigms, wherein the function is defined precisely at the point of its invocation and is employed immediately to process inputs without the encumbrance of a persistent identifier.

The elegance of inline anonymous functions lies in their capacity to mirror mathematical abstraction while simultaneously providing the flexibility requisite for dynamic computation. Their adoption within higher-level expressions underscores an economy of syntax and semantics that elevates the clarity of functional transformations. In this manner, the transient binding captures both the operational intent and the environmental context, yielding a closure that encapsulates the surrounding lexical scope for subsequent evaluation.

Higher-Order Function Constructs

Higher-order function constructs extend the notion of function manipulation by treating functions as first-class citizens within the computational framework. A higher-order function is distinguished by its ability to either accept one or more functions as arguments or to return a function as its result. Formally, if one considers a function H such that $H : (A \to B) \to C$, the abstraction delineates an operator that transforms a function mapping elements of set A to set B into an element of set C. This elevated level of abstraction is reflective of the core principles in functional programming and mathematical logic.

Within these constructs, inline anonymous functions find extensive utility. Their integration enables the direct insertion of ad hoc mappings into the syntactic structure of function application, thereby realizing a seamless composition of behaviors. The rigorous hierarchy of these higher-order functions is further enriched by corresponding mathematical methodologies such as currying and partial application, which decompose multi-argument functions into sequences of single-argument functions. The attendant closure properties inherent in the anonymous definitions allow these composite entities to maintain a consistent reference to the lexical environment in which they were defined, ensuring a deterministic evaluation strategy.

The theoretical framework supporting higher-order functions provides insights into the mechanisms by which computational processes may be composed, decomposed, and subsequently reassembled. Such a framework not only describes the transformational capabilities of functions but also delineates the precise binding and scope rules that preserve data integrity across asynchronous operations.

Function Factories and Dynamic Function Generation

Function factories constitute a refined architectural pattern wherein a generating function yields a new function, effectively serving as a

131

blueprint for dynamic function creation. A function factory can be formally described by a mapping of the form $F : P \to (A \to B)$, where a set of parameters P determines the behavior of the resulting function that maps elements from A to B. This paradigm leverages the concept of closure, as the newly minted function retains an association with the lexical environment in which it was created.

By encapsulating specific contextual information at the time of their generation, function factories enable the production of customized functions tailored to particular computational tasks. The generated function carries with it a snapshot of the local environment, thereby ensuring that state-specific parameters remain invariant during subsequent invocations. This mechanism offers a controlled means of deferring computation until such time as the generated function is explicitly executed, with the environmental conditions preserved by the closure mechanism.

The interplay between parameterization and closure in function factories provides a potent framework for crafting dynamic, reusable abstractions. The resultant functions are not merely static mappings but are imbued with a rich contextual heritage that informs their operation. This confluence of dynamic function generation and higher-order abstraction plays a pivotal role in advancing both theoretical and practical aspects of modern computation, as it synthesizes flexible, context-aware behavior within a rigorously defined mathematical structure.

R Code Snippet

```
# -----------------------------------------------------------------
# This code snippet demonstrates key concepts from the chapter:
#
# 1. Inline Anonymous Functions (Lambda Expressions)
#    - Defined on the fly without being assigned a global name.
#    - Mirrors the lambda calculus notion of x.f(x).
#
# 2. Higher-Order Functions
#    - Functions that accept other functions as arguments or return
↪    them.
#
# 3. Function Factories (Dynamic Function Generation)
#    - Functions that produce other functions based on parameters,
#      maintaining a closure on their local environment.
# -----------------------------------------------------------------
```

```r
# Example 1: Inline Anonymous Functions
# Directly applying an anonymous function to compute the square of a
↪   number
square_result <- (function(x) x^2)(5)   # Equivalent to x.x^2 applied
↪   to 5
print(paste("Square of 5 =", square_result))


# Example 2: Higher-Order Function using Anonymous Function
# Define a higher-order function that applies a function twice to an
↪   input.
apply_twice <- function(f, x) {
  # Applies the function f to x two times: f(f(x))
  return(f(f(x)))
}
# Using an inline lambda (anonymous function) to add 3
result_twice <- apply_twice(function(x) x + 3, 10)   # 10 + 3 + 3 =
↪   16
print(paste("Result of applying function twice:", result_twice))


# Example 3: Function Factory for Creating Multipliers
# This function factory returns a new function that multiplies its
↪   argument by a fixed factor.
multiplier_factory <- function(factor) {
  # Closure: The inner function remembers the 'factor' from its
  ↪   creation environment.
  generated_function <- function(x) {
    return(x * factor)
  }
  return(generated_function)
}
# Generate a doubling function (i.e., multiply by 2)
double <- multiplier_factory(2)
print(paste("Double of 7 =", double(7)))


# Generate a tripling function (i.e., multiply by 3)
triple <- multiplier_factory(3)
print(paste("Triple of 7 =", triple(7)))


# Example 4: Function Factory for Creating Power Functions
# This demonstrates dynamic function generation where a generated
↪   function
# raises a number to a specified exponent (capturing the exponent
↪   via closure).
make_power_function <- function(exponent) {
  # Returns a function that computes (x ^ exponent)
  function(x) {
    return(x ^ exponent)
  }
}
# Create functions for square and cube using the factory
square_func <- make_power_function(2)
cube_func <- make_power_function(3)
print(paste("Square of 4 =", square_func(4)))
```

```r
print(paste("Cube of 4 =", cube_func(4)))

# Example 5: Combining Higher-Order Functions with Factory-Generated
↪  Functions
# Define a function that applies a generated function repeatedly.
apply_n_times <- function(f_factory, n, value) {
  # f_factory is expected to be a function that returns a function.
  f <- f_factory()  # Generate the function (e.g., an incrementer)
  result <- value
  for(i in 1:n) {
    result <- f(result)
  }
  return(result)
}
# Define a simple increment function factory that produces a
↪  function to add 1
increment_factory <- function() {
  return(function(x) x + 1)
}
# Apply the increment function 5 times to the starting value 10: 10
↪  + 1*5 = 15
incremented_value <- apply_n_times(increment_factory, 5, 10)
print(paste("10 incremented 5 times =", incremented_value))

# Example 6: Vectorized Operation with an Inline Anonymous Function
# Use sapply to compute factorial values for numbers 1 through 10.
# (Note: gamma(n+1) gives n! for integer n)
numbers <- 1:10
factorial_values <- sapply(numbers, function(x) gamma(x + 1))
print("Factorial values for 1 to 10:")
print(factorial_values)
```

Chapter 26

The Apply Family: Lapply and Sapply

Conceptual Foundations

The apply family represents a refined abstraction in functional programming paradigms, particularly within the context of operating on list-like and vector-like structures. Its formulation is grounded in the principles of higher-order functions, where functions serve as first-class objects and can be manipulated in a manner analogous to mathematical mappings. Consider a function $f : X \to Y$, defined on an arbitrary set X and producing outputs in Y. For a finite collection $L = \{x_1, x_2, \ldots, x_n\}$, the operation performed by an apply function encapsulates the mapping

$$L \mapsto \{f(x_1), f(x_2), \ldots, f(x_n)\}.$$

This encapsulation not only abstracts away the underlying iteration mechanism but also enforces a clean separation between the data structure and the functional operation applied to its elements. The methodology adheres strictly to the mathematical formalism of function composition and transformation, thereby enabling efficient manipulation of collections without recourse to explicit looping constructs.

Detailed Examination of *lapply*

The function *lapply* implements the previously outlined mapping paradigm with a pronounced emphasis on preserving the structural characteristics of the input. When applied to a list or similar aggregate, *lapply* returns a new list whose elements are the result of applying a transformation function to each corresponding element of the original list. Formally, for a list $L = \{x_1, x_2, \ldots, x_n\}$ and a transformation function f, the operation is defined as

$$lapply(L, f) = \{f(x_1), f(x_2), \ldots, f(x_n)\}.$$

This definition guarantees a one-to-one correspondence between the elements of the input list and those of the output list, irrespective of the complexity or heterogeneity of the individual elements. In scenarios where the constituent elements of the list belong to diverse classes or contain varying data structures, *lapply* maintains a consistent output format by confining the results within the list construct. This reliability in structural preservation is particularly vital in large-scale computational settings, where the integrity of the data pipeline is maintained by ensuring that transformations yield predictable and uniformly accessible results.

Detailed Examination of *sapply*

The function *sapply* builds upon the foundational principles of *lapply* but introduces an augmented mechanism aimed at simplifying the structure of the resultant output. When the outcomes of a function f applied over a list $L = \{x_1, x_2, \ldots, x_n\}$ are amenable to unification into an atomic vector or a matrix, *sapply* performs this collapse in a manner that respects the homogeneity of the outputs. Specifically, if each application $f(x_i)$ yields a scalar or an identically dimensioned array, then

$$sapply(L, f) = \phi\big(\{f(x_1), f(x_2), \ldots, f(x_n)\}\big),$$

where the operator ϕ denotes the simplification function that coerces the list structure into a more canonical form. The transformation executed by *sapply* is contingent upon stringent checks for type consistency and dimensional congruence, ensuring that the simplicity of the output structure does not compromise the fidelity of the computational result. This simplification process mirrors the search for homomorphisms within algebraic systems, where a collection of elements is restructured into a form that preserves the intrinsic properties of the original mapping while achieving a higher degree of computational efficiency.

Comparative Analysis of *lapply* and *sapply*

The distinct operational characteristics of *lapply* and *sapply* underscore a pivotal dichotomy in the design of the apply family. On one hand, *lapply* is predicated on the principle of structural fidelity; it uniformly returns a list regardless of the inherent uniformity of its constituent elements. On the other hand, *sapply* endeavors to reconcile structural uniformity with computational efficiency by introducing a conditional simplification mechanism. Mathematically, if one considers the mapping

$$L \xrightarrow{f} \{f(x_1), f(x_2), \ldots, f(x_n)\},$$

then *lapply* preserves this mapping in its raw form, while *sapply* applies the simplification transformation ϕ, resulting in

$$sapply(L, f) = \phi\big(\{f(x_1), f(x_2), \ldots, f(x_n)\}\big).$$

The choice between employing *lapply* or *sapply* is thus informed by the need for either unadulterated structural replication or the desire for a streamlined, simplified output. This decision is deeply rooted in the underlying properties of the transformation function and the nature of the data at hand, with significant implications for both the performance and the expressiveness of the final computational model.

R Code Snippet

```
# The following R code snippet demonstrates the key concepts and
↪    algorithms
# discussed in this chapter on the apply family (lapply and sapply).
#
# Mathematically, let L = {x1, x2, ..., xn} be a collection and let
↪    f be a
# transformation function (f: X -> Y). The apply functions execute
↪    the mapping:
#
#        L  -->  { f(x1), f(x2), ..., f(xn) }
```

```r
#
# The function lapply preserves the structure of L by returning a
↪    list, whereas
# sapply attempts to simplify the result (to a vector or matrix) if
↪    possible.
#
# Example 1: Apply a transformation function to a list of numeric
↪    vectors

# Create a list of numeric vectors
data_list <- list(
    vector1 = c(1, 2, 3),
    vector2 = c(4, 5, 6),
    vector3 = c(7, 8, 9)
)

# Define a transformation function: for each element, compute f(x) =
↪    x^2 + 1
transform_fun <- function(x) {
    return(x^2 + 1)
}

# Using lapply: Applies transform_fun to each element and returns a
↪    list
lapply_result <- lapply(data_list, transform_fun)
print("Lapply Result (List Structure):")
print(lapply_result)

# Using sapply: Applies transform_fun and simplifies output if
↪    possible
sapply_result <- sapply(data_list, transform_fun)
print("Sapply Result (Simplified Structure):")
print(sapply_result)


# Example 2: Transformation function returning scalar outputs

# Create a list of single numeric values
num_list <- list(a = 1, b = 2, c = 3, d = 4)

# Define a function that computes the square of a number: f(x) = x^2
square_fun <- function(x) {
    return(x^2)
}

# Apply the function using lapply to preserve individual outputs as
↪    list elements
lapply_num <- lapply(num_list, square_fun)
# Apply the function using sapply to simplify the result into a
↪    numeric vector
sapply_num <- sapply(num_list, square_fun)

print("Lapply on num_list (List of Scalars):")
```

```r
print(lapply_num)
print("Sapply on num_list (Simplified to Vector):")
print(sapply_num)


# Example 3: Function returning a fixed-length vector output

# Define a function that returns a vector of summary statistics
#   [mean, sum]
stats_fun <- function(x) {
    m <- mean(x)
    s <- sum(x)
    # f(x) returns: [mean, sum]
    return(c(mean = m, sum = s))
}

# When applied to data_list, each element produces a vector of
#   length 2.
# sapply simplifies this into a 2 x n matrix.
stats_matrix <- sapply(data_list, stats_fun)
print("Sapply Result for stats_fun (Matrix Output):")
print(stats_matrix)


# Example 4: Handling heterogeneous list elements

# Create a mixed-type list demonstrating heterogeneity in structure
mixed_list <- list(
    numbers = c(10, 20, 30),
    chars   = c("a", "b", "c"),
    nested  = list(subitem = c(5, 15))
)

# Define a function to return the length of an element
length_fun <- function(x) {
    return(length(x))
}

lapply_mixed <- lapply(mixed_list, length_fun)
sapply_mixed <- sapply(mixed_list, length_fun)

print("Lapply on mixed_list (Returns a List):")
print(lapply_mixed)
print("Sapply on mixed_list (Simplified to Vector):")
print(sapply_mixed)

# End of comprehensive R code demonstration for using lapply and
#   sapply.
```

Chapter 27

Object Classes and Type Checking

Object Representation and Class Structures

Within the programming environment of R, the object system is underpinned by a multifaceted representation mechanism that encapsulates both data and metadata. Every entity within this environment is instantiated as an object endowed with a set of attributes that define its structural and behavioral properties. At its core, the notion of a class is introduced through a designated class attribute which can comprise either a single identifier or a vector of identifiers. This mechanism accommodates various object systems such as the $S3$ system, where class designation is achieved through informal tagging, and the $S4$ system, which imposes stringent formal definitions via explicit slot declarations and inheritance hierarchies. The duality between these systems illustrates a tradeoff between flexibility and rigorous type enforcement, where the $S3$ system favors expedience and the $S4$ approach endows objects with an architecture that anticipates and mitigates unintended semantic discrepancies. The structural representation of objects is thus not solely a function of the contained data but also an intricate mapping of metadata that facilitates subsequent method dispatch and introspection.

Dynamic Type Checking Mechanisms

The dynamic nature of R's type system necessitates robust mechanisms for runtime type verification and validation. In this context, objects are subjected to type inquiry procedures that assess their conformity to specific primitive or composite types. These procedures are formulated as predicate functions which, upon evaluation, yield boolean outcomes that confirm the object's adherence to expected type constructs. The intrinsic heterogeneity among objects—ranging from atomic vectors and matrices to more elaborate list structures—mandates that type checking be both precise and flexible. The runtime environment, therefore, leverages a combination of introspective functions to interrogate properties such as class membership and storage mode, ensuring that every operation invoked matches the semantic contract dictated by the object's type. In the absence of compile-time type enforcement, this dynamic type checking protocol plays a pivotal role in preserving both computational consistency and the integrity of method resolution.

Strategies for Type Management and Coercion

An integral aspect of the object system involves not only the verification of an object's type but also its transformation and management across varied contexts. Type management in R is frequently conceptualized through conversion operations that enact a mapping of the form $f : C_1 \to C_2$, where an object of class C_1 is methodically coerced into an object of class C_2. Such transformations are governed by a set of predefined coercion rules that aim to preserve the essential properties of the object while rendering it compatible with operations that necessitate a particular type. Implicit transformations may occur in function invocations, yet the precision required in complex computational scenarios often demands explicit coercion strategies. The existence of a comprehensive type management framework ensures that objects retain their semantic integrity during these conversions, thereby mitigating issues related to data misinterpretation or loss of structure. By embedding detailed metadata within each object, the system facilitates rigorous type validation and controlled interconversion, thereby maintaining a coherent and reliable computational paradigm.

R Code Snippet

```r
#----------------------------------------------------
# S3 Object System Example: Define a "Person" class
#----------------------------------------------------

# Constructor for S3 Person object
createPerson <- function(name, age) {
  person <- list(name = name, age = age)
  class(person) <- "Person"  # assign S3 class attribute
  return(person)
}

# Custom print method for S3 Person objects
print.Person <- function(x, ...) {
  cat("Person Object:\n")
  cat("  Name:", x$name, "\n")
  cat("  Age: ", x$age, "\n")
}

#----------------------------------------------------
# S4 Object System Example: Define an "Employee" class
#----------------------------------------------------

# Define S4 class with explicit slot declarations
setClass("Employee",
         slots = c(
           name     = "character",
           age      = "numeric",
           position = "character"
         ))

# Constructor function for S4 Employee objects
createEmployee <- function(name, age, position) {
  new("Employee", name = name, age = age, position = position)
}

# Define a show method for the Employee S4 class
setMethod("show", "Employee", function(object) {
  cat("Employee Object:\n")
  cat("  Name:    ", object@name, "\n")
  cat("  Age:     ", object@age, "\n")
  cat("  Position:", object@position, "\n")
})

#----------------------------------------------------
# Dynamic Type Checking Functions
#----------------------------------------------------

# Function to check and report the type and class of any object
checkObjectType <- function(obj) {
  cat("Runtime Type Information:\n")
```

```r
  cat("  typeof: ", typeof(obj), "\n")
  cat("  class:  ", class(obj), "\n")

  if (is.atomic(obj)) {
    cat("  The object is atomic.\n")
  } else {
    cat("  The object is not atomic.\n")
  }

  # Check for S3 class inheritance
  if (inherits(obj, "Person")) {
    cat("  Detected S3 class: Person\n")
  }

  # Check for S4 object structure
  if (isS4(obj)) {
    cat("  Detected S4 object.\n")
  }
}


#--------------------------------------------------
# Type Management and Coercion Examples
#--------------------------------------------------

# Coerce an S3 Person object into a detailed list with metadata
convertPersonToList <- function(person) {
  if (!inherits(person, "Person")) {
    stop("Provided object is not of class Person!")
  }
  result <- list(
    Name     = person$name,
    Age      = person$age,
    Class    = "Person",
    Verified = TRUE
  )
  return(result)
}


# Coerce an S4 Employee object into a list representation
convertEmployeeToList <- function(employee) {
  if (!isS4(employee)) {
    stop("Provided object is not an S4 Employee!")
  }
  emp_list <- list(
    Name     = employee@name,
    Age      = employee@age,
    Position = employee@position,
    Class    = "Employee"
  )
  return(emp_list)
}


#--------------------------------------------------
```

```r
# Demonstration: Object Creation, Type Checking, and Coercion
#-------------------------------------------------

# Create an S3 Person Object
person1 <- createPerson("Alice", 30)
print(person1)
checkObjectType(person1)

# Convert S3 Person to a detailed list
personMetadata <- convertPersonToList(person1)
cat("\nConverted Person Metadata:\n")
print(personMetadata)

# Create an S4 Employee Object
employee1 <- createEmployee("Bob", 40, "Manager")
print(employee1)
checkObjectType(employee1)

# Convert S4 Employee to a list format
employeeList <- convertEmployeeToList(employee1)
cat("\nConverted Employee List:\n")
print(employeeList)

#-------------------------------------------------
# Additional Dynamic Type Checking and Data Processing
#-------------------------------------------------

# Example: Working with numeric vectors and handling missing values
numericVector <- c(10, 20, NA, 40, 50)
cat("\nInitial Numeric Vector:\n")
print(numericVector)

# Check basic type predicates
cat("Is numeric:", is.numeric(numericVector), "\n")
cat("Are all elements non-missing:", all(!is.na(numericVector)),
↪   "\n")

# Replace NA values with the mean of non-missing elements using
↪   ifelse()
calculatedMean <- mean(numericVector, na.rm = TRUE)
numericVectorClean <- ifelse(is.na(numericVector), calculatedMean,
↪   numericVector)
cat("Numeric Vector after NA replacement:\n")
print(numericVectorClean)
```

144

Chapter 28

Handling Missing Values

Missing Data Representations

Within modern data analysis frameworks, missing entries are typically denoted by the symbols NA and NaN, which, despite superficial similarity, represent distinct concepts. The symbol NA is employed as a general indicator for values that are absent or undefined within a dataset, whereas NaN (Not a Number) specifically encapsulates results from indeterminate numerical operations such as divisions of zero by zero or operations yielding undefined arithmetic outcomes. This dichotomy is central to the structural integrity of computational representations, as the underlying metadata associated with each element includes type and legitimacy markers that govern subsequent processing and analysis.

Detection Techniques for Missing Values

The identification of missing data is a fundamental operation that underlies robust data preprocessing pipelines. Methods for detecting missing values are predicated on the evaluation of individual data elements to ascertain conformity with the constructs NA and NaN. Such evaluation processes are typically executed via predicate functions, which rigorously test each element against the criteria of absence or numerical indeterminacy. The detection algorithm

145

must account for the heterogeneous nature of data structures—ranging from atomic vectors to multi-dimensional arrays—ensuring that the presence of missing values is accurately reported irrespective of an object's complexity. The precise discrimination between NA and NaN is essential, as the propagation of these values through arithmetic or statistical operations can yield results that compromise the integrity of inferential conclusions.

Strategies for Managing and Imputing Missing Data

Once detected, missing data require meticulous handling to preserve the statistical validity and overall consistency of the dataset. Management strategies typically bifurcate into deletion techniques and imputation methodologies. Deletion techniques, though straightforward, run the risk of reducing sample size and potentially introducing bias through non-random omission. Imputation strategies, on the other hand, involve the substitution of missing entries with statistically derived estimates. Approaches in imputation vary from simple replacement methods, such as substitution with central tendency measures, to more elaborate algorithms that leverage the covariance structure among variables. These imputation methods aim to construct a surrogate dataset in which the underlying distributional properties remain largely intact. The efficacy of a chosen strategy is intrinsically linked to the missing data mechanism itself, necessitating a rigorous assessment of whether values are missing completely at random, missing at random, or missing not at random. This theoretical framework informs the depth of imputation required and the potential impact on subsequent analysis.

Theoretical Implications in Missing Data Analysis

The presence of missing values exerts significant influence upon the theoretical underpinnings of statistical models and computational algorithms. Unaddressed or improperly managed missing data may induce bias in parameter estimation, distort variance computations, and alter the covariance matrix of the observed data. The integrity of inferential procedures is contingent upon the assumption that the dataset accurately reflects the phenomenon under study;

deviations introduced by missing observations can therefore lead to substantively erroneous conclusions. Furthermore, the integration of missing data handling within the computational workflow necessitates an appreciation of its effects on convergence properties and the stability of optimization routines. Mathematical formulations governing likelihood estimates and error propagation are sensitive to the distributional modifications induced by imputation or data deletion, thereby demanding a comprehensive theoretical treatment that reconciles the underlying statistical assumptions with the practical exigencies of data processing.

Considerations in Data Preprocessing

In the context of comprehensive data preprocessing, the detection and management of missing values constitute a critical procedural step. The establishment of a robust framework for missing data handling ensures that downstream analytical procedures are not compromised by inadvertent data distortions. This framework typically integrates systematic detection protocols, rigorous classification criteria, and adaptive strategies for imputation or exclusion. Such an approach underscores the necessity of maintaining consistency across diverse data types while also accommodating the inherent uncertainties that missing values introduce. The careful orchestration of these techniques is paramount in preserving the semantic integrity of the dataset, thereby fostering analyses that reliably reflect the underlying informational content.

R Code Snippet

```
# ----------------------------------------------------------------
# This script demonstrates detection, deletion, and imputation of
↪    missing values
# (NA and NaN) in R, along with a simple linear regression model
↪    using imputed data.
# ----------------------------------------------------------------

# 1. Create a sample vector containing both NA and NaN values.
sample_vector <- c(1, 2, NA, 4, NaN, 6, NA, 8)
cat("Sample Vector:\n")
print(sample_vector)

# Detect missing values in the vector.
total_missing <- sum(is.na(sample_vector))
```

```r
nan_count <- sum(is.nan(sample_vector))
na_only_count <- sum(is.na(sample_vector) & !is.nan(sample_vector))
cat("Total missing (NA and NaN):", total_missing, "\n")
cat("NaN count:", nan_count, "\n")
cat("NA count (excluding NaN):", na_only_count, "\n\n")

# 2. Create a sample data frame with missing values.
df <- data.frame(
  ID     = 1:10,
  Age    = c(25, NA, 30, 22, NA, 40, 28, NaN, 35, 27),
  Income = c(50000, 55000, NA, 58000, 60000, NA, 52000, 54000,
  ↪  61000, 63000),
  Score  = c(85, 90, 88, NA, 92, 87, NaN, 91, 89, 90)
)
cat("Original Data Frame:\n")
print(df)

# 3. Function to provide a summary of missing data per column.
missing_summary <- function(data) {
  summary_matrix <- sapply(data, function(x) {
    total <- length(x)
    missing <- sum(is.na(x))
    percent_missing <- round(missing / total * 100, 2)
    na_only <- sum(is.na(x) & !is.nan(x))
    nan_count <- sum(is.nan(x))
    c(Total = total, Missing = missing, Percent = percent_missing,
      NA_only = na_only, NaN = nan_count)
  })
  return(as.data.frame(t(summary_matrix)))
}

cat("Missing Data Summary:\n")
print(missing_summary(df))

# 4. Deletion Technique: Remove rows that contain any missing
↪  values.
df_complete <- df[complete.cases(df), ]
cat("\nData after Deletion (Complete Cases):\n")
print(df_complete)

# 5. Imputation Technique: Replace missing values with the column
↪  mean.
impute_mean <- function(data) {
  data_imputed <- data  # Copy original data.
  for (col in names(data_imputed)) {
    if (is.numeric(data_imputed[[col]])) {
      mean_value <- mean(data_imputed[[col]], na.rm = TRUE)
      # Replace both NA and NaN values with the computed column
      ↪  mean.
      data_imputed[[col]][is.na(data_imputed[[col]])] <- mean_value
    }
  }
  return(data_imputed)
```

```
}

df_imputed_mean <- impute_mean(df)
cat("\nData after Mean Imputation:\n")
print(df_imputed_mean)

# 6. Imputation Technique: Replace missing values with the column
↪   median.
impute_median <- function(data) {
  data_imputed <- data    # Copy original data.
  for (col in names(data_imputed)) {
    if (is.numeric(data_imputed[[col]])) {
      median_value <- median(data_imputed[[col]], na.rm = TRUE)
      # Replace both NA and NaN values with the computed column
      ↪   median.
      data_imputed[[col]][is.na(data_imputed[[col]])] <-
        ↪   median_value
    }
  }
  return(data_imputed)
}

df_imputed_median <- impute_median(df)
cat("\nData after Median Imputation:\n")
print(df_imputed_median)

# 7. Linear Regression Example using the Mean Imputed Data.
# The formula Score ~ Age + Income represents the model equation:
#    Score = beta0 + beta1 * Age + beta2 * Income + error
lm_model <- lm(Score ~ Age + Income, data = df_imputed_mean)
cat("\nLinear Regression Model Summary (using Mean Imputed
↪   Data):\n")
print(summary(lm_model))
```

Chapter 29

Sorting and Ordering Data

Foundational Concepts in Sorting

The operation of sorting constitutes the systematic rearrangement of elements within a data structure according to a well-defined order relation. In the context of computer science and statistical computing, sorting methodologies are evaluated in terms of their computational complexity, with many algorithms achieving an average-case performance of $O(n \log n)$. The categorization into stable and unstable sorting techniques is determined by whether the relative positioning of elements deemed equivalent is preserved. Such properties have critical ramifications for subsequent data manipulation and analysis, particularly in environments where reproducibility and data integrity are paramount.

Sorting of Vectors

Vectors, representing one-dimensional collections of elements, form the elemental building blocks of more complex data structures. The process of ordering vectors requires the specification of a comparison operator that imposes a total order on the contained elements. The simplicity of this data structure allows for the adoption of classical sorting algorithms, including but not limited to recursive divide-and-conquer strategies, which partition the vector into smaller subarrays. The operational efficiency, coupled with the preservation of type integrity, is essential when vectors represent fundamental units of numerical, character, or logical data. The consideration of stability in the sorting process further ensures that implicit relationships among identical elements remain intact throughout reordering.

Ordering of Matrices

Matrices, as two-dimensional arrays, introduce an added layer of complexity in the sorting process due to the need to maintain the structural demarcation between rows and columns. When arranging matrix components, one common approach involves independently sorting along one axis—either the row or column dimension—so that the inherent organization of data is not compromised. Alternatively, matrices may be conceptually transformed into one-dimensional arrays for ordering, with the stipulation that the original dimensional framework can be reconstructed post-sort. In both strategies, it is imperative to establish coherent criteria for comparison across the targeted dimensions, thereby ensuring that the resultant ordered matrix accurately reflects both the distributional characteristics and the underlying relational structure of the data.

Sorting and Ordering of Data Frames

Data frames embody a tabular structure wherein each column encapsulates a distinct variable and each row corresponds to an observational unit. The ordering of data frames is achieved by determining key columns that dictate the lexicographical sequence of the entire table. This operation necessitates the coordinated reordering of multiple columns while preserving the interdependencies across diverse data types. In practice, the sorting mechanism applied to data frames must account for heterogeneous formats, such as numeric and categorical data, and implement ordering rules that are both comprehensive and efficient. The challenge is compounded in large-scale datasets, where optimization of sorting algorithms is crucial in order to adhere to stringent performance criteria. The methodological rigor in establishing multi-dimensional sort operations is central to ensuring that data frames remain consistent and analytically robust throughout the sorting process.

R Code Snippet

```r
# R Code Demonstrating Sorting and Ordering Operations

###########################
## 1. Sorting of Vectors ##
###########################

# Create a numeric vector
num_vector <- c(34, 7, 23, 32, 5, 62)
cat("Original vector:\n", num_vector, "\n")

# Sort vector in ascending order
sorted_vector <- sort(num_vector)
cat("Sorted vector (ascending):\n", sorted_vector, "\n")

# Sort vector in descending order
sorted_vector_desc <- sort(num_vector, decreasing = TRUE)
cat("Sorted vector (descending):\n", sorted_vector_desc, "\n")

# Retrieve the order indices that would sort the vector
order_indices <- order(num_vector)
cat("Order indices for sorting the vector:\n", order_indices, "\n")

###################################
## 2. Ordering of Matrices       ##
###################################

# Set seed for reproducibility and create a matrix
set.seed(1)
matrix_data <- matrix(sample(1:100, 12, replace = TRUE), nrow = 3)
cat("\nOriginal Matrix:\n")
print(matrix_data)

# (a) Sorting each row individually while maintaining the row
#     structure
sorted_rows_matrix <- t(apply(matrix_data, 1, sort))
cat("\nMatrix with each row sorted:\n")
print(sorted_rows_matrix)

# (b) Sorting each column individually
sorted_cols_matrix <- apply(matrix_data, 2, sort)
cat("\nMatrix with each column sorted:\n")
print(sorted_cols_matrix)

# (c) Global sorting: Flatten the matrix, sort the elements, and
#     reshape back
global_sorted <- sort(as.vector(matrix_data))
global_sorted_matrix <- matrix(global_sorted, nrow =
    nrow(matrix_data))
cat("\nMatrix globally sorted (flatten -> sort -> reshape):\n")
print(global_sorted_matrix)
```

```
#####################################
## 3. Ordering of Data Frames      ##
#####################################

# Create a data frame with mixed data types
df <- data.frame(
  ID = c("A3", "A1", "A2", "A4"),
  Value = c(100, 200, 100, 50),
  Category = c("X", "Z", "Y", "X")
)
cat("\nOriginal Data Frame:\n")
print(df)

# Order the data frame first by 'Value' then by 'Category'
↪  lexicographically
ordered_df <- df[order(df$Value, df$Category), ]
cat("\nData Frame ordered by Value then Category:\n")
print(ordered_df)

# Another example: Lexicographical ordering with multiple columns
df2 <- data.frame(
  Name = c("Zoe", "Adam", "Eve", "Bob"),
  Age = c(23, 45, 23, 45),
  Score = c(88, 92, 85, 92)
)
cat("\nAnother Data Frame before ordering:\n")
print(df2)

ordered_df2 <- df2[order(df2$Age, df2$Name), ]
cat("\nData Frame ordered lexicographically by Age then Name:\n")
print(ordered_df2)

##########################################
## 4. Custom QuickSort Algorithm        ##
##########################################

# A custom implementation of the QuickSort algorithm for vectors
quickSort <- function(x) {
  if (length(x) <= 1) {
    return(x)
  } else {
    pivot <- x[1]
    less <- quickSort(x[x < pivot])
    equal <- x[x == pivot]
    greater <- quickSort(x[x > pivot])
    return(c(less, equal, greater))
  }
}

cat("\nCustom QuickSort Output:\n")
custom_sorted_vector <- quickSort(num_vector)
```

```
cat("Custom sorted vector using QuickSort:\n", custom_sorted_vector,
↪   "\n")
```

Chapter 30

Merging and Joining Data Frames

Fundamental Concepts of Data Frame Merging

Data frames constitute structured, two-dimensional tabular data where each column represents a variable and each row corresponds to an observation. The process of merging involves the synthesis of two or more data frames into a single, unified data structure. This operation is defined mathematically through set-theoretic principles, where rows are paired based on an equivalence relation established on one or more key attributes. In the abstract, given data frames D_1 and D_2, the merged data set can be articulated as a relation

$$D = \{(r_1, r_2) : r_1 \in D_1, \ r_2 \in D_2, \ \text{and} \ key(r_1) = key(r_2)\},$$

with $key(r)$ denoting the value or tuple of values that uniquely identify each record. This fundamental concept traces its origins to relational algebra where operations such as the natural join form the theoretical basis for merging procedures. The integrity of the resulting data frame is inherently dependent upon the precision of the key matching process and the adherence to the underlying ordering principles of the contributing datasets.

Key Matching and Merge Operations

Central to the merging process is the mechanism of key matching, wherein specific columns or combinations of columns are designated as identifiers. These identifiers serve as the pivot around which rows from disparate data frames are aligned. The specification of a key can range from a singular attribute exhibiting unique values to composite keys constructed from multiple variables. Formally, if K_1 and K_2 represent the sets of key values in data frames D_1 and D_2, respectively, the condition $K_1 \cap K_2 \neq \emptyset$ guarantees the feasibility of a join operation. Merges based on these keys are often categorized into several types, including inner joins—defined by the intersection $K_1 \cap K_2$—and outer joins, which incorporate elements from the union $K_1 \cup K_2$. The rigorous enforcement of key equality ensures that the resultant data frame retains a logical consistency, thereby validating the integrity of subsequent analytical endeavors.

Techniques for Joining Data Frames

Joining techniques in data processing are characterized by the method through which rows are consolidated based on overlapping key attributes. Among the various methodologies, the inner join operates on the premise that only records exhibiting a shared key membership are preserved in the merged output. In contrast, outer joins accommodate a more inclusive approach by reintegrating all records, with the absence of a corresponding match manifested as a placeholder for missing data. Additional variants, such as left and right joins, impose an asymmetric structure wherein the ordering of the key sets plays a significant role in determining the output. The selection of a joining technique reflects a balance between data completeness and computational efficiency; each method introduces specific implications with respect to the inclusion of unmatched rows and the preservation of intrinsic data order. The theoretical underpinnings of these techniques are deeply rooted in set operations and relational mapping, and they provide a robust framework for combining datasets while maintaining rigorous standards for data consistency.

Algorithmic Considerations and Data Integrity

The computational complexity embodied in merge and join operations is closely tied to the algorithms employed for key matching and record reordering. Hash-based methods, for instance, can achieve average-case performance on the order of $O(n)$, where the uniform distribution of keys is a critical factor in mitigating hash collisions. Alternate approaches, such as sort-merge joins, hinge on the preliminary ordering of data frames—a process that incurs a computational overhead of $O(n \log n)$—yet these methods exhibit strengths in scenarios where partial ordering has already been established. Beyond computational speed, the meticulous handling of anomalies such as duplicate keys, missing values, and data type inconsistencies is of paramount importance. Such discrepancies necessitate the implementation of auxiliary strategies to ensure that the merge operation yields a data frame with verifiable integrity. The interplay between algorithmic efficiency and data consistency forms the cornerstone of effective merging techniques, and an in-depth analysis of these principles provides critical insights into the systematic amalgamation of complex datasets.

R Code Snippet

```
# This R code snippet demonstrates various merge and join operations
# corresponding to the theoretical formulations discussed in the
↪   chapter.
# The central equation:
#   D = {(r1, r2) : r1  D1, r2  D2, and key(r1) = key(r2)}
# is implemented here through different types of joins using R's
↪   merge function
# and data.table for enhanced performance and efficiency.

# Create two example data frames with a common key column 'ID'
D1 <- data.frame(
  ID = c(1, 2, 3, 4),
  Name = c("Alice", "Bob", "Charlie", "David"),
  Score = c(85, 90, 78, 88)
)

D2 <- data.frame(
  ID = c(3, 4, 5, 6),
  Age = c(23, 27, 30, 22),
  Department = c("IT", "HR", "Finance", "Marketing")
```

```r
)

# 1. Inner Join: Only records with matching keys in both D1 and D2
#    are retained.
inner_join_result <- merge(D1, D2, by = "ID")
cat("Inner Join Result:\n")
print(inner_join_result)

# 2. Left Join: All records from D1 are retained.
# Non-matching records from D2 are filled with NA.
left_join_result <- merge(D1, D2, by = "ID", all.x = TRUE)
cat("\nLeft Join Result:\n")
print(left_join_result)

# 3. Right Join: All records from D2 are retained.
# Non-matching records from D1 are filled with NA.
right_join_result <- merge(D1, D2, by = "ID", all.y = TRUE)
cat("\nRight Join Result:\n")
print(right_join_result)

# 4. Outer Join: All records from both D1 and D2 are included.
# Unmatched records are filled with NA.
outer_join_result <- merge(D1, D2, by = "ID", all = TRUE)
cat("\nOuter Join Result:\n")
print(outer_join_result)

# Advanced: Efficient Merge Using data.table for larger datasets.
# This is analogous to a hash-based join which typically achieves
#    average-case O(n) performance.
library(data.table)

# Convert data frames to data.tables
DT1 <- as.data.table(D1)
DT2 <- as.data.table(D2)

# Set keys on data.table objects to enable fast join operations.
setkey(DT1, ID)
setkey(DT2, ID)

# Fast inner join using data.table syntax (hash-based join)
dt_inner_join <- DT1[DT2, nomatch = 0]
cat("\nFast Inner Join using data.table:\n")
print(dt_inner_join)

# Note:
# The code above illustrates different types of merge operations.
# The join operations are based on key matching, as outlined by the
#    equation:
#    D = {(r1, r2) : r1 in D1, r2 in D2, key(r1) = key(r2)}
# It also highlights computational algorithm considerations,
# such as the use of hash-based methods (via data.table) for
#    efficient joins.
```

Chapter 31

Data Reshaping with Base R

Conceptual Framework of Data Reshaping

Data reshaping encompasses the systematic transformation of a dataset's structure without altering its intrinsic informational content. In many analytical workflows, the original configuration of data does not optimally represent the underlying relationships among observations and variables. A typical wide-format dataset can be conceptualized as a matrix X, where each element X_{ij} corresponds to the measurement associated with observation i and variable j. Reshaping operations reorient this structure into alternative layouts, thereby enabling more efficient data manipulation and subsequent analysis. This process is inherently mathematical, as it involves the reorganization of indexed data points and the preservation of data integrity under a bijective mapping between its original and reshaped configurations.

Melting: Converting Wide Format to Long Format

The melting operation transforms a wide-format dataset into a long-format representation, thereby collapsing multiple columns that contain related measurements into a more compact set of key and value pairs. In this conversion, identifiers that characterize distinct observations are isolated from the measured variables. Formally, given a wide-format dataset represented by a set of ordered pairs $\{(i, j, X_{ij}) : i \in I, j \in J\}$, the melting process restructures the data into a long-format table where each row encapsulates the observation index i, the variable identifier j, and the corresponding value X_{ij}. This structural transformation facilitates applications that require data in a normalized form, allowing for operations such as aggregation, filtering, and statistical modeling to be performed on a uniform data layout. The base R functions for reshaping implement these operations by leveraging explicit specification of identifier and measured variable sets, thereby abstracting the underlying matrix transposition logic.

Casting: Reconstituting the Data Structure

Casting is the inverse operation to melting and aims to reassemble a long-format dataset back into its wide format. In this context, casting redistributes the key-value pairs into an array-like structure by spreading the variable identifiers across distinct columns. This transformation is guided by a set of grouping variables that serve to uniquely identify each observation. Mathematically, if the long-format representation is denoted by the set

$$L = \{(i, j, X_{ij}) : i \in I, \ j \in J\},$$

then casting seeks a function $f : I \to X$ that reestablishes the original matrix form where each row is indexed by an element of I and each column by an element of J. The process demands precise alignment of keys and necessitates that the grouping variables are consistent across the data entries. Base R's reshaping mechanisms offer the capacity to perform these complex structural transformations through a single, coherent interface, thus maintaining the fidelity of the original dataset during the conversion process.

Theoretical and Methodological Considerations

Reshaping operations in base R are grounded in the theoretical principles of relational data theory and matrix algebra. The operations of melting and casting are essentially bijective mappings that preserve the cardinality and integrity of the dataset under transformation. The methodological framework underlying these operations requires the explicit identification of primary keys, which serve as the unifying basis for the reassembly of data during casting. Moreover, attention to the ordering of observations and variables is paramount; any deviation from the established ordering protocol can lead to ambiguity in the reshaped result. The computational strategies employed by base R functions optimize data manipulation by systematically managing variable roles, ensuring that identifiers and measurement variables are rigorously partitioned. This disciplined approach not only facilitates predictable and replicable outcomes but also underpins advanced statistical analyses that necessitate consistent data schemas.

R Code Snippet

```
# Create a sample wide-format data frame representing the matrix X,
# where each row corresponds to an observation (i) and each column
↪   to a variable (j)
df_wide <- data.frame(
  id = 1:5,
  score_A = c(90, 85, 88, 95, 80),
  score_B = c(75, 80, 70, 85, 78),
  score_C = c(88, 90, 92, 85, 84)
)

# Display the original wide-format data
print("Original Wide-format Data:")
print(df_wide)

#
↪   ----------------------------------------------------------------------
# Melting: Converting Wide Format to Long Format
#
# The wide-format dataset is represented by:
#   { (i, j, X_ij) : i in I, j in J }
# Here, we use the 'reshape' function in base R to collapse multiple
# measurement columns (score_A, score_B, score_C) into key-value
↪   pairs,
# where 'id' is the identifier, 'variable' is the key (corresponding
↪   to j),
# and 'score' is the observed value X_ij.
#
↪   ----------------------------------------------------------------------

df_long <- reshape(df_wide,
```

```
                    varying = list(c("score_A", "score_B",
                    ↪  "score_C")),
                    v.names = "score",
                    timevar = "variable",
                    times = c("A", "B", "C"),
                    idvar = "id",
                    direction = "long")

# Order the data by 'id' and 'variable' for clarity
df_long <- df_long[order(df_long$id, df_long$variable), ]

print("Long-format Data (After Melting):")
print(df_long)

#
↪  --------------------------------------------------------------------------
# Casting: Reconstituting the Data Structure (Long to Wide)
#
# Casting is the inverse operation where the long-format dataset,
# L = { (i, j, X_ij) : i in I, j in J },
# is transformed back into the wide-format (matrix) by assigning
↪  each
# unique observation id to a row and spreading variable identifiers
↪  into columns.
#
↪  --------------------------------------------------------------------------

df_wide_cast <- reshape(df_long,
                    timevar = "variable",
                    idvar = "id",
                    direction = "wide")

# Clean up column names for consistency (replace 'score.' with
↪  'score_')
names(df_wide_cast) <- gsub("score\\.", "score_",
↪  names(df_wide_cast))

print("Reconstituted Wide-format Data (After Casting):")
print(df_wide_cast)

#
↪  --------------------------------------------------------------------------
# Verification: Ensuring Data Integrity via Bijective Mapping
#
# Extract the measurement matrix X (excluding the identifier column)
↪  from
# both the original wide-format and the recast wide-format data
↪  frames.
# According to the theoretical bijective mapping, these matrices
↪  should be identical.
#
↪  --------------------------------------------------------------------------
```

162

```r
matrix_original <- as.matrix(df_wide[, -1])
matrix_recast   <- as.matrix(df_wide_cast[, -1])

print("Original Matrix X:")
print(matrix_original)

print("Recast Matrix X:")
print(matrix_recast)

if (identical(matrix_original, matrix_recast)) {
  print("Validation: The original and recast matrices are identical.
  ↪ Data integrity preserved.")
} else {
  print("Validation: There is a discrepancy between the original and
  ↪ recast matrices!")
}

# End of comprehensive R code snippet demonstrating:
# 1. Representation of data as a matrix X.
# 2. Melting (wide-to-long conversion) using the 'reshape' function.
# 3. Casting (long-to-wide reconstitution) to restore original data
↪ layout.
# 4. Verification of the bijective mapping that preserves data
↪ integrity.
```

Chapter 32

Reading Data from Files

Foundations of File-Based Data Structures

Data files are regarded as sequential assemblies of textual records, each of which encapsulates a collection of field values. Such files are frequently interpreted as matrices, wherein each row is associated with a distinct observation and each column corresponds to a unique variable. In this framework, the file is understood as a manifestation of a matrix X, where an element X_{ij} represents the data value found at the intersection of the ith record and jth attribute. This perception facilitates the systematic transformation of raw text into a structured internal representation that accurately preserves the source schema.

Mechanisms for Parsing Delimited Files

Within the base R environment, functions such as *read.csv* and *read.table* serve as fundamental instruments for importing data from files. These functions operate on the principle of delimiter-based tokenization, whereby the content of a file is segmented into discrete tokens based on a specified separator, whether it is a comma, a tab, or another character. The delimiter separates individual fields, which are then aggregated into a tabular form. The parsing process integrates rigorous string manipulation and pattern matching techniques, ensuring that the continuous stream of characters is partitioned correctly into rows and columns. This mechanism effectively transforms a raw text file into a structured object that mirrors the logical organization of the original dataset.

Parameterization and Data Type Inference

The import functions provide an extensive set of parameters to fine-tune their behavior. Parameters governing the presence of a header, the exact nature of the delimiter, and the identification of characters to be interpreted as missing values are critical in guiding the parsing process. In addition, these functions implement data type inference mechanisms; by examining a subset of the input records, they deduce appropriate data types for each column. The conversion process maps textual representations to canonical types such as numeric, character, or categorical, thereby aligning the imported data with the requirements of subsequent analyses. This inferential procedure is essential for ensuring both the semantic integrity and the computational viability of the data structure.

Handling Imperfections within Source Data

Files of a practical nature may exhibit a range of irregularities, including inconsistent field counts, embedded delimiters within field values, or unanticipated line breaks. Robust parsing algorithms incorporate error detection and correction strategies to address such imperfections. These functions undertake consistency checks during the import process to identify anomalies and, where possible, substitute missing or corrupted entries with appropriate placeholder values. The mechanisms for dealing with extraneous spaces, escape characters, and other formatting challenges are embedded within the parsing logic to ensure that the resulting data frame maintains a high degree of fidelity to the intrinsic structure of the source file.

Advanced Considerations and Optimization Strategies

When dealing with voluminous data files, performance and efficiency become paramount concerns. The data import functions provide several optimization features designed to mitigate memory overhead and enhance reading speed. Techniques such as buffered reading, preallocation of memory, and selective column parsing contribute to the efficient transformation of large files into structured datasets. Furthermore, provisions exist for handling locale-specific formatting, which may include variations in decimal markers or thousands separators. The balancing act between algorithmic complexity and computational efficiency is achieved through careful parameter tuning, ensuring that the methods applied are both scalable and robust under resource-constrained conditions.

R Code Snippet

```
# Set locale for consistent numeric formatting if required
# Uncomment and modify the following lines according to your system
# Sys.setlocale("LC_ALL", "English_United States.UTF-8")   # For
↪    Windows
# Sys.setlocale("LC_ALL", "en_US.UTF-8")                    # For
↪    Unix/Linux

# Define the file path to the CSV file
file_path <- "data/sample_data.csv"

# Function: read_file_data
# Description: Imports a delimited file into R using specified
↪    parameters.
# It performs data type inference, error handling, and prints the
↪    structure of the imported data.
read_file_data <- function(file, header = TRUE, sep = ",",
                      na.strings = c("", "NA", "NULL"),
                      ↪    stringsAsFactors = FALSE) {

    # Using tryCatch to manage potential errors or warnings during
    ↪    file import
    data <- tryCatch({
        # Import data using read.csv; this reads the file into a
        ↪    data.frame
        df <- read.csv(file, header = header, sep = sep,
                    na.strings = na.strings, stringsAsFactors =
                    ↪    stringsAsFactors)
```

```r
  # Print the structure of the imported data to inspect data type
  ↪  inference
  cat("Data structure after import:\n")
  str(df)
  return(df)
}, warning = function(w) {
  message("Warning encountered: ", conditionMessage(w))
  return(NULL)
}, error = function(e) {
  message("Error encountered: ", conditionMessage(e))
  return(NULL)
})

  return(data)
}


# Import the data using the defined function
data_frame <- read_file_data(file_path)

# If data was imported successfully, proceed with transformations
↪  and checks
if (!is.null(data_frame)) {

  # Convert the data.frame to a matrix representation to mimic file
  ↪  matrix X
  data_matrix <- as.matrix(data_frame)
  cat("\nMatrix representation of the data:\n")
  print(data_matrix)

  # Check for consistency: all rows in a data.frame should have the
  ↪  same number of columns
  # (This is more a conceptual check as data.frames inherently have
  ↪  consistent column counts)
  if (nrow(data_frame) > 0 && any(sapply(data_frame, length) !=
  ↪  nrow(data_frame))) {
    warning("Inconsistent row lengths detected. Verify the source
    ↪  data for anomalies.")
  }

  # Handling Missing Data:
  # Replace NA values in numeric columns with a placeholder (e.g.,
  ↪  -999)
  numeric_cols <- sapply(data_frame, is.numeric)
  data_frame[numeric_cols] <- lapply(data_frame[numeric_cols],
  ↪  function(col) {
    col[is.na(col)] <- -999
    return(col)
  })

  cat("\nSummary statistics after handling missing values:\n")
  print(summary(data_frame))

  # Selective Column Parsing:
```

```
# Demonstrate processing only the first three columns if available
if (ncol(data_frame) >= 3) {
  selected_columns <- data_frame[, 1:3]
  cat("\nPreview of the first three columns:\n")
  print(head(selected_columns))
}

# Advanced: Optimize reading large files using the 'data.table'
↪   package's fread function.
# fread is well-suited for buffered reading and improved
↪   performance.
if (requireNamespace("data.table", quietly = TRUE)) {
  cat("\nReading data using data.table::fread for optimized
  ↪   performance:\n")
  library(data.table)
  dt_data <- fread(file_path, header = TRUE, sep = ",", na.strings
  ↪   = c("", "NA", "NULL"))
  print(head(dt_data))
} else {
  cat("\ndata.table package not available. Skipping optimized file
  ↪   reading demonstration.\n")
}

} else {
  cat("\nData import failed. Please verify the file path, format,
  ↪   and delimiter used.\n")
}
```

Chapter 33

Writing Data to Files

Conceptual Foundations of Data Exportation

The process of exporting data in a programming environment represents a critical phase in the lifecycle of data processing and analysis. In this context, the transformation of an internal data structure, typically represented as a data frame or matrix, into an external representation is formalized through functions such as write.csv and write.table. These functions facilitate the conversion of in-memory objects into a delimited text format, thereby establishing a bridge between computational results and persistent storage. The exported file can be envisioned as a two-dimensional array X, where each element X_{ij} encodes the value corresponding to the ith observation and the jth variable. This abstraction provides a rigorous foundation for subsequent operations, including data sharing, archival, and interoperability with external systems.

Specification of Export Functions in R

The functionalities inherent in write.csv, write.table, and analogous functions are underpinned by a series of parameters that dictate the explicit formatting of the output file. Each function adheres to a systematic protocol for parsing a structured object into a sequential assembly of text. The role of these functions extends beyond the mere serialization of data; they execute complex operations that include the conversion of data types, the treatment of special characters, and the arrangement of delimiters to ensure compatibility with external applications. The systematic mapping from the internal representation to a textual matrix is embodied in the algorithmic structure of these functions, thus ensuring that the inherent properties of the data, such as numerical precision and categorical distinctions, are preserved in the output format.

Parameterization and Customization Techniques

A detailed examination of the configurable parameters reveals a multidimensional approach that governs data export. Parameters such as the choice of delimiter, the enclosure of character strings, and the inclusion of a header row are instrumental in determining the structure of the exported file. Further refinement is achieved through options that control the handling of missing values, the specification of decimal markers, and the suppression of row names. The parameterization effectively allows the exported file to be tailored to the requirements of downstream applications, thereby offering a high degree of flexibility. This customization is paramount when interfacing with diverse data ecosystems where consistency in data representation is essential for maintaining semantic integrity.

Considerations for Data Integrity and Formatting

Data integrity during the export phase is maintained through meticulous handling of various formatting challenges. The precise definition of field separators must accommodate cases where the delimiter might appear as a part of the field content, necessitating the use of escape sequences or quotation marks. The verification of data types is ensured by a thorough analysis of the underlying structure, where numerical values, character strings, and categorical labels are subjected to explicit conversion rules. This careful treatment prevents loss of information and minimizes rounding errors or truncations, particularly in the presence of high-precision numeric data. The resulting file adheres to a stringent format that guarantees consistency with the original data semantics.

Optimization Strategies for High-Volume Data Output

In scenarios involving extensive datasets, the efficiency of the export process becomes paramount. The implementation of write.csv, write.table, and similar functions incorporates optimization strategies that address the constraints of memory allocation and I/O bandwidth. Buffering techniques, preallocation of storage, and selective formatting options are systematically utilized to expedite the writing process without compromising data accuracy. Such optimizations enable the execution of data export operations in resource-intensive environments, ensuring that the computational overhead remains within acceptable limits while delivering a robust and scalable output format.

R Code Snippet

```
# Example R Code Snippet for Writing Data to Files
# This script demonstrates the conversion of an in-memory data
↪   structure (data.frame)
# into a delimited text file representation, closely following the
↪   conceptual model where
# each element X_{ij} represents the value at the i-th observation
↪   and j-th variable.

# Set the seed for reproducibility
set.seed(123)

# Generate a sample data frame with 100 observations
n_obs <- 100
X <- data.frame(
  Observation = 1:n_obs,
  NumericVar1 = round(rnorm(n_obs, mean = 50, sd = 10), 2),   #
  ↪   Random normally distributed numbers with rounding for
  ↪   precision
  NumericVar2 = round(runif(n_obs, min = 20, max = 80), 2),     #
  ↪   Random uniformly distributed numbers
  Category    = sample(c("A", "B", "C"), n_obs, replace = TRUE) #
  ↪   Categorical variable
)

# Introduce missing values into the numeric columns for
↪   demonstration purposes
X$NumericVar1[sample(1:n_obs, 5)] <- NA
X$NumericVar2[sample(1:n_obs, 3)] <- NA
```

```r
# Display the first few rows of the data to verify content
print(head(X))

# The following steps illustrate the transformation of the data
↪ frame (internal representation)
# into an external textual matrix where each field corresponds to
↪ X_{ij}.

# Exporting data using write.csv:
# - 'row.names = FALSE' ensures that row names are not included in
↪ the exported file.
# - 'na = ""' converts any NA values to empty strings to maintain
↪ formatting integrity.
csv_filename <- "exported_data.csv"
write.csv(X, file = csv_filename, row.names = FALSE, na = "")

# Exporting data using write.table with customization:
# This example uses a tab as field separator and encloses character
↪ strings in quotes.
table_filename <- "exported_data.tsv"
write.table(X, file = table_filename, sep = "\t", col.names = TRUE,
↪ row.names = FALSE,
            quote = TRUE, na = "")

# Optimization Strategies for High-Volume Data Output:
# For large datasets, it is critical to monitor I/O performance.
# The system.time function helps benchmark the export process.
benchmark_csv <- system.time({
  write.csv(X, file = "benchmark_export.csv", row.names = FALSE, na
  ↪ = "")
})
print(benchmark_csv)

# End of data export demonstration.
```

172

Chapter 34

Basic Plotting with Base R

Foundations of the Base Graphics System

Within the computational framework of R, the base graphics system provides a fundamental apparatus for creating visual representations of data. This system operates under an immediate mode paradigm, whereby each plotting command directly influences the graphical device and contributes to a cumulative output. The design adheres to a rigorous abstract specification that defines graphical primitives, coordinate mappings, and the delineation of plotting regions. Data values are mapped onto a two-dimensional space via the x and y axes, ensuring that numerical and categorical information is rendered in a spatially coherent manner.

Structural Components and Visual Elements

The graphical representation within the base system is organized into well-defined regions, including the central plotting area and the surrounding margins that host supplementary elements such as axis labels, titles, and annotations. Each plot is constructed upon a coordinate system that defines the spatial positions of points, lines, and other geometric markers. The system partitions the visual field into components that are parameterized independently, yet inter-

173

dependently contribute to the overall graphical composition. This partitioning is achieved through a precise mapping from abstract data structures to rendered elements, ensuring that visual components maintain their intended proportionality and alignment.

Parameterization and Aesthetic Customization

Customization of visual output in the base graphics environment is accomplished through an extensive array of graphical parameters. These parameters govern attributes such as color, point shape, line type, and font size, and may be specified on a global scale or applied locally to individual plotting directives. The underlying mechanism employs a systematic approach to parameter propagation, in which aesthetic properties are dynamically adjusted to reflect both the intrinsic characteristics of the data and the desired stylistic presentation. Such parameterization enables a nuanced control over the graphic's appearance, thereby facilitating a precise and faithful depiction of data relationships.

Rendering Pipeline and Graphical Devices

The transition from abstract plotting instructions to a concrete visual output is managed by the rendering pipeline, which operates within the confines of a designated graphical device—be it a display screen, a window, or an external file. The pipeline initiates with the establishment of a plotting frame and proceeds through the computation of spatial coordinates for all graphical elements. Subsequent stages of the pipeline execute low-level drawing operations that convert these coordinates and parameter specifications into pixel representations. Optimization strategies integrated into the pipeline ensure efficient memory management and input/output processing, thus accommodating the demands of rendering even in scenarios involving extensive datasets.

Conceptual Interpretation of Data Visualizations

The base graphics system in R enables the transformation of complex data sets into intelligible visual constructs by mapping quantitative measurements onto a spatial medium. The visual representations produced reflect key relationships, trends, and variations inherent in the data, conveyed through elements such as axes, grid lines, and plotted points. The careful selection and configuration of graphical parameters support the accurate translation of abstract data into visual metaphors, thereby bridging the gap between numerical analysis and perceptual comprehension. The process embodies principles of computational geometry and statistical reasoning, culminating in visualizations that encapsulate both the precision of data and the elegance of design.

R Code Snippet

```
# ------------------------------------------------------
# R Code Snippet: Comprehensive Example of Base R Plotting
# Demonstrating equations, parameterization, and algorithmic
↪    constructs
# ------------------------------------------------------

# 1. Setting Global Graphical Parameters and Layout
par(mfrow = c(2, 2))            # create a 2x2 plot layout
par(mar = c(5, 4, 4, 2) + 0.1)  # set margins: bottom, left, top,
↪    right


# ------------------------------------------------------
# 2. Plotting a Quadratic Function with Mathematical Annotation
# Define the quadratic function: y = a*x^2 + b*x + c, here a=1, b=0,
↪    c=0 (y = x^2)
quad_func <- function(x, a = 1, b = 0, c = 0) {
  return(a * x^2 + b * x + c)
}
# Generate x values
x <- seq(-10, 10, length.out = 200)
y <- quad_func(x)
# Plot the quadratic function (curve) with customizations
plot(x, y, type = "l", col = "blue", lwd = 2,
     main = "Quadratic Function: y = x^2",
     xlab = "x", ylab = expression(x^2))
# Add a grid for better readability
grid(col = "gray", lty = "dotted")
# Annotate the graph with the equation text
```

175

```r
text(0, 50, labels = expression(y == x^2), col = "red", cex = 1.2)


# ----------------------------------------------------
# 3. Scatter Plot with Linear Regression and Equation Annotation
# Generate noisy data for demonstration
set.seed(123)
x_data <- seq(0, 10, length.out = 50)
y_data <- 3 * x_data + rnorm(50, mean = 0, sd = 3)
# Create scatter plot with data points
plot(x_data, y_data, pch = 19, col = "darkgreen",
    main = "Scatter Plot with Linear Regression",
    xlab = "Independent Variable", ylab = "Dependent Variable")
# Fit a linear model to the data
fit <- lm(y_data ~ x_data)
# Draw the regression line on the plot
abline(fit, col = "red", lwd = 2)
# Create a mathematical annotation for the regression equation
eq <- substitute(italic(y) == a + b %.% italic(x),
                 list(a = round(coef(fit)[1], 1), b =
                 ↪  round(coef(fit)[2], 1)))
legend("topleft", legend = as.expression(eq), bty = "n", text.col =
↪  "red")


# ----------------------------------------------------
# 4. Advanced Plotting: Histogram with Density Curve and Boxplot
# Histogram with Density Overlay
hist_data <- rnorm(1000, mean = 0, sd = 1)
hist(hist_data, breaks = 30, prob = TRUE, col = "lightblue",
    main = "Histogram with Density Curve", xlab = "Value")
lines(density(hist_data), col = "darkblue", lwd = 2)

# Boxplot for Stratified Data
group <- rep(c("Group 1", "Group 2"), each = 50)
values <- c(rnorm(50, mean = 5, sd = 1), rnorm(50, mean = 7, sd =
↪  1.5))
boxplot(values ~ group, col = c("orange", "lightgreen"),
        main = "Boxplot by Group", xlab = "Group", ylab = "Values")


# ----------------------------------------------------
# 5. Direct Mathematical Function Plot using curve()
# Plot the sinc function: f(x) = sin(x)/x (handling x=0 is implicit)
curve(sin(x)/x, from = -10, to = 10, col = "purple", lwd = 2,
    main = "Plot of sin(x)/x", xlab = "x", ylab =
    ↪  expression(frac(sin(x), x)))
abline(h = 0, col = "gray", lty = "dashed")
# Add an annotation with a mathematical label
text(5, 0.3, labels = expression(frac(sin(x), x)), col = "purple")


# ----------------------------------------------------
```

```
# 6. Reset Graphical Parameters to Default (Single Plot)
par(mfrow = c(1, 1))
```

Chapter 35

Plot Customization

Graphical Parameterization in the Base Graphics Paradigm

The customization of plot aesthetics is governed by a robust system of graphical parameters that enable precise control over visual elements. Within this paradigm, attributes such as

$mathrm colors$,

$mathrm linetype$,

$mathrm pointshape$, and

$mathrm fontstyle$ may be adjusted through a collection of well-defined settings. These parameters are integrated into the plotting framework in a manner that permits both global and local modifications, thereby ensuring consistent rendering of components across a variety of graphical outputs. The configuration process involves mapping abstract parameter values onto concrete visual representations, a procedure that is essential for achieving a harmonious balance between informational content and aesthetic refinement.

Color Schemes and Palette Considerations

The selection and manipulation of color schemes constitute a fundamental aspect of plot customization. Colors function as both discriminators of data classes and as tools for emphasizing critical information within a visualization. The comprehensive support for color specification allows for the use of predetermined color names as well as customized hexadecimal codes, with the possibility of

incorporating transparency parameters via indices such as
alpha. The interplay between background and foreground color
choices, together with the appropriate adjustment of brightness
and contrast, contributes to the effective communication of quantitative relationships and categorical distinctions within the graphical output.

Customizing Textual Elements: Titles, La-
bels, and Annotations

Textual components, including plot titles, axis labels, and annotations, serve as indispensable vehicles for conveying context and
nuance. The integration of mathematical expressions into these
textual elements necessitates rigorous adherence to formatting conventions, such as the enclosure of mathematical symbols—e.g., x,
mu, or
sigma—within dollar signs to ensure proper typesetting. A variety of font attributes, including size, style, and color, are available
to format such textual items so that they not only enhance the
overall visual appeal but also maintain clarity and precision in the
conveyance of quantitative information. This systematic approach
to text customization facilitates the clear delineation of data dimensions and supports the interpretability of the plot.

Axes Formatting and Scaling Techniques

Axes constitute the structural backbone of any graphical representation by delineating the coordinate space in which data are displayed. Customizing these elements involves the meticulous adjustment of parameters that govern the positioning and appearance of
tick marks, the specification of axis limits, and the implementation
of scaling transformations. The configuration of axes may include
both linear and non-linear (e.g., logarithmic) scaling techniques to
accurately represent data distributions that exhibit complex behavior. Special attention is given to the alignment and spacing of
tick marks, which must be calibrated to ensure that the mapping
of data points onto the two-dimensional plane yields an intelligible
and coherent plot structure.

Advanced Aesthetic Refinements

The pursuit of an optimal balance between informational density and visual elegance often warrants advanced refinement techniques that extend beyond basic parameter adjustments. Layering multiple graphical elements with varying degrees of opacity and prominence enables the construction of plots that exhibit both depth and clarity. The precise arrangement of plot components—ranging from background grids to overlaid data markers—requires a well-considered calibration to ensure that each element contributes meaningfully to the overall visual narrative. This advanced approach to aesthetic customization leverages an iterative process of parameter tuning, whereby the graphical output is continually refined to achieve a state of both expressive complexity and stylistic cohesion.

R Code Snippet

```r
# Comprehensive R Code for Plot Customization Demonstration

# Clear current workspace variables
rm(list = ls())

# Set seed for reproducibility
set.seed(123)

# Generate sample data: a noisy sine wave
x <- seq(0, 2 * pi, length.out = 100)
y <- sin(x) + rnorm(100, mean = 0, sd = 0.1)

# Save current graphical parameters and configure margins
op <- par(no.readonly = TRUE)
par(mar = c(5, 5, 4, 2) + 0.1)  # bottom, left, top, right margins

# Create base plot with customized graphical parameters
plot(x, y,
     type = "p",               # Scatter plot type
     pch = 21,                 # Point type that supports
     ↪ background color
     bg = adjustcolor("steelblue", alpha.f = 0.6),  #
     ↪ Semi-transparent fill for points
     col = "darkblue",         # Border color for points
     cex = 1.2,                # Increase point size
     main = expression("Customized Plot of " * sin(x) * " + Noise"),
     xlab = expression("Angle (" * theta * ")"),
     ylab = "Sinusoidal Value",
```

```r
    frame.plot = FALSE,          # Remove the default box frame
    ↪ around the plot
    las = 1,                     # Make axis labels horizontal
    cex.lab = 1.2,               # Increase axis label font size
    cex.axis = 0.9)              # Axis tick label size

# Add a light dotted grid to enhance readability
grid(col = "grey80", lty = "dotted")

# Customize the X-axis with specific tick positions and mathematical
↪ labels
axis(1,
    at = seq(0, 2 * pi, by = pi / 2),
    labels = c("0", expression(pi/2), expression(pi),
               expression(3*pi/2), expression(2*pi)),
    col.axis = "darkgreen",
    font.axis = 2)

# Customize the Y-axis ticks with alternate coloring
axis(2,
    at = seq(min(y, na.rm = TRUE), max(y, na.rm = TRUE), length.out
    ↪ = 5),
    col.axis = "darkred",
    font.axis = 2)

# Use a moving average (rolling mean) to smooth the data points
# Install and load the 'zoo' package if not already installed
if (!require("zoo")) {
  install.packages("zoo")
  library(zoo)
} else {
  library(zoo)
}

# Compute a rolling mean with a window size of 5
y_smooth <- rollmean(y, k = 5, fill = NA)

# Overlay the smoothed trend line with custom line type and color
lines(x, y_smooth, col = "firebrick", lwd = 2, lty = 2)

# Add a legend to the plot with custom symbols and line styles
legend("topright",
       legend = c("Raw Data", "Smoothed Trend"),
       pch = c(21, NA),                    # Only raw data has a
       ↪ point symbol
       pt.bg = c(adjustcolor("steelblue", alpha.f = 0.6), NA),
       col = c("darkblue", "firebrick"),
       lty = c(NA, 2),                     # Trend line style only
       ↪ for the smoothed line
       lwd = c(NA, 2),                     # Line width for the
       ↪ smoothed line
       bty = "n")                          # No border around the
       ↪ legend
```

```r
# Annotate the plot with text, including a mathematical expression
text(pi, max(y, na.rm = TRUE),
     labels = expression(paste("Peak at ", pi, " radians")),
     pos = 3, cex = 0.9, col = "purple")

# Demonstrate usage of a custom color palette for additional points
# Generating extra data points to highlight on the plot
additional_points <- data.frame(
  x = seq(0, 2 * pi, length.out = 10),
  y = sin(seq(0, 2 * pi, length.out = 10)) + 0.3
)

# Plot these additional points with a distinct point shape and a hex
↪    color with transparency
points(additional_points$x, additional_points$y,
       pch = 24,                          # Use a triangle point shape
       col = "black",
       bg = "#FF573380",                  # Custom hexadecimal color with
       ↪    alpha transparency
       cex = 1.5)

# Restore original graphical parameters
par(op)

# End of Comprehensive Plot Customization Script
```

Chapter 36

Histograms and Density Plots

Fundamental Concepts of Data Distribution Visualization

The graphical representation of data distributions provides a framework for examining the statistical properties inherent in empirical datasets. Histograms and density plots are deployed as complementary visualization techniques that facilitate a rigorous understanding of data behavior. Histograms discretize the range of observations into contiguous intervals and quantify the frequency or relative frequency with which data points fall within each interval. In contrast, density plots employ kernel smoothing techniques to estimate a continuous probability density function over the domain of the data. Each method encapsulates essential characteristics of variability, central tendency, and dispersion, thereby furnishing a structured avenue for analyzing modality and shape without reliance on extraneous inferential assumptions.

Histograms: Structure, Binning, and Interpretation

Histograms are constructed by partitioning the data range into discrete segments, commonly referred to as bins, wherein the frequency counts are computed for each segment. The normalized frequency within a bin is often determined by dividing the count by the product of the total number of observations and the bin width (h). Various heuristic criteria, including Scott's rule and the Freedman-Diaconis rule, are employed to ascertain an optimal value for h, aiming to balance resolution against statistical noise. The visual arrangement of bins, with each bin reflecting an aggregated summary of data, allows for an immediate appraisal of the distribution's shape and structure. The inherent simplicity of the histogram renders it a valuable tool for preliminary data analysis as it both highlights empirical concentrations and delineates potential outlier behavior.

Density Plots: Kernel Estimation and Smoothing Techniques

Density plots are generated through the process of kernel density estimation, whereby a smooth approximation of the underlying probability density function is derived from a finite set of observations. The density estimate at a point x is typically expressed as

$$f(x) = \frac{1}{n \cdot h} \sum_{i=1}^{n} K\left(\frac{x - x_i}{h}\right),$$

where n denotes the total number of data points, x_i represents the individual observations, h is the bandwidth parameter, and K is the kernel function, often selected as the Gaussian kernel. The choice of bandwidth is crucial; a small value of h produces a density estimate that may overfit the sample data, capturing noise as structure, whereas a larger h imposes a higher degree of smoothness that can obscure subtle features. The continuous nature of density plots, derived from the summation of weighted kernel functions, provides a refined representation of data distribution that facilitates the detection of multimodal structures and local fluctuations.

Comparative Analysis: Histograms Versus Density Plots

Histograms and density plots, while both aimed at visualizing data distributions, convey complementary aspects of the underlying information. The discrete binning of histograms emphasizes the count-based representation of data, thereby making them particularly effective for identifying frequency concentrations and abrupt changes in distributional levels. In contrast, density plots yield a continuous narrative through the aggregation of kernel functions, which smooth the data in a manner that accentuates the overall trend and the finer nuances of distributional variability. The integration of these perspectives enables a multifaceted exploration of data, wherein the histogram provides a direct manifestation of empirical frequencies and the density plot offers insight into the probabilistic structure shaped by the inherent variability of the dataset.

Parameter Considerations for Visual Data Representation

The efficacy of histograms and density plots is contingent upon the meticulous selection of parameters governing their construction. For histograms, the determination of the bin width (h) and the alignment of bin boundaries are pivotal factors that influence the clarity and accuracy of data portrayal. In the context of density plots, the kernel function K and the bandwidth h form the core of the estimation process; the bandwidth must be judiciously calibrated to strike a balance between overfitting and oversmoothing. The interplay of these parameters demands rigorous statistical consideration, as subtle adjustments can profoundly affect the visual representation of the distribution. This parameterization process is instrumental in ensuring that the visualization faithfully encapsulates the statistical properties of the dataset while mitigating the introduction of artifacts or distortions.

R Code Snippet

```
# R code snippet for illustrating Histogram and Density Plot
↪  concepts

# Set seed for reproducibility
set.seed(123)

# Generate synthetic data (normally distributed)
n <- 1000
data <- rnorm(n, mean = 0, sd = 1)
```

185

```r
#----------------------------------------------------------------------
# Determine Optimal Bin Widths for Histograms
#----------------------------------------------------------------------
# Freedman-Diaconis rule:
#   fd_bin_width = 2 * IQR(data) / n^(1/3)
fd_bin_width <- 2 * IQR(data) / (n^(1/3))
# Number of bins based on FD rule:
bins_fd <- ceiling((max(data) - min(data)) / fd_bin_width)

# Scott's rule:
#   scott_bin_width = 3.5 * sd(data) / n^(1/3)
scott_bin_width <- 3.5 * sd(data) / (n^(1/3))
bins_scott <- ceiling((max(data) - min(data)) / scott_bin_width)

# Print bin width and bin count results
cat("Freedman-Diaconis bin width:", fd_bin_width, "\n")
cat("Number of bins (FD rule):", bins_fd, "\n")
cat("Scott bin width:", scott_bin_width, "\n")
cat("Number of bins (Scott rule):", bins_scott, "\n")


#----------------------------------------------------------------------
# Plot Histogram with Kernel Density Overlay
#----------------------------------------------------------------------
# Create a histogram using FD rule bins, with probability densities
hist(data, breaks = bins_fd, probability = TRUE,
     main = "Histogram with Freedman-Diaconis Bins",
     xlab = "Data Values", col = "lightblue", border = "black")

# Overlay density estimation using R's built-in density() function
dens <- density(data)  # default uses Gaussian kernel
lines(dens, col = "red", lwd = 2)

#----------------------------------------------------------------------
# Manual Kernel Density Estimation (Using Gaussian Kernel)
#----------------------------------------------------------------------
# Define the Gaussian kernel function:
#   K(u) = (1/sqrt(2*pi)) * exp(-0.5 * u^2)
gaussian_kernel <- function(u) {
  (1 / sqrt(2 * pi)) * exp(-0.5 * u^2)
}

# Define manual density estimation function based on:
#   f(x) = (1/(n * h)) * sum_{i=1}^{n} K((x - x_i) / h)
manual_density <- function(x, data, h) {
  n <- length(data)
  kernel_values <- gaussian_kernel((x - data) / h)
  sum(kernel_values) / (n * h)
}

# Use the bandwidth from the built-in density estimate for
#   consistency
h <- dens$bw
```

186

```r
# Create a grid of x values covering the data range
x_grid <- seq(min(data) - 1, max(data) + 1, length.out = 200)

# Compute manual density estimates across the grid
density_manual <- sapply(x_grid, manual_density, data = data, h = h)

#-------------------------------------------------------------------
# Plot Comparison of Manual and Built-in Density Estimates
#-------------------------------------------------------------------
# Plot the manual density estimate
plot(x_grid, density_manual, type = "l", lwd = 2, col = "blue",
     main = "Manual Kernel Density Estimation vs. Built-in",
     xlab = "Data Values", ylab = "Density")
# Overlay the built-in density estimate (dashed red line)
lines(dens$x, dens$y, col = "red", lwd = 2, lty = 2)
# Add a legend to differentiate the estimates
legend("topright", legend = c("Manual Estimate", "Built-in
↪   density()"),
       col = c("blue", "red"), lty = c(1, 2), lwd = 2)
```

Chapter 37

Bar Plots and Pie Charts

Fundamental Aspects of Categorical Visualizations

Categorical visualizations encapsulate the representation of discrete data into structured graphical formats, wherein each category is assigned a distinct visual element. The quantitative information underlying each category may be expressed in absolute counts or normalized proportions, mathematically defined by $p_i = n_i/N$, where n_i denotes the frequency for category i and N is the aggregate of all observations. This transformation affords a clear depiction of the data distribution while maintaining a proportional correspondence among the individual categories. Such representations are instrumental in scenarios where the elucidation of compositional structure is paramount.

Bar Plots: Construction and Configuration

Bar plots materialize categorical data through the construction of rectangular elements, each of which is aligned along a common axis. The magnitude of each bar is typically proportional to either the raw count or a normalized measure, with the latter being computed as n_i/N. The spatial arrangement of these bars, whether oriented vertically or horizontally, is determined by the nature of the underlying data and the intended emphasis on discrete versus continuous comparisons. The delineation of inter-bar spacing and the width of each bar are parameterized carefully to optimize the balance between granularity and clarity. Furthermore, the absence of continuous interpolation between discrete bars reinforces the categorical nature of the data, ensuring that each bar stands as an isolated testament to its corresponding numerical value.

Pie Charts: Geometric and Proportional Analysis

Pie charts provide an alternative approach to displaying categorical distributions by partitioning a circular plane into sectors, with each sector's central angle reflecting its proportional contribution. Mathematically, the conversion of the relative frequency p_i into an angular measure is accomplished via the relation $\theta_i = 360° \cdot p_i$, ensuring that the sum of all sectors satisfies the constraint $\sum_i \theta_i = 360°$. The geometric configuration of pie charts inherently appeals to a holistic interpretation of the data, where the area of each sector, and consequently its associated angle, symbolizes the magnitude of each category in relation to the entirety of the dataset. This continuous angular framework affords a visual synthesis that emphasizes comparative proportions and the distributional balance across the segmented circular domain.

Comparative Analysis of Bar Plots and Pie Charts

The two visualization methods diverge in their approach to encoding categorical information. Bar plots are characterized by their discrete, linear representation, where the height or length of each bar is directly indicative of the underlying numerical value. This modality allows for the immediate identification of quantitative differences across categories and is particularly effective when precise comparative measurements are desired. In contrast, pie charts adopt a circular framework that distributes the data proportionately around a central point. The translation of numerical proportions into angular measures yields a visual narrative that emphasizes the compositional equilibrium inherent in the dataset. The choice between employing bar plots or pie charts is frequently dictated by the specific attributes of the data and the intended mode of interpretation; while bar plots excel in scenarios that require exact quantification, pie charts offer a more integrated visualization that encapsulates the overall structure of the categorical distribution without recourse to explicit numerical demarcation.

R Code Snippet

```
# R Code Snippet: Visualizing Categorical Data with Bar Plots and
↪   Pie Charts
# This script demonstrates:
# 1. The computation of normalized proportions (p_i = n_i / N)
# 2. The conversion of these proportions into angular measures for a
↪   pie chart (theta_i = 360 * p_i)
# 3. The construction of both a bar plot and a pie chart to
↪   represent the categorical data

# Step 1: Define Categorical Data
categories <- c("Category A", "Category B", "Category C", "Category
↪   D")
# Frequency counts for each category (n_i)
counts <- c(50, 30, 10, 10)

# Step 2: Compute Total Observations and Normalized Proportions
total <- sum(counts)              # Total count (N)
proportions <- counts / total     # Normalized proportions: p_i = n_i
↪   / N

# Step 3: Compute Sector Angles for Pie Chart
angles <- 360 * proportions       # Angular measure for each category:
↪   theta_i = 360 * p_i

# Display the computed values in the console for verification
cat("Frequencies (n_i):", counts, "\n")
cat("Total Observations (N):", total, "\n")
cat("Normalized Proportions (p_i):", proportions, "\n")
cat("Sector Angles (theta_i in degrees):", angles, "\n\n")

# Step 4: Constructing the Bar Plot
# The height of each bar represents the frequency (n_i) directly.
barplot(counts,
        names.arg = categories,
        col = "skyblue",
        main = "Bar Plot of Categorical Data",
        xlab = "Categories",
        ylab = "Frequency",
        ylim = c(0, max(counts) + 10))
```

```
# Step 5: Constructing the Pie Chart
# In the pie chart, each sector's angle is proportional to p_i;
↪   labels include percentage values.
pie(counts,
    labels = paste(categories, "\n", sprintf("%.1f%%", proportions *
    ↪ 100)),
    col = rainbow(length(categories)),
    main = "Pie Chart of Categorical Data")

# End of Script
```
_____

Chapter 38

Scatter Plots and Line Graphs

Scatter Plots: Representing Bivariate Relationships

Scatter plots provide a graphical representation of the interdependence between two continuous variables. In this representation, each observation is denoted by a point plotted according to its coordinates (x_i, y_i) in a Cartesian coordinate system. The spatial distribution of these points facilitates the identification of patterns, clusters, and potential anomalies. The placement of each point is governed by the underlying joint probability distribution of the variables, and the aggregation of points often serves as a precursor to the estimation of statistical measures such as the Pearson correlation coefficient, denoted by ρ. This visual form is particularly adept at revealing the degree of linear association as well as nonlinear phenomena that may arise from complex interactions between variables.

The geometry of a scatter plot is further compounded by considerations of scale and dimensionality. Appropriate selection of axis limits ensures that the inherent variability in the data is neither obscured by truncation nor diluted by overextension. In cases where the range of values spans several orders of magnitude, transformations such as $y = \log(y)$ or $x = \log(x)$ are employed to render the distribution more uniform and enhance interpretability. The isolated nature of each marker underscores the discrete sampling of what is essentially a continuous phenomenon, allowing for an unmediated view of the variability and the potential linear or curvilinear trends that characterize the data.

Line Graphs: Depicting Sequential Trends

Line graphs are constructed by sequentially connecting individual data points with line segments, thereby emphasizing continuity across a series of observations. Each point, typically represented as (x_i, y_i), is linked to its neighbor to form a continuous trajectory that mirrors the evolution of the variable of interest. This form of visualization is particularly effective in contexts where the independent variable exhibits an intrinsic order, such as time or a sequential index. The continuous lines not only highlight local fluctuations but also reveal overarching trends, gradients, and the potential presence of periodic behavior.

The construction of a line graph involves a careful balance between the visual representation of discrete data points and the interpolation of intermediate values. The connected line segments act as approximations of an underlying continuous function $f(x)$, thereby providing a visual estimate of the rate of change. This rate, which may be interpreted as an empirical derivative, is critical for the identification of acceleration or deceleration trends. Moreover, the use of line graphs often entails the incorporation of scaling strategies that ensure the plotted trends are not distorted by the distribution of the independent variable. In applications where the sequential dependency is paramount, the line graph serves as an indispensable tool for visualizing the dynamic interplay between variables over a continuum.

Comparative Examination of Graphical Representations

The distinct mechanisms underlying scatter plots and line graphs underscore a fundamental paradigm in data visualization: the trade-off between discrete representation and continuous interpolation. Scatter plots, by virtue of their isolated point markers, inherently emphasize the individuality of each observed pair (x_i, y_i), thereby facilitating an unembellished exploration of the statistical dispersion and the clustering of the data. This quality is particularly advantageous when the objective is to detect outliers or to examine the variability inherent in the observed phenomena.

In contrast, line graphs integrate the discrete observations into a coherent visual trajectory, thereby accentuating the sequential progression and trend estimation within the dataset. The continuous lines serve to smooth over the randomness that may be apparent in a scatter plot, offering instead a synthesized view of the trend dynamics. Such synthesis is especially pertinent when the data is expected to follow a gradual evolution, as the connected markers provide a visual narrative that is sensitive to both gradual shifts and abrupt changes. The choice between employing a scatter plot or a line graph is thus intrinsically linked to the specific characteristics of the data and the nature of the relationship that is intended to be depicted.

Geometric and Statistical Underpinnings

The visual paradigms of scatter plots and line graphs are deeply rooted in the principles of geometry and statistical inference. In scatter plots, the mapping of each data point to a coordinate (x_i, y_i) is a direct manifestation of the statistical sampling process, where the spatial distribution of points encapsulates measures of central tendency, dispersion, and the correlation coefficient ρ. The geometrical arrangement enables the evaluation of the joint variability between the variables and supports inferential procedures aimed at hypothesis testing regarding linearity and association.

Line graphs, by stitching together sequential observations, perform an implicit form of interpolation that approximates an underlying continuous function. The contiguous nature of the line segments provides a visual analogue to the concept of differentiation, wherein the slope of a segment approximates the instantaneous rate of change. This geometric continuity not only enhances the interpretability of trends but also facilitates the estimation of derivative measures, thereby bridging the visual representation with rigorous statistical analysis. Both graphical forms underscore the importance of precise axis scaling and the judicious use of transformations to ensure that the depiction of the data remains faithful to its statistical properties, hence providing a robust framework for the analysis of inter-variable relationships.

R Code Snippet

```
# Set a seed for reproducibility
set.seed(123)

# -------------------------------
# Generate synthetic data for scatter plots
# -------------------------------
n <- 100
x <- rnorm(n, mean = 5, sd = 2)
y <- 3 * x + rnorm(n, mean = 0, sd = 2)

# Calculate the Pearson correlation coefficient ()
pearson_rho <- cor(x, y)
cat("Pearson Correlation Coefficient ():", round(pearson_rho, 3),
↪    "\n")

# -------------------------------
# Scatter Plot: Representing Bivariate Relationships
# -------------------------------
plot(x, y,
     main = "Scatter Plot of x vs. y",
     xlab = "Variable x",
     ylab = "Variable y",
     pch = 19,
     col = "blue")
# Adding a regression line to highlight the linear association
abline(lm(y ~ x), col = "red", lwd = 2)

# -------------------------------
# Log Transformation Example
# (If the range spans several orders of magnitude)
# -------------------------------
# Shift data to ensure positive values for log transformation
x_adj <- x - min(x) + 1
y_adj <- y - min(y) + 1

# Create scatter plot with both axes transformed using logarithm
plot(log(x_adj), log(y_adj),
     main = "Scatter Plot with Log-Log Transformation",
     xlab = "log(x_adj)",
     ylab = "log(y_adj)",
     pch = 19,
     col = "darkgreen")

# -------------------------------
# Line Graph: Depicting Sequential Trends
# -------------------------------
# Generate synthetic sequential data (e.g., time series)
time <- 1:n
# Create a trend with a sinusoidal component and a slight linear
↪    drift
```

```r
temperature <- sin(time / 10) + 0.05 * time + rnorm(n, sd = 0.2)

# Plot the time series data as a line graph, emphasizing continuity
plot(time, temperature, type = "o",
    main = "Line Graph of Temperature Over Time",
    xlab = "Time",
    ylab = "Temperature",
    col = "purple")

# Fit a linear model to the temperature data and add the trend line
trend_model <- lm(temperature ~ time)
abline(trend_model, col = "red", lwd = 2)
cat("Linear Trend Model Summary:\n")
print(summary(trend_model))

# -------------------------------
# Approximate Derivative: Estimating Rate of Change
# -------------------------------
# Compute the approximate derivative (dy/dt) using finite
↪ differences
rate_of_change <- diff(temperature) / diff(time)

# Plot the approximate derivative to assess
↪ acceleration/deceleration trends
plot(time[-1], rate_of_change, type = "o",
    main = "Approximate Derivative of Temperature",
    xlab = "Time",
    ylab = "Rate of Change",
    col = "orange")

# End of R Code Snippet
```

196

Chapter 39

Boxplots and Violin Plots

Boxplots: A Framework for Summarizing Distributional Characteristics

Boxplots, also designated as box-and-whisker plots, encapsulate key statistical aspects of a univariate distribution through a compact visual representation. The construction of a boxplot commences with the computation of the first quartile Q_1, the median M, and the third quartile Q_3, which together delineate the interquartile range, given by $IQR = Q_3 - Q_1$. These quantiles form the basis of the graphical box that spans from Q_1 to Q_3, with the internal division of the box by a line corresponding to the median M. Whiskers extend from the boundaries of the box to pre-defined limits, commonly set to $1.5 \times IQR$ beyond the quartiles, thereby providing a criterion for the identification of outlying observations. This visual mechanism succinctly conveys symmetry, skewness, and the presence of atypical data points within the dataset, while maintaining a robust abstraction of the underlying distributional properties.

Violin Plots: Visualizing the Underlying Density

Violin plots advance the conveyance of distributional information by augmenting the traditional boxplot with a depiction of the estimated probability density function. The methodology employs kernel density estimation to generate a smooth probability density function $f(x)$ that is displayed symmetrically about a central axis. This dual presentation not only encapsulates conventional summary statistics—often including the median and quartile bounds—but also reveals intricate patterns such as multimodality and subtle variations in the spread of the data. The rendered shape of the violin plot provides an immediate visual approximation of the distribution's morphology, including regions of concentration and sparsity, thus affording a comprehensive view of data variability that extends beyond the capabilities of standard boxplots.

Comparative Analysis of Graphical Representations

The inherent differences between boxplots and violin plots illuminate distinct aspects of data characterization. The boxplot offers a parsimonious summary by abstracting the dataset into a handful of robust quantiles, thereby facilitating rapid visual assessments of central tendency and spread. However, such summarization may entail the loss of granular information regarding the distribution's detailed shape or the emergence of multiple modes. In contrast, the violin plot, through its integration of kernel density estimation, accentuates the comprehensive structure of the data distribution. This representation not only retains essential summary statistics but also elucidates characteristics such as asymmetry, bimodality, or other complex distributional features. Accordingly, the adoption of either graphical form is influenced by the analytical objectives, with boxplots favoring succinct statistical abstraction and violin plots enabling an in-depth exploration of the distributional intricacies and variability inherent to the dataset.

R Code Snippet

```r
# Set seed for reproducibility
set.seed(123)

# Generate sample data: 100 random numbers from a normal
↪   distribution with mean = 50 and sd = 10
data <- rnorm(100, mean = 50, sd = 10)

# Compute summary statistics: Q1, Median, and Q3
# Q1: 25th percentile, Median: 50th percentile, Q3: 75th percentile
Q1 <- as.numeric(quantile(data, 0.25))
median_val <- median(data)
Q3 <- as.numeric(quantile(data, 0.75))

# Calculate the Interquartile Range (IQR)
# Equation: IQR = Q3 - Q1
IQR_val <- Q3 - Q1

# Compute whisker limits for the boxplot
# Lower whisker = Q1 - 1.5 * IQR
# Upper whisker = Q3 + 1.5 * IQR
lower_whisker <- Q1 - 1.5 * IQR_val
upper_whisker <- Q3 + 1.5 * IQR_val

# Identify outliers: values outside the whisker limits
outliers <- data[data < lower_whisker | data > upper_whisker]

# Print computed statistics
cat("Q1:", round(Q1, 2), "\n")
cat("Median:", round(median_val, 2), "\n")
cat("Q3:", round(Q3, 2), "\n")
cat("IQR:", round(IQR_val, 2), "\n")
cat("Lower Whisker:", round(lower_whisker, 2), "\n")
cat("Upper Whisker:", round(upper_whisker, 2), "\n")
cat("Outliers:", outliers, "\n\n")

# Plot the Boxplot with custom annotations
boxplot(data, main = "Custom Boxplot", horizontal = TRUE,
        col = "lightblue", xlab = "Value", ylab = "Boxplot")
# Add a red line for the median
abline(v = median_val, col = "red", lwd = 2)
# Add dashed purple lines for the whisker limits
abline(v = lower_whisker, col = "purple", lwd = 2, lty = 2)
abline(v = upper_whisker, col = "purple", lwd = 2, lty = 2)

# Generate a Violin Plot using ggplot2 to visualize the density
↪   estimation
library(ggplot2)
# Create a data frame for ggplot2
df <- data.frame(Value = data)
```

```r
# Construct the violin plot with an overlaid boxplot
p <- ggplot(df, aes(x = factor(0), y = Value)) +
  geom_violin(fill = "lightgreen", color = "darkgreen", adjust = 1)
  ↪  +
  geom_boxplot(width = 0.1, fill = "white", outlier.color = "red") +
  labs(title = "Violin Plot with Boxplot Overlay", x = "", y =
  ↪  "Value") +
  theme_minimal()

# Print the violin plot
print(p)

# Additionally, perform Kernel Density Estimation manually and plot
↪  the density curve
# This demonstrates the kernel density estimation f(x) used in
↪  constructing a violin plot.
density_est <- density(data, kernel = "gaussian")
plot(density_est, main = "Kernel Density Estimation",
     xlab = "Value", ylab = "Density", col = "blue", lwd = 2)
polygon(density_est, col = rgb(0.1, 0.1, 0.8, 0.3), border = "blue")

# End of comprehensive R code snippet demonstrating:
# 1. Calculation of key statistics (Q1, Median, Q3, IQR)
# 2. Determination of boxplot whisker limits and outlier detection
# 3. Construction of boxplots and violin plots (with kernel density
↪  estimation)
```

Chapter 40

Plot Layouts and Multiplots

Matrix-Based Layouts

Arranging multiple plots within a single graphical window can be formulated using a matrix paradigm that explicitly defines spatial partitions. In this framework, an integer matrix is employed such that each element, for instance, L_{ij} in a matrix $L \in \mathbb{Z}^{r \times c}$, designates a unique plotting region. The mapping of these indices onto the device area enables nonuniform and asymmetrical allocations, wherein groups of cells can be merged to form larger, contiguous regions for plots that require expanded dimensions. This method permits a deliberate assignment of spatial attributes, allowing for refinements in border delineation and relative sizing. The matrix-based approach is particularly advantageous when the visualization demands precise geometric configurations that reflect underlying data heterogeneity.

Graphical Parameterization with $par()$ Settings

In parallel with layout functions, the utilization of $par()$ settings presents a robust mechanism for orchestrating multiple plots within a composite display. Parameters such as $mfrow$ and $mfcol$ are instrumental for decomposing the plotting canvas into a predetermined grid defined by a tuple $(n_{\text{rows}}, n_{\text{cols}})$. Beyond this structural partitioning, ancillary parameters—namely mar, mai, and oma—grant the capacity to finely calibrate margins and inter-panel spacing. The adjustment of these settings ensures that each individual plot attains a balanced allocation of space while maintaining consistency in axis alignment, scaling, and overall aesthetics. Through the deliberate modulation of these variables, the graphical object is rendered with enhanced clarity and a disciplined visual hierarchy.

Hybrid Approaches to Multiplot Arrangement

The integrative application of matrix-based layouts and $par()$ parameterization yields a versatile system for complex plot arrangements. Initially, the layout function establishes a global partitioning scheme by distributing available device area into discrete regions as dictated by an underlying matrix construct. Subsequently, the modification of local graphical parameters via $par()$ refines this structure by dictating intrinsic properties such as margin widths, interstitial spacing, and the allocation of subregions within each designated cell. This dual-stage methodology functions as a form of two-tier optimization: the global layout decisively allocates spatial domains while the subsequent local adjustments, executed through meticulous tuning of $par()$ settings, ensure that the internal characteristics of each panel adhere to rigorous visualization standards. Such a hybrid approach accommodates complex plotting scenarios where heterogeneous plot dimensions and intricate arrangements underscore a commitment to precision in data presentation.

R Code Snippet

```
# Comprehensive R code snippet demonstrating matrix-based layout,
# graphical parameterization via par() settings, and a hybrid
↪   approach
# to arranging multiple plots in a single graphics device.

# ----------------------------
# Step 1: Define a custom layout matrix
# This matrix specifies the plotting regions with nonuniform,
↪   asymmetrical allocations.
```

202

```r
# In the matrix below:
# - Regions with the same number merge cells into a single plotting
↪    area.
# - Plot 1 spans the top-left two-by-two block.
# - Plots 2 and 3 occupy the top-right and middle-right cells
↪    respectively.
# - Plots 4, 5, and 6 are arranged in the bottom row, each occupying
↪    one cell.
layout_matrix <- matrix(c(
  1, 1, 2,
  1, 1, 3,
  4, 5, 6
), nrow = 3, byrow = TRUE)

# Optionally, define relative widths and heights for each column and
↪    row
layout(widths = c(2, 2, 1), heights = c(1, 1, 0.8))
layout(layout_matrix)

# Set overall outer margins (oma argument) for the entire device
par(oma = c(3, 3, 3, 3))   # bottom, left, top, right outer margins

# ----------------------------
# Region 1: Large plot (matrix-based spanning region)
# Adjust margins using par(mar) for this individual plot
par(mar = c(4, 4, 2, 1))   # bottom, left, top, right margins
# Plot a sine wave demonstrating a continuous function
x <- seq(0, 2 * pi, length.out = 300)
y <- sin(x)
plot(x, y, type = 'l', col = 'blue', lwd = 2,
     main = "Sine Wave", xlab = "x", ylab = "sin(x)")

# ----------------------------
# Region 2: Scatter Plot
par(mar = c(3, 3, 2, 1))
set.seed(42)   # for reproducibility
x_scatter <- rnorm(50)
y_scatter <- rnorm(50)
plot(x_scatter, y_scatter, pch = 19, col = 'red',
     main = "Scatter Plot", xlab = "X", ylab = "Y")

# ----------------------------
# Region 3: Histogram
par(mar = c(3, 3, 2, 1))
data_hist <- rnorm(100)
hist(data_hist, col = 'green', main = "Histogram",
     xlab = "Values", breaks = 10)

# ----------------------------
# Region 4: Boxplot
par(mar = c(3, 3, 2, 1))
# Generate sample data for two groups
group_A <- rnorm(20, mean = 0, sd = 1)
```

```r
group_B <- rnorm(20, mean = 1, sd = 1.2)
boxplot(list(A = group_A, B = group_B), col = c("lightblue",
↪   "pink"),
        main = "Boxplot", ylab = "Value")

# ----------------------------
# Region 5: Bar Plot
par(mar = c(3, 3, 2, 1))
# Create a categorical frequency table from random samples
categories <- sample(letters[1:5], 100, replace = TRUE)
counts <- table(categories)
barplot(counts, col = "orange", main = "Bar Plot",
        xlab = "Category", ylab = "Frequency")

# ----------------------------
# Region 6: Regression Plot with fitted line
par(mar = c(3, 3, 2, 1))
# Simulate data for linear regression
x_reg <- rnorm(100)
y_reg <- 2 * x_reg + rnorm(100)
plot(x_reg, y_reg, pch = 16, col = "purple",
     main = "Regression Plot", xlab = "X", ylab = "Y")
# Fit a linear model and add the regression line
fit <- lm(y_reg ~ x_reg)
abline(fit, col = "black", lwd = 2)
# Display model summary in the console
print(summary(fit))

# ----------------------------
# Reset layout to default (single plot region)
layout(1)
```

204

dation. For instance, the representation of a line segment may be parametrized as

$$L(t) = (1 - t) P_0 + t P_1, \quad t \in [0, 1],$$

where P_0 and P_1 denote the endpoints. Such a formulation underlines the continuous nature of the encoding, in contrast to the discrete sampling intrinsic to raster methods. The mathematical rigor inherent in these formats ensures that transformations, such as rotations and translations, can be applied uniformly across the entire graphical object without loss of fidelity.

The encoding of curves frequently employs Bézier representations, in which a cubic curve is defined by

$$B(t) = (1-t)^3 P_0 + 3(1-t)^2 t P_1 + 3(1-t) t^2 P_2 + t^3 P_3,$$

with $t \in [0, 1]$ and control points P_0, P_1, P_2, P_3. The smoothness and scalability afforded by such parametric descriptions render vector formats particularly suitable for graphical output that must be reproduced at arbitrary magnifications.

2 Raster-Based Formats

Raster-based file formats, exemplified by PNG and $JPEG$, represent images as a finite grid of discrete picture elements, or pixels. Each pixel is assigned a numerical value encoding its color and intensity, so that the complete image is stored as a two-dimensional array

$$I : \{1, \ldots, M\} \times \{1, \ldots, N\} \to C,$$

where M and N denote the pixel dimensions and C is the color space. The fidelity of such representations is inherently bounded by the resolution, since enlargement beyond the native pixel density introduces interpolation artifacts and a consequent degradation of visual quality.

The storage requirements of raster formats scale with the product $M \times N$, and compression schemes are frequently employed to reduce the attendant data volume. Lossless methods preserve the exact pixel values, whereas lossy methods discard perceptually insignificant information to achieve greater compression ratios.

dation. The intrinsic compatibility of these formats with linear transformations, as described by affine mappings in computational geometry, ensures that the fidelity of the visual content is maintained under a variety of scaling and rotation operations.

2   Raster-Based Formats

Raster-based file formats, such as *PNG* and *JPEG*, represent graphical outputs as arrays of pixels. The resolution of these images is dictated by parameters including the dots per inch (*dpi*) and the physical dimensions of the plotting device. In raster rendering, each pixel serves as a discrete unit of visual information, and the overall image is constructed as a finite grid. Consequently, the preservation of fine details is contingent on the initial resolution settings, and scaling operations may introduce artifacts if the underlying pixel density is not sufficiently high. The trade-off between file size and visual clarity is a central concern when selecting a raster-based format for plots intended for both digital dissemination and print reproduction.

File Format Selection and Characterization

The choice of an appropriate file format for exporting plots is governed by several criteria, including the target medium, the complexity of the visual content, and the requirements for subsequent post-processing. When the primary objective is to ensure absolute scalability and precision, vector-based formats are preferred due to their inherent capacity to describe shapes via mathematical equations. Conversely, scenarios that involve the presentation of detailed textures or images with substantial color variation may benefit from the efficiency of raster-based formats. This selection process requires an evaluation of the content's geometric and chromatic attributes, balanced against factors such as file size, interoperability, and the standards governing the publication medium.

Optimization Techniques for Exported Graphics

The exportation of graphical content involves a series of optimizations aimed at balancing aesthetic quality with computational efficiency. Central to this process is the calibration of parameters that control resolution, color mapping, and compression. The resolution, often specified in terms of *dpi*, must be adjusted to ensure that the exported figure meets the precision requirements of the target output device. Concurrently, the configuration of margin sizes, inter-element spacing, and font scaling is critical to maintaining the structural coherence of the visualization. The optimization strategy is further refined by considering the effects of affine transformations on the graphical elements, thereby ensuring that the final output, denoted by I, satisfies properties of invariance such that $T(\mathcal{G}) = I$ under the prescribed transformation parameters. This meticulous adjustment of graphical settings is instrumental in producing high-fidelity exports that are well-suited for reporting and sharing across diverse computational and publication environments.

R Code Snippet

```r
# Function to perform an affine transformation on (x, y)
↪   coordinates.
# The transformation follows:
# [x_new] = [ a  b ] [x] + [tx]
# [y_new]   [ c  d ] [y]   [ty]
affine_transform <- function(x, y, matrix, translation = c(0, 0)) {
  new_x <- matrix[1, 1] * x + matrix[1, 2] * y + translation[1]
  new_y <- matrix[2, 1] * x + matrix[2, 2] * y + translation[2]
  return(list(x = new_x, y = new_y))
}


# Plot function that demonstrates the original data points and their
↪   transformed version.
# This function also conceptually illustrates the mapping T:   → F,
# where   represents the set of graphical parameters (e.g., line
↪   colors, marker styles,
# line weights, axis annotations, etc.) and F represents the final
↪   file output.
plot_transformation <- function() {
  # Ensure reproducibility
  set.seed(123)
```

```r
# Generate random data points
x <- runif(50, min = 0, max = 10)
y <- runif(50, min = 0, max = 10)

# Define parameters for an affine transformation:
# Rotate by 30 degrees and scale by a factor of 1.2, then
↪   translate by (2, 3)
theta <- pi / 6        # 30 degrees in radians
scaling <- 1.2         # Scaling factor

# Create the affine transformation matrix combining rotation and
↪   scaling:
# [a, b]
# [c, d]
a <- scaling * cos(theta)
b <- -scaling * sin(theta)
c <- scaling * sin(theta)
d <- scaling * cos(theta)
T_matrix <- matrix(c(a, b, c, d), nrow = 2, byrow = TRUE)

# Define the translation vector (tx, ty)
translation <- c(2, 3)

# Compute the transformed coordinates using the affine
↪   transformation
transformed <- affine_transform(x, y, T_matrix, translation)

# Plot the original points using blue filled circles
plot(x, y,
     pch = 16,
     col = "blue",
     xlab = "X",
     ylab = "Y",
     main = "Original and Transformed Points",
     xlim = c(0, 15), ylim = c(0, 15))

# Overlay the transformed points using red triangles
points(transformed$x, transformed$y, pch = 17, col = "red")

# Add a legend to distinguish between the two sets of points
legend("topleft",
       legend = c("Original", "Transformed"),
       col = c("blue", "red"),
       pch = c(16, 17))

# The above plotting process embodies the concept:
# T:  → F, where the set of graphical attributes
# (color, marker style, etc.) is mapped to the final file
↪   representation F.
}

# Function to export any plot to a file with adequate
↪   parametrization.
```

```r
# It allows selection of file format (PDF for vector-based exports,
# PNG for raster-based exports, or SVG for scalable vector
↪  graphics).
export_plot <- function(plot_fun, filename, file_format = "pdf", dpi
↪  = 300,
                              width = 6, height = 4, ...) {
  if (file_format == "pdf") {
    pdf(filename, width = width, height = height, ...)
  } else if (file_format == "png") {
    png(filename, width = width, height = height, res = dpi, units =
    ↪  "in", ...)
  } else if (file_format == "svg") {
    svg(filename, width = width, height = height, ...)
  } else {
    stop("Unsupported file format: choose 'pdf', 'png', or 'svg'.")
  }

  # Execute the plotting function to generate the plot.
  plot_fun()

  # Close the file device to finalize and save the file.
  dev.off()
}

# Usage Example:
# Export the plot as a PDF file (vector-based format,
↪  resolution-independent)
export_plot(plot_transformation, "TransformedPlot.pdf", file_format
↪  = "pdf", width = 6, height = 4)

# Export the same plot as a PNG file (raster-based format, requires
↪  setting dpi)
export_plot(plot_transformation, "TransformedPlot.png", file_format
↪  = "png", dpi = 300, width = 6, height = 4)
```

Chapter 42

Basic Linear Regression with lm()

Mathematical Formulation and Model Structure

A linear regression model constitutes a fundamental statistical framework for elucidating the relationship between a dependent variable y and one or more independent variables. In the simplest form, the model is posited as

$$y = \beta_0 + \beta_1 x + \epsilon,$$

where β_0 characterizes the intercept, β_1 represents the slope of the linear association, and ϵ signifies an error term assumed to follow a distribution with zero mean and constant variance. The model encapsulates the hypothesis that the expected value of the response variable, denoted as $E(y)$, is linearly dependent on the predictor variable x. Within this basic framework, the error term is generally presumed to be independently and identically distributed, thereby facilitating the derivation of estimators under standard assumptions.

Parameter Estimation via Ordinary Least Squares

The estimation of parameters within the specified linear model is typically achieved through the method of ordinary least squares (OLS). This approach involves the minimization of the sum of the squared differences between the observed values y_i and the values predicted by the model $\beta_0 + \beta_1 x_i$, for $i = 1, \ldots, n$, where n denotes the number of observations. Mathematically, the estimation problem is expressed as

$$\min_{\beta_0, \beta_1} \sum_{i=1}^{n} (y_i - \beta_0 - \beta_1 x_i)^2 .$$

The solution to this minimization yields the estimators $\hat{\beta}_0$ and $\hat{\beta}_1$, which are interpreted respectively as the baseline level of the response variable when $x = 0$ and the incremental change in y per unit increase in x. Functions such as $lm()$ in statistical software encapsulate these computations, ensuring that the estimation process is both robust in execution and optimized for numerical accuracy.

Statistical Inference and Model Evaluation

Subsequent to the determination of parameter estimates, a rigorous statistical evaluation is undertaken to assess model adequacy and the significance of the regression coefficients. Standard errors for the estimators $\hat{\beta}_0$ and $\hat{\beta}_1$ are derived in the context of the underlying distributional assumptions of the error term. Inference is typically conducted via t-tests to examine whether each coefficient deviates significantly from zero, thereby assessing the existence of an association between the predictor and response variables. Moreover, the coefficient of determination, R^2, quantifies the proportion of total variability in the dependent variable that is explained by the independent variable, offering a succinct metric for model performance. Additional diagnostic procedures, including analyses of residuals and formal tests for heteroscedasticity, are employed to verify that the foundational assumptions of the linear regression model hold, thereby lending credence to the subsequent interpretations and conclusions derived from the analysis.

R Code Snippet

```r
# Set seed for reproducibility
set.seed(123)

# Generate sample data for linear regression
n <- 100                    # number of observations
x <- rnorm(n, mean = 10, sd = 2)  # independent variable

# Define true model parameters
beta0 <- 5    # intercept
beta1 <- 3    # slope

# Generate error term (noise) from a normal distribution with mean 0
↪ and sd 1
epsilon <- rnorm(n, mean = 0, sd = 1)

# Construct dependent variable y using the linear model: y = beta0 +
↪ beta1 * x + epsilon
y <- beta0 + beta1 * x + epsilon

# Create a data frame with the generated data
data <- data.frame(x = x, y = y)

# Fit a linear regression model using Ordinary Least Squares (OLS)
model <- lm(y ~ x, data = data)

# Display the summary of the model
summary_output <- summary(model)
print(summary_output)

# Plot the observed data and add the fitted regression line
plot(data$x, data$y,
    main = "Scatter Plot with Fitted Regression Line",
    xlab = "Independent Variable (x)",
    ylab = "Dependent Variable (y)",
    pch = 19, col = "blue")
abline(model, col = "red", lwd = 2)

# Calculate predicted values and residuals
predictions <- predict(model, newdata = data)
residuals <- data$y - predictions

# Plot residuals vs fitted values to assess model assumptions (e.g.,
↪ homoscedasticity)
plot(predictions, residuals,
    main = "Residuals vs Fitted Values",
    xlab = "Fitted Values",
    ylab = "Residuals",
    pch = 19, col = "darkgreen")
abline(h = 0, col = "black", lwd = 2)
```

```r
# Manually compute the R-squared value for model validation
ss_total <- sum((data$y - mean(data$y))^2)
ss_res <- sum(residuals^2)
r_squared_manual <- 1 - (ss_res / ss_total)
cat("Manual R-squared:", r_squared_manual, "\n")
```

Chapter 43

Analyzing Model Summaries

Components of a Model Summary

The output produced by model summary functions constitutes a detailed compendium of diagnostic information that characterizes the performance and validity of a fitted regression model. Such summaries typically enumerate parameter estimates, accompanied by their corresponding standard errors, t-statistics, and p-values, arranged systematically in tabular form. Embedded within this output are global measures of model performance, including metrics such as the coefficient of determination, R^2, its adjusted variant, and the F-statistic. Each of these elements is derived from underlying statistical theory and contributes to a comprehensive portrait of the model's explanatory power and precision. In particular, the reported standard errors reflect the variability inherent in the estimation process, while the t-statistics and p-values assess the evidence against the null hypotheses that the true coefficients are zero.

Interpretation of Coefficient Estimates and Inference Metrics

The core of any regression analysis resides in the interpretation of the estimated coefficients. Each coefficient, denoted as $\hat{\beta}_i$ for

214

a given predictor, represents the quantified impact of a one-unit change in the predictor variable on the response, under the assumption that all other variables are held constant. The precision of these estimates is indicated by their standard errors, $s(\hat{\beta}_i)$, which are computed based on the variability observed in the data and the design of the model. The ratio $\frac{\hat{\beta}_i}{s(\hat{\beta}_i)}$ yields the t-statistic, a value that follows a t-distribution under the assumption of normally distributed errors. This statistic provides an objective basis for testing the null hypothesis that the true coefficient, β_i, is zero. In tandem with the associated p-value, these inference metrics facilitate a rigorous evaluation of the statistical significance of each predictor. The structure of the model summary thereby allows for an assessment of the individual contributions of explanatory variables, as well as the overall coherence of the model as a representation of the underlying data-generating process.

Residual Diagnostics and Global Model Fit Measures

An integral part of model summary diagnostics is the analysis of residuals, defined as the differences between the observed responses and their corresponding predicted values, $e_i = y_i - \hat{y}_i$. The distribution and behavior of these residuals offer insight into the validity of the fundamental assumptions of the regression model, namely the premises of homoscedasticity and normality. The residual standard error, which is often reported in the model summary, is calculated as

$$\text{RSE} = \sqrt{\frac{1}{n-p} \sum_{i=1}^{n} (y_i - \hat{y}_i)^2},$$

where n denotes the number of observations and p represents the number of parameters estimated, including the intercept. This measure furnishes an estimate of the typical deviation of observed values from those predicted by the model. In addition to these localized diagnostics, global measures such as the coefficient of determination, R^2, and its adjusted version encapsulate the proportion of total variability in the response variable that is accounted for by the predictors. The F-statistic provided in the summary further evaluates the joint significance of the predictors, testing the null hypothesis that the model with no predictors fits the data as

well as the proposed model. Together, these diagnostic outputs
create a robust framework for scrutinizing both the fidelity of the
estimated parameters and the overarching explanatory adequacy
of the regression model.

R Code Snippet

```r
# Simulate Data for Linear Regression Analysis
set.seed(123)        # Ensure reproducibility
n <- 100             # Number of observations

# Generate predictor variable from a normal distribution
x <- rnorm(n, mean = 5, sd = 2)

# Define true model parameters
beta0 <- 2           # Intercept
beta1 <- 3           # Slope coefficient
sigma <- 2           # Standard deviation of the error term

# Generate random error term
epsilon <- rnorm(n, mean = 0, sd = sigma)

# Create response variable: y = beta0 + beta1 * x + error
y <- beta0 + beta1 * x + epsilon

# Combine the variables into a data frame
data <- data.frame(y = y, x = x)

# Fit a linear regression model
model <- lm(y ~ x, data = data)

# Obtain the model summary which includes coefficients, standard
↪  errors, t-statistics, p-values,
# as well as global measures like R-squared and the F-statistic
model_summary <- summary(model)
print(model_summary)

# Extract the coefficient matrix from the model summary.
# Columns: Estimate, Std. Error, t value, Pr(>|t|)
coeff_matrix <- model_summary$coefficients
print("Coefficients and Inference Metrics:")
print(coeff_matrix)

# Manually compute t-statistics for each coefficient using:
# t = Estimate / Std. Error
t_statistics_manual <- coeff_matrix[, "Estimate"] / coeff_matrix[,
↪  "Std. Error"]
print("Manual Computation of t-statistics:")
print(t_statistics_manual)
```

```r
# Manual Calculation of the Residual Standard Error (RSE)
# RSE = sqrt( sum((y - y_pred)^2) / (n - p) )
n_obs <- length(model$residuals)                    # Total number of
↪  observations
p_params <- length(coeff_matrix[, "Estimate"])       # Number of
↪  estimated parameters (intercept + predictors)
rse_manual <- sqrt(sum(model$residuals^2) / (n_obs - p_params))
print(sprintf("Manual Residual Standard Error (RSE): %.4f",
↪  rse_manual))
print(sprintf("RSE from Model Summary: %.4f", model_summary$sigma))

# Extract Global Model Fit Measures:
# - R-squared: Proportion of variance in the response explained by
↪  the model
# - Adjusted R-squared: Adjusted measure that accounts for the
↪  number of predictors
# - F-statistic: Test statistic for the overall significance of the
↪  model
r_squared <- model_summary$r.squared
adj_r_squared <- model_summary$adj.r.squared
f_statistic <- model_summary$fstatistic[1]          # The
↪  F-statistic value
print(sprintf("R-squared: %.4f", r_squared))
print(sprintf("Adjusted R-squared: %.4f", adj_r_squared))
print(sprintf("F-statistic from summary: %.4f", f_statistic))

# In simple linear regression, the F-statistic is equivalent to the
↪  square of the t-statistic
# for the slope coefficient. We verify this by calculating:
f_stat_manual <- t_statistics_manual["x"]^2
print(sprintf("Manual F-statistic (t^2 for predictor 'x'): %.4f",
↪  f_stat_manual))

# Plotting Diagnostic Plots
# Generate diagnostic plots to assess:
# 1. Residuals vs Fitted values,
# 2. Normal Q-Q plot,
# 3. Scale-Location plot,
# 4. Residuals vs Leverage plot.
par(mfrow = c(2, 2))
plot(model)
```

Chapter 44

Working with Formulas in R

Fundamental Syntax and Structural Components

In the realm of statistical modeling within R, the formula object serves as a concise and expressive specification of model structure. At its core, the formula is an expression that delineates the relationship between one or more response variables and a collection of predictors. The central element of this notation is the tilde symbol, denoted as $\sim$, which partitions the expression into a left-hand side (LHS) and a right-hand side (RHS). The LHS is reserved for the dependent variable whose behavior or distribution is to be explained, whereas the RHS encompasses the independent variables, whose linear or non-linear contributions are to be modeled. This syntactic arrangement ensures that the structure of a statistical model is clearly articulated, facilitating subsequent operations such as the construction of design matrices and the evaluation of parameter estimates.

Operators and Notational Nuances

A variety of operators imbue the formula syntax with substantial flexibility, allowing for both the inclusion and exclusion of model terms in a succinct manner. The additive operator, represented by $+$, is employed to concatenate individual predictors, thereby articulating an additive relationship among them. In contrast, the subtraction operator, indicated by $-$, permits the exclusion of specific terms from the complete model specification. Special attention is warranted for the colon operator, :, which explicitly signifies interaction effects between predictor variables without automatically including the corresponding main effects. Moreover, the multiplication operator, typically rendered as $*$, invokes a more expansive treatment by simultaneously incorporating both the main effects and their interaction. In cases where an arithmetic computation or transformation is to be directly embedded within the formula, the function-like notation $I(\cdot)$ is utilized to denote that the enclosed expression is to be interpreted literally. Such notational distinctions allow for the precise and unambiguous declaration of complex relationships within statistical models.

Evaluation and Environmental Context in Formula Objects

The formula object in R is not merely a static expression but also an encapsulation of an evaluative environment. When a formula is processed by a modeling function, it is interpreted within a specific data context that determines the scope over which variables and functions are resolved. This environment plays a pivotal role in ensuring that any transformations or computations specified in the formula are executed with the correct bindings. In essence, the formula is parsed into an intermediate representation that delineates both the structure of the model and the manner in which variables are to be sourced and manipulated. This duality enables the formulation to serve as a bridge between abstract mathematical specifications and concrete computational implementations, thereby enhancing both the clarity and reproducibility of statistical analyses.

Inclusion of Transformations and Interaction Modeling

The expressive power of R's formula syntax is further exemplified by its capacity to incorporate transformations and model intricate interactions directly within the specification. Transformations of predictor variables, whether linear or non-linear in nature, may be seamlessly integrated via embedded function calls. For instance, polynomial terms, logarithmic transformations, or other mathematical manipulations can be encapsulated within the formula, thereby obviating the need for external preprocessing. Interaction effects, integral to capturing the synergistic influence of variables, may be specified either explicitly using the colon operator or implicitly by employing the multiplication operator to generate a comprehensive set of terms, which includes both main effects and their interactions. This facility for in situ transformation and interaction modeling endows R's formula framework with a level of versatility that is essential for accurately representing the multifaceted relationships inherent in complex data structures.

R Code Snippet

```
# Set seed for reproducibility
set.seed(123)

# Create a sample dataset with continuous predictors and a
↪   categorical group variable
n <- 100
df <- data.frame(
  y     = rnorm(n),              # Response variable
  x1    = runif(n, 1, 10),        # Predictor 1: Uniform
  ↪   distribution
  x2    = rnorm(n),              # Predictor 2: Normal
  ↪   distribution
  group = factor(sample(c("A", "B"), n, replace = TRUE))  #
  ↪   Categorical predictor
)

# --------------------------------------------------
# Example 1: Simple Linear Regression
#   Using the tilde (~) to separate the response from predictors.
#   This model includes x1 and x2 as additive predictors.
model1 <- lm(y ~ x1 + x2, data = df)
print(summary(model1))

# --------------------------------------------------
# Example 2: Linear Regression without an Intercept
#   The "-1" in the formula removes the intercept term.
model2 <- lm(y ~ x1 + x2 - 1, data = df)
print(summary(model2))

# --------------------------------------------------
# Example 3: Explicit Interaction via Colon Operator
#   The ":" operator specifies the interaction between x1 and x2
↪   without automatic inclusion of main effects.
```

```r
model3 <- lm(y ~ x1 + x2 + x1:x2, data = df)
print(summary(model3))


# -------------------------------------------------
# Example 4: Interaction Using Multiplication Operator
#    The "*" operator includes both main effects (x1 and x2) and
# ↪  their interaction.
model4 <- lm(y ~ x1 * x2, data = df)
print(summary(model4))


# -------------------------------------------------
# Example 5: Incorporating Transformations Within the Formula
#    The log() function transforms x1, and I(x2^2) indicates that x2
# ↪  should be squared literally.
model5 <- lm(y ~ log(x1) + I(x2^2), data = df)
print(summary(model5))


# -------------------------------------------------
# Example 6: Using Polynomial Terms in the Formula
#    poly(x1, 2) creates a second-degree polynomial basis for x1.
model6 <- lm(y ~ poly(x1, 2) + x2, data = df)
print(summary(model6))


# -------------------------------------------------
# Example 7: Generating the Design Matrix from a Formula
#    The model.matrix() function expands the formula to show all
# ↪  terms, including interactions and transformations.
design_matrix <- model.matrix(~ poly(x1, 2) * x2, data = df)
print(head(design_matrix))


# -------------------------------------------------
# Example 8: Formula with an Embedded Function and Environment
# ↪  Evaluation
#    Here the formula uses a sine transformation of x2 via
# ↪  I(sin(x2)).
fml <- y ~ x1 + I(sin(x2))
# Create the corresponding design matrix within the data environment
design_matrix2 <- model.matrix(fml, data = df)
print(head(design_matrix2))

# Display the internal structure of the formula object
print(str(fml))


# -------------------------------------------------
# Example 9: Updating Formulas Dynamically
#    The update() function adds 'group' as an additional predictor to
# ↪  the existing formula.
updated_formula <- update(fml, . ~ . + group)
model7 <- lm(updated_formula, data = df)
print(summary(model7))
```

Chapter 45

Generating Random Data and Sampling

Foundations of Random Number Generation

Random data generation is grounded in the production of sequences that approximate the properties of true randomness. Central to this process is the concept of a pseudo-random number generator (PRNG), which produces numbers that are statistically indistinguishable from independent and identically distributed samples. The outputs of most PRNGs are computed in a deterministic fashion based on an initial seed and are typically distributed uniformly over the interval $[0, 1]$. Many algorithms, such as the Linear Congruential Generator defined by

$$X_{n+1} = (aX_n + c) \bmod m,$$

and the Mersenne Twister with its long period and high-dimensional equidistribution, have been instrumental in simulations across computational fields. The quality of such generators is evaluated in terms of period length, distributional uniformity, and the absence of detectable correlations, all of which are pivotal when these sequences are subsequently transformed to simulate data from other distributions.

Distribution Transformations for Simulated Data

The uniform random variables produced by PRNGs serve as a basis for simulating data from a wide variety of probability distributions. The fundamental methodology employed in this transformation is the probability integral transform. For a given cumulative distribution function (CDF) F, the transformation

$$x = F^{-1}(u)$$

guarantees that the variable x will follow the distribution characterized by F, provided that u is uniformly distributed over the interval $(0, 1)$. This method, known as inverse transform sampling, exploits the monotonic nature of CDFs and rests on the theorem that if U is a uniform random variable on $(0, 1)$, then the variable $X = F^{-1}(U)$ has CDF F. In additional cases, when the inverse of the CDF is not tractable, alternative methods such as rejection sampling or transformation approaches like the Box-Muller method for normal distributions offer robust mechanisms to simulate the desired statistical behavior.

Sampling Techniques in Simulated Environments

In the simulation of datasets, sampling techniques are employed to mimic a variety of data collection methodologies. Simple random sampling, where each member of a dataset has an equal chance of selection, is often used to generate baseline datasets that reflect homogeneity in sampling probability. Alternatively, sampling without replacement, mathematically characterized by the probability

$$P(\text{sample}) = \frac{1}{\binom{N}{n}},$$

for a population of size N and a sample of size n, addresses scenarios in which each selected unit is unique. More structured approaches, such as stratified sampling, partition the data into distinct subpopulations before selection, thereby ensuring that subgroups are represented in the generated sample. These techniques are critical for simulating datasets that accurately reflect the variability and inherent structure present in empirical data, thereby permitting rigorous analysis of statistical properties such as bias, variance, and confidence intervals.

Theoretical and Practical Considerations in Data Simulation

The rigorous application of random data generation and sampling methods necessitates careful attention to both theoretical underpinnings and practical implications. The statistical properties of simulations are profoundly influenced by the quality of the random number sequences, as deficiencies in the randomness can lead to biased estimations and erroneous inferences. Reproducibility, achieved through the controlled initialization of the random seed, ensures that experimental results are verifiable and comparable across replicated studies. Moreover, the interplay between distribution transformation and sampling methodology demands a nuanced understanding of the underlying mathematical structures. Considerations such as convergence in distribution, the ergodic properties of the process, and the preservation of correlation structures become paramount when simulating data intended to inform complex models. Every component of the simulation process, from the generation of uniform variates to their meticulous transformation into target distributions, must be orchestrated to maintain the integrity and validity of the resultant analysis.

R Code Snippet

```r
# Linear Congruential Generator (LCG) Function
lcg <- function(seed, n, a = 1664525, c = 1013904223, m = 2^32) {
  # Initialize vector to store random numbers
  nums <- numeric(n)
  x <- seed
  for (i in 1:n) {
    # Compute the next random value using the LCG recurrence
    ↪ relation
    x <- (a * x + c) %% m
    # Normalize to [0,1] by dividing by m
    nums[i] <- x / m
  }
  return(nums)
}

# Demonstration of LCG:
```

```r
set.seed(42)   # Setting global seed for reproducibility in our demo
lcg_numbers <- lcg(seed = 123456, n = 10)
cat("LCG Generated Uniform Random Numbers:\n")
print(lcg_numbers)

# Inverse Transform Sampling for the Exponential Distribution
# The inverse transformation for the exponential distribution (rate
↪    parameter ) is:
#      x = -log(u)/, where u ~ Uniform(0,1)
inverse_transform_exp <- function(n, rate = 1) {
  u <- runif(n)   # Generate n uniform random numbers between 0 and 1
  exp_samples <- -log(u) / rate
  return(exp_samples)
}

# Generate 10 random samples from an exponential distribution with
↪    rate = 0.5
exp_samples <- inverse_transform_exp(n = 10, rate = 0.5)
cat("\nExponential Samples (rate = 0.5):\n")
print(exp_samples)

# Box-Muller Method for Generating Standard Normal Random Variables
# This method transforms pairs of uniform random variables into
↪    normally distributed ones.
box_muller <- function(n) {
  # Ensure n is even; if odd, increment n by 1 to use complete pairs
  if (n %% 2 == 1) {
    n <- n + 1
  }
  u1 <- runif(n / 2)
  u2 <- runif(n / 2)
  z1 <- sqrt(-2 * log(u1)) * cos(2 * pi * u2)
  z2 <- sqrt(-2 * log(u1)) * sin(2 * pi * u2)
  normals <- c(z1, z2)
  return(normals[1:n])
}

# Generate 10 standard normal samples using Box-Muller
↪    transformation
normal_samples <- box_muller(n = 10)
cat("\nNormal Samples via Box-Muller:\n")
print(normal_samples)

# Sampling Techniques
# --------------------
# 1. Simple Random Sampling:
data_vector <- 1:100
set.seed(123)   # Ensure reproducibility
simple_random_sample <- sample(data_vector, size = 10, replace =
↪    FALSE)
cat("\nSimple Random Sample from 1:100:\n")
print(simple_random_sample)
```

```r
# 2. Stratified Sampling:
# Create a data frame with a grouping variable.
df <- data.frame(
  id = 1:100,
  group = rep(c("A", "B"), each = 50)
)

set.seed(123)   # Reproducible stratified sampling

# Split the data frame by 'group', sample 5 observations from each
↪   subgroup and recombine.
strat_sample <- do.call(rbind, lapply(split(df, df$group),
↪   function(subdf) {
  subdf[sample(nrow(subdf), 5), ]
}))
cat("\nStratified Sample (5 from each group A and B):\n")
print(strat_sample)
```

Chapter 46

Probability Distributions and Their Functions

Density Functions

In the realm of probability theory, density functions provide the fundamental description of continuous random variables. For a random variable X, the probability density function (PDF) $f_X(x)$ is defined over the real line, satisfying the conditions

$$f_X(x) \geq 0 \quad \text{for all } x \in \mathbb{R} \quad \text{and} \quad \int_{-\infty}^{\infty} f_X(x)\, dx = 1.$$

This formulation encapsulates the distribution's local behavior, facilitating the derivation of probabilistic properties through integration. The analytical properties of $f_X(x)$, such as continuity and differentiability, play a critical role in the rigorous development of inferential techniques. When addressing discrete random variables, the probability mass function (PMF) assumes a comparable role; however, the focus here remains on the continuous setting. The density function forms the cornerstone in applications ranging from likelihood estimation to the asymptotic analysis of stochastic processes.

Cumulative Distribution Functions

The cumulative distribution function (CDF) $F_X(x)$ is defined for any random variable X by

$$F_X(x) = \mathbb{P}(X \leq x),$$

which, in the case of a continuous random variable, can be expressed as

$$F_X(x) = \int_{-\infty}^{x} f_X(t)\, dt.$$

This function is non-decreasing and right-continuous, properties that are indispensable in the proofs of several fundamental results, such as the Helly-Bray theorem and the Glivenko-Cantelli theorem. The CDF summarizes the entire distributional behavior of X, rendering it an essential tool for both theoretical scrutiny and practical applications. Its structure allows for an immediate assessment of the probability mass accumulated up to any given point, thereby aiding in the analysis of tail behavior and central tendency.

Quantile Functions

The quantile function, typically denoted as $Q(p)$ for probabilities $0 < p < 1$, serves as the inverse to the CDF in a generalized sense. Formally, it is defined by

$$Q(p) = \inf\{x \in \mathbb{R} : F_X(x) \geq p\}.$$

This function maps the unit interval onto the support of X, and its properties, such as monotonicity and almost-everywhere continuity, are fundamental to the study of order statistics and non-parametric inference. The quantile function is central to inverse transform sampling, a method that transforms uniformly distributed random variates into observations that follow the target distribution. Its rigorous mathematical treatment provides insight into the structure of distributions and serves as a gateway for analytical derivations in robust statistics, where percentiles and medians are of primary interest.

Random Generation Functions

Random generation functions are designed to produce pseudo-random samples that adhere to a specified probability law. These functions are underpinned by principles stemming from density and cumulative distribution functions. Given a target distribution with known characteristics, the inverse transform method utilizes the quantile function to generate samples by mapping values from a uniform distribution on the interval $(0, 1)$ to the desired distribution. When inverse transformation is computationally infeasible, alternative methods—such as rejection sampling or Markov chain Monte Carlo techniques—are employed.

The theoretical analysis of these algorithms involves intricate considerations of convergence properties, computational complexity, and efficiency. Measures such as variance reduction and error bounds are analyzed rigorously to ensure that the generated samples accurately reflect the underlying distributional assumptions. Through a synthesis of probability theory and algorithm analysis, random generation functions bridge the gap between abstract distributional models and their empirical counterparts, thereby playing a pivotal role in simulation experiments and the validation of statistical models.

R Code Snippet

```
# Comprehensive R Code Snippet Demonstrating Density, CDF, Quantile
↪    and Random Generation Functions

#
↪    ------------------------------------------------------------------
# 1. Custom Density Function for the Standard Normal Distribution
#
↪    ------------------------------------------------------------------
# Define a custom probability density function (PDF) for a standard
↪    normal variable.
my_pdf <- function(x) {
  1 / sqrt(2 * pi) * exp(-0.5 * x^2)
}

# Generate a sequence of x values for plotting the density
x <- seq(-4, 4, length.out = 400)
pdf_values <- my_pdf(x)

# Plot the custom density function
plot(x, pdf_values, type = "l", lwd = 2, col = "blue",
     main = "Standard Normal Density Function (PDF)",
     xlab = "x", ylab = "Density")

# Verify normalization: the integral of the PDF over (-Inf, Inf)
↪    should be 1
```

```r
integral_result <- integrate(my_pdf, lower = -Inf, upper = Inf)
cat("Integral of PDF over the entire range:", integral_result$value,
↪   "\n")


#
↪   ----------------------------------------------------------------------
# 2. Cumulative Distribution Function (CDF)
#
↪   ----------------------------------------------------------------------
# Build a CDF by numerically integrating the PDF from -Inf to x.
my_cdf <- function(x_vals) {
  sapply(x_vals, function(xi) {
    integrate(my_pdf, lower = -Inf, upper = xi)$value
  })
}

# Compute the CDF values for the sequence x and plot the CDF.
cdf_values <- my_cdf(x)
plot(x, cdf_values, type = "l", lwd = 2, col = "red",
     main = "Standard Normal Cumulative Distribution Function
     ↪   (CDF)",
     xlab = "x", ylab = "Cumulative Probability")


#
↪   ----------------------------------------------------------------------
# 3. Quantile Function and Inverse Transform Sampling
#
↪   ----------------------------------------------------------------------
# Demonstrate the quantile function using built-in qnorm for
↪   selected probabilities.
probs <- c(0.025, 0.5, 0.975)
quantiles <- qnorm(probs)
cat("Quantiles for probabilities 0.025, 0.5, 0.975:", quantiles,
↪   "\n")

# Inverse Transform Sampling:
# Generate pseudo-random samples from the standard normal
↪   distribution.
set.seed(123)   # For reproducibility
n_samples <- 10000
uniform_samples <- runif(n_samples)   # Generate uniform samples
↪   between 0 and 1
normal_samples <- qnorm(uniform_samples)   # Transform via the
↪   quantile function (inverse CDF)

# Visualize the generated samples with a histogram overlaid with the
↪   theoretical density.
hist(normal_samples, breaks = 30, probability = TRUE,
     col = "lightgray", border = "white",
     main = "Histogram of Generated Normal Samples",
     xlab = "Value")
lines(x, dnorm(x), col = "blue", lwd = 2)
```

```r
# Perform a Kolmogorov-Smirnov test to statistically compare the
↪  generated samples with the normal distribution.
ks_result <- ks.test(normal_samples, "pnorm")
cat("Kolmogorov-Smirnov test result:\n")
print(ks_result)

#
↪  -------------------------------------------------------------------
# 4. Rejection Sampling Example for a Custom Distribution
#
↪  -------------------------------------------------------------------
# Target Distribution: f(x) = (3/4) * (1 - x^2) for x in [-1, 1]
# This defines a valid probability density function on the interval
↪  [-1, 1].

target_density <- function(x) {
  ifelse(x >= -1 & x <= 1, (3/4) * (1 - x^2), 0)
}

# Proposal Distribution: Use a Uniform distribution over [-1, 1]
↪  with density g(x) = 1/2.
proposal_density <- function(x) {
  ifelse(x >= -1 & x <= 1, 1/2, 0)
}

# Determine the rejection constant M.
# For x in [-1, 1]: f(x)/g(x) = (3/4)*(1 - x^2) / (1/2) = (3/2) * (1
↪  - x^2)
# The maximum value occurs at x = 0, so M = 3/2.
M <- 3/2

# Implement the Rejection Sampling Algorithm.
set.seed(456)  # For reproducibility
n_target <- 5000  # Number of desired samples from the target
↪  distribution
samples_target <- numeric(0)  # Initialize vector to collect
↪  accepted samples

while(length(samples_target) < n_target) {
  # Draw a candidate sample from the proposal distribution
  ↪  (Uniform[-1, 1])
  candidate <- runif(1, min = -1, max = 1)
  # Draw a uniform random number for acceptance decision
  u <- runif(1)
  # Accept the candidate if it satisfies the acceptance probability
  ↪  criterion.
  if(u < target_density(candidate) / (M *
  ↪  proposal_density(candidate))) {
    samples_target <- c(samples_target, candidate)
  }
}

# Plot histogram of the samples obtained via rejection sampling.
```

231

```r
hist(samples_target, breaks = 30, probability = TRUE,
     col = "lightblue", border = "white",
     main = "Rejection Sampling: Target Distribution",
     xlab = "x")
# Overlay the theoretical target density curve.
x_target <- seq(-1, 1, length.out = 400)
lines(x_target, target_density(x_target), col = "red", lwd = 2)

# End of the comprehensive R code snippet.
```

Chapter 47

Statistical Testing Basics

Foundations of Statistical Hypothesis Testing

Statistical hypothesis testing constitutes a rigorous framework for evaluating conjectures regarding population parameters and distributional attributes. Within this framework, a null hypothesis, denoted by H_0, encapsulates a baseline assumption, while an alternative hypothesis, denoted by H_1, represents a competing claim. The methodology relies on calculated test statistics, which are derived from sample data and whose distributions under H_0 are theoretically known. Critical to the formulation are the concepts of Type I error, defined as the probability of rejecting H_0 when it is true, and Type II error, which represents the failure to reject H_0 when H_1 is true. The statistical significance level, typically expressed as α, serves as a threshold for determining whether the observed data provide sufficient evidence for a deviation from the null hypothesis.

Implementation of R's Built-In Statistical Tests

R provides an extensive suite of built-in functions that encapsulate a multitude of statistical tests through robust, well-optimized algorithms. These functions are designed to seamlessly execute computations that integrate theoretical distributions with numerical methods, thus automating the process of evaluating hypotheses. The implementations adhere to standard mathematical formulations and often incorporate adjustments for small sample sizes or deviations from ideal assumptions. By abstracting the underlying computations, these routines allow for the practical application of classical tests, ensuring that the computed results maintain fidelity to the rigorous statistical underpinnings. Such built-in functionalities are essential for replicability and computational efficiency in data-driven research contexts.

Calculation and Interpretation of p-values and Test Statistics

The test statistic serves as a quantitative measure summarizing the deviation between observed data and the expectation under H_0. Its analytical distribution, often characterized by known probability density functions such as the normal, t, or χ^2 distributions, allows for the derivation of tail probabilities. The resulting p-value quantifies the probability of obtaining a test statistic at least as extreme as the one observed, assuming the null hypothesis is true. Mathematically, the p-value can be expressed as

$$p = \mathbb{P}(T \geq t_{\text{obs}} \mid H_0)$$

for an appropriate test statistic T and observed value t_{obs}. The computed p-value is compared against a predetermined significance level α, and a p-value smaller than α is interpreted as evidence against H_0. This process of quantification and subsequent decision-making is central to the inferential procedures implemented within R's testing functions.

Comparative Analysis of Parametric and Non-Parametric Methods

Parametric statistical tests, such as the one-sample and two-sample t-tests or analysis of variance (ANOVA), rest on the assumption that the data are sampled from populations that adhere to specific distributions, typically the normal distribution. These methods

234

exploit known functional forms and make use of estimates of central tendency and variability, thereby enabling the derivation of exact or asymptotic distributions for the test statistics. In contrast, non-parametric tests dispense with stringent distributional assumptions, relying instead on the ordinal or rank-order information inherent in the data. Techniques such as the Wilcoxon rank-sum test and the Kruskal-Wallis test exemplify this approach, offering robust alternatives in situations where parametric assumptions might be untenable. The comparative analysis of these methodologies involves a consideration of statistical power, sensitivity to underlying assumptions, and applicability to different types of data. R's built-in functions provide efficient execution for both classes of tests, ensuring that theoretical rigor is maintained while accommodating a wide array of practical scenarios.

R Code Snippet

```
# Set seed for reproducibility
set.seed(123)

# -----------------------------
# One-Sample t-Test and Manual Calculation
# -----------------------------

# Generate sample data: 30 observations from a normal distribution
↪   with mean=5 and sd=2
n <- 30
data <- rnorm(n, mean = 5, sd = 2)

# Conduct a one-sample t-test against the null hypothesis H0: mu = 5
t_test_result <- t.test(data, mu = 5)
cat("One-sample t-test result:\n")
print(t_test_result)

# Manual Calculation of the t-statistic and corresponding p-value
# Formula: t = (x - mu0) / (s / sqrt(n))
sample_mean <- mean(data)
sample_sd   <- sd(data)
t_stat      <- (sample_mean - 5) / (sample_sd / sqrt(n))
df          <- n - 1  # degrees of freedom

# Calculate the two-tailed p-value manually using the t-distribution
p_value_manual <- 2 * (1 - pt(abs(t_stat), df = df))
cat("\nManual Calculation:\n")
cat("  Sample Mean        :", sample_mean, "\n")
cat("  Sample SD          :", sample_sd, "\n")
cat("  Calculated t-Statistic :", t_stat, "\n")
```

```
cat(" Degrees of Freedom   :", df, "\n")
cat(" Manual p-value       :", p_value_manual, "\n\n")

# -----------------------------
# Analysis of Variance (ANOVA)
# -----------------------------

# Generate data for two groups with a subtle mean difference
group <- rep(c("A", "B"), each = n)
# Group A: mean = 5, Group B: mean = 6
values <- c(rnorm(n, mean = 5, sd = 2), rnorm(n, mean = 6, sd = 2))
anova_data <- data.frame(Group = factor(group), Value = values)

# Perform ANOVA to test if the group means are significantly
↪ different
anova_result <- aov(Value ~ Group, data = anova_data)
cat("ANOVA result:\n")
print(summary(anova_result))

# -----------------------------
# Non-Parametric Test: Wilcoxon Rank Sum Test
# -----------------------------

# Generate two independent samples for non-parametric comparison
group_A <- rnorm(n, mean = 5, sd = 2)
group_B <- rnorm(n, mean = 6, sd = 2)

# Conduct the Wilcoxon rank sum test for comparing group_A and
↪ group_B
wilcox_result <- wilcox.test(group_A, group_B)
cat("\nWilcoxon Rank Sum Test result:\n")
print(wilcox_result)

# -----------------------------
# Monte Carlo Simulation for p-value Approximation
# -----------------------------

# Number of simulations for Monte Carlo approximation
num_simulations <- 10000

# Simulate t-statistics under the null hypothesis (mu = 5)
simulated_t_stats <- replicate(num_simulations, {
  sim_sample <- rnorm(n, mean = 5, sd = 2)
  (mean(sim_sample) - 5) / (sd(sim_sample) / sqrt(n))
})

# Approximate the p-value as the proportion of simulations where the
↪ absolute
# simulated t-statistic exceeds the observed absolute t_stat from
↪ our sample.
mc_p_value <- mean(abs(simulated_t_stats) >= abs(t_stat))
cat("\nMonte Carlo Simulation p-value approximation:\n")
```

236

```
cat("  Approximated p-value:", mc_p_value, "\n")
```

Chapter 48

Correlation and Covariance Functions

Fundamental Concepts

Let X and Y be two random variables characterized by their respective probability distributions. The concept of covariance serves as a measure of the joint variability of these variables. In precise mathematical terms, the covariance between X and Y is defined by

$$\operatorname{cov}(X, Y) = E\big[(X - E[X])(Y - E[Y])\big],$$

where $E[X]$ and $E[Y]$ denote the expected values of X and Y, respectively. This measure captures the directional relationship between the deviations of each variable from its mean. A positive value indicates that, on average, deviations of X from its mean are accompanied by deviations of Y in the same direction, while a negative value implies an inverse relationship between their deviations.

In contrast, the correlation coefficient quantifies the linear association on a standardized scale. By normalizing the covariance with respect to the standard deviations of the variables, the resulting measure is rendered dimensionless and bounded. This normalization facilitates comparison across different pairs of variables regardless of the original units of measurement.

Mathematical Formulation

For a pair of random variables X and Y, the covariance is computed via the expectation

$$\text{cov}(X, Y) = E\big[(X - E[X])(Y - E[Y])\big],$$

which, in the context of finite samples, is typically estimated by

$$\hat{\text{cov}}(X, Y) = \frac{1}{n - 1} \sum_{i=1}^{n} (x_i - \bar{x})(y_i - \bar{y}),$$

where x_i and y_i represent observed values from the respective samples, $\bar{x}$ and $\bar{y}$ denote the sample means, and n is the number of observations.

The correlation coefficient, customarily denoted by $\rho_{X,Y}$ for the underlying population or by r in sample-based analyses, is mathematically expressed as

$$\rho_{X,Y} = \frac{\text{cov}(X, Y)}{\sigma_X \, \sigma_Y},$$

where $\sigma_X = \sqrt{\text{var}(X)}$ and $\sigma_Y = \sqrt{\text{var}(Y)}$ are the standard deviations of X and Y, respectively. This formulation ensures that $\rho_{X,Y}$ is confined to the interval $[-1, 1]$, thereby providing a consistent scale for the assessment of linear dependency between the variables.

Statistical Properties and Interpretation

The covariance and correlation possess several mathematical properties that are central to their application in statistical inference. Covariance is a symmetric measure; that is, $\text{cov}(X, Y)$ is equal to $\text{cov}(Y, X)$. Moreover, the variance of a variable can be viewed as a special case of covariance, since $\text{var}(X) = \text{cov}(X, X)$. Despite these appealing theoretical properties, the magnitude of covariance is inherently dependent on the scales of X and Y, rendering direct interpretation difficult when variables are measured in disparate units.

In contrast, the correlation coefficient, being a standardized measure, provides an intuitive gauge for the strength and direction of the linear relationship. A correlation value of 1 signifies a perfect positive linear association, while a value of -1 indicates a perfect inverse relationship. A value that approximates 0 implies little or no linear association between the variables. It is important to note that a zero correlation does not necessarily imply independence; rather, it indicates the absence of a linear pattern in the relationship between X and Y.

Practical Considerations in Correlation and Covariance Analysis

The calculation of covariance and correlation is fundamental in disciplines that require the analysis of multivariate data. Due to the sensitivity of covariance to the units of measurement, its direct usage is often limited to scenarios where the variables share a common scale. The correlation coefficient circumvents this limitation by eliminating the influence of scale, thus permitting robust comparisons across diverse datasets.

In the process of empirical analysis, the utilization of these measures is augmented by their inherent properties such as symmetry and the direct relationship between variance and covariance. The interpretation of such measures benefits from a solid understanding of their mathematical formulations. For instance, the normalization inherent in the computation of the correlation coefficient underlines its role as a measure of relative linear association, unencumbered by the absolute magnitudes of the underlying variabilities. The theoretical framework provided by these functions underpins numerous advanced statistical methodologies, where the interpretation of inter-variable relationships is of paramount significance.

R Code Snippet

```
# Comprehensive R code snippet for Covariance and Correlation
↪    Analysis

# Setting seed for reproducibility
set.seed(123)

# Generate sample data for two random variables X and Y
n <- 100
X <- rnorm(n, mean = 50, sd = 10)        # X ~ N(50, 10^2)
```

```r
Y <- 1.5 * X + rnorm(n, mean = 0, sd = 20)   # Y has a linear
↪   relationship with X

# Compute sample means for X and Y
mean_X <- mean(X)
mean_Y <- mean(Y)

# Manually calculate sample covariance using the formula:
# cov(X,Y) = (1/(n-1)) * sum((X - mean(X)) * (Y - mean(Y)))
cov_manual <- sum((X - mean_X) * (Y - mean_Y)) / (n - 1)

# Calculate sample covariance using the built-in cov() function
cov_builtin <- cov(X, Y)

# Compute standard deviations for X and Y
sd_X <- sd(X)
sd_Y <- sd(Y)

# Manually calculate the correlation coefficient:
# cor(X,Y) = cov_manual / (sd(X) * sd(Y))
cor_manual <- cov_manual / (sd_X * sd_Y)

# Calculate the correlation coefficient using the built-in cor()
↪   function
cor_builtin <- cor(X, Y)

# Display the calculated results
cat("Manual Covariance: ", cov_manual, "\n")
cat("Built-in Covariance: ", cov_builtin, "\n\n")
cat("Manual Correlation: ", cor_manual, "\n")
cat("Built-in Correlation: ", cor_builtin, "\n\n")

# Create a scatter plot to visualize the relationship between X and
↪   Y
plot(X, Y,
     main = "Scatter Plot of X vs Y",
     xlab = "X",
     ylab = "Y",
     pch = 19,
     col = "blue")
# Add a regression line to the scatter plot
abline(lm(Y ~ X), col = "red", lwd = 2)

# Define a function to compute covariance and correlation from two
↪   numeric vectors
compute_stats <- function(vec1, vec2) {
  if (length(vec1) != length(vec2)) {
    stop("Vectors must be of the same length.")
  }
  n <- length(vec1)
  mean1 <- mean(vec1)
  mean2 <- mean(vec2)
  covariance <- sum((vec1 - mean1) * (vec2 - mean2)) / (n - 1)
```

241

```r
  correlation <- covariance / (sd(vec1) * sd(vec2))
  return(list(covariance = covariance, correlation = correlation))
}

# Test the compute_stats function using the sample data
stats_result <- compute_stats(X, Y)
cat("Function Output - Covariance: ", stats_result$covariance, "\n")
cat("Function Output - Correlation: ", stats_result$correlation,
↪  "\n")

# Monte Carlo Simulation: Evaluate the distribution of covariance
↪  estimates

# Number of simulations
num_simulations <- 1000
cov_estimates <- numeric(num_simulations)

# Perform the simulation
for (i in 1:num_simulations) {
  # Generate new random samples for X and Y
  X_sample <- rnorm(n, mean = 50, sd = 10)
  Y_sample <- 1.5 * X_sample + rnorm(n, mean = 0, sd = 20)

  # Calculate and store the covariance using the built-in function
  cov_estimates[i] <- cov(X_sample, Y_sample)
}

# Plot histogram of covariance estimates to examine their
↪  distribution
hist(cov_estimates,
     breaks = 30,
     main = "Distribution of Covariance Estimates",
     xlab = "Covariance",
     col = "lightgreen",
     border = "gray")

# Overlay a density curve on the histogram
lines(density(cov_estimates), col = "red", lwd = 2)
```

Chapter 49

Basic Simulation with sample() and Monte Carlo Methods

Simulation Framework and Definitions

Basic simulation techniques provide a systematic approach for exploring stochastic phenomena through synthetic data generation. In this framework, a function such as sample() is employed to draw random elements from a finite set, thereby forming the basis for constructing simulated experiments. Consider a collection of independent draws $X_1, X_2, \ldots, X_n$ from a given distribution F. The empirical approximation of the expected value of a random variable is expressed as

$$\hat{E}[X] = \frac{1}{n} \sum_{i=1}^{n} X_i,$$

which converges to the true expectation as the number of samples increases. Such formulations serve to rigorously define the relationship between theoretical probabilities and their empirical counterparts obtained through simulation.

Mechanisms of the sample() Function in Stochastic Modeling

The sample() function constitutes a fundamental tool in simulation-based methodologies due to its capacity to generate random selections from a predefined set of elements. When applied to a vector $V = \{v_1, v_2, \ldots, v_m\}$, the function performs random sampling according to specified probability weights, thereby establishing a discrete probability distribution over V. Formally, if the probability of selecting element v_i is given by $P(v_i)$, then repeated invocation of sample() yields an ensemble of outcomes that closely approximates the underlying discrete distribution. This mechanism of sampling provides the structural foundation upon which further simulation-based analyses are constructed, enabling the empirical investigation of variability and uncertainty intrinsic to complex systems.

Principles of Monte Carlo Estimation

Monte Carlo simulation capitalizes on the statistical law of large numbers by performing a vast number of independent trials to approximate deterministic quantities. Considering an arbitrary function g defined on the sample space, the expected value of $g(X)$ can be estimated via

$$\hat{E}[g] = \frac{1}{N} \sum_{i=1}^{N} g(x_i),$$

where each x_i represents an independent sample drawn from the distribution of interest, and N denotes the total number of simulation trials. The efficiency and accuracy of this estimation process are directly linked to the central limit theorem, which guarantees that the distribution of the estimator approximates a normal distribution in the limit of large N. Moreover, the variance of the estimator is characterized by

$$\mathrm{Var}(\hat{E}[g]) = \frac{\mathrm{Var}(g(X))}{N},$$

thus quantifying the degree of statistical uncertainty associated with the simulation. This mathematical underpinning elucidates the rigorous basis upon which Monte Carlo techniques are founded, permitting numerical approximations of complex integrals and optimization criteria that are otherwise analytically intractable.

Modeling Variability through Simulation Techniques

In applied computational research, variability often embodies the intrinsic fluctuations and stochastic behavior of complex systems. The combination of sample()-based random selection and Monte Carlo methodologies facilitates a detailed examination of such variability. By constructing numerous simulated datasets through repeated random sampling, it is possible to capture the distributional properties of key parameters. For instance, empirical distributions of means, variances, or other statistical moments can be derived and analyzed to assess the robustness and sensitivity of modeled phenomena. The dispersion observed across simulation trials provides critical insight into the reliability and precision of statistical estimates, effectively mapping out the uncertainty landscape inherent in the system under study. This simulation-based approach enables a quantitative evaluation of risk and variability, thereby offering a substantive means for the numerical exploration of complex probabilistic models.

R Code Snippet

```
# Set the seed for reproducibility
set.seed(123)

# Define a discrete distribution:
# We consider a finite set of values and associated probabilities.
x_values <- c(-2, -1, 0, 1, 2)
probabilities <- c(0.1, 0.2, 0.4, 0.2, 0.1)

# Number of independent draws (simulation trials)
N <- 10000

# Define a function g(x) for which we wish to estimate the expected
↪   value.
# For example, let g(x) = x^2.
g <- function(x) {
  return(x^2)
}

#----------------------------------------------------------------
# Monte Carlo Simulation Framework:
#
# 1. Draw N independent samples from the discrete distribution using
↪   sample().
```

```
# 2. Estimate the expected value of X using:
#        hat{E}[X] = (1/N) * sum_{i=1}^N X_i
# 3. Estimate the expected value of g(X) using:
#        hat{E}[g] = (1/N) * sum_{i=1}^N g(x_i)
# 4. Calculate the sample variance of g(X) and then derive the
↪ variance of the
#    estimator using:
#        Var(hat{E}[g]) = Var(g(X)) / N
#-----------------------------------------------------------------


# Draw samples from x_values with replacement using the specified
↪ probability weights.
samples <- sample(x_values, size = N, replace = TRUE, prob =
↪ probabilities)

# Compute the Monte Carlo estimator for the expected value of X.
est_mean_X <- mean(samples)
# This corresponds to: (1/N)*sum(samples)

# Compute the Monte Carlo estimator for the expected value of g(X).
est_mean_g <- mean(g(samples))
# This corresponds to: (1/N)*sum(g(samples))

# Compute the sample variance of g(X)
var_g <- var(g(samples))
# According to the theory, the variance of the estimator is: var_g /
↪ N.
var_est_mean_g <- var_g / N

# Output the simulation results
cat("Monte Carlo estimation based on", N, "samples:\n")
cat("Estimated E[X]      =", est_mean_X, "\n")
cat("Estimated E[g(X)]   =", est_mean_g, "\n")
cat("Sample Var(g(X))    =", var_g, "\n")
cat("Variance of hat{E}[g] =", var_est_mean_g, "\n")


#-----------------------------------------------------------------
# Demonstrating Convergence of the Estimators:
#
# Compute the running average for both X and g(X) to visualize
↪ convergence.
# Running average for X: running_mean[t] = (sum of first t samples)
↪ / t
# Running average for g(X): running_mean_g[t] = (sum of first t g(x)
↪ values) / t
#-----------------------------------------------------------------
running_mean   <- cumsum(samples) / seq_along(samples)
running_mean_g <- cumsum(g(samples)) / seq_along(samples)

# Plot the convergence of the running means for both E[X] and
↪ E[g(X)]
# Set up a 1x2 plotting layout.
par(mfrow = c(1, 2))
```

246

```
# Plot convergence for the expected value of X
plot(running_mean, type = "l", col = "blue",
    main = "Convergence of E[X]", xlab = "Number of Samples", ylab
    ↪  = "Running Mean of X")
abline(h = est_mean_X, col = "red", lty = 2)

# Plot convergence for the expected value of g(X)
plot(running_mean_g, type = "l", col = "blue",
    main = "Convergence of E[g(X)]", xlab = "Number of Samples",
    ↪  ylab = "Running Mean of g(X)")
abline(h = est_mean_g, col = "red", lty = 2)
```

Chapter 50

Writing Custom Scripts and Functions for Reusability

Foundations of Code Reusability

Within the realm of computational research and software development, the systematic construction of custom scripts and modular functions is underpinned by well-established theoretical principles. Code reusability entails designing software components that, once defined with clear semantics and rigorously specified behavior, can be applied across multiple applications with minimal modification. The abstraction of a function can be formally expressed as

$$f : \mathcal{D} \rightarrow \mathcal{R},$$

where $\mathcal{D}$ represents the domain of inputs and $\mathcal{R}$ denotes the corresponding range of outputs. This formalism ensures that each function behaves as a deterministic and predictable mapping, which, in turn, enhances modularity, reduces redundancy, and fosters long-term maintainability in large-scale systems.

Modular Architecture and Separation of Concerns

The implementation of modular architecture is central to enabling effective code reusability. This design philosophy advocates for the decomposition of a complex program into discrete, self-contained modules, each responsible for a singular aspect of functionality. Such separation of concerns reduces interdependencies among different segments of code and limits the propagation of errors when adjustments are made. By encapsulating logic within distinct scripts and functions, the system adheres to principles that allow each module to operate independently while contributing to the overall computational objective. This refined organization not only simplifies the process of testing and debugging but also supports the seamless integration of individual components, thereby creating a robust framework that is resilient to future changes and extensions.

Principles of Custom Function Design

Designing custom functions with reusability in mind requires adherence to stringent principles that promote clarity, robustness, and predictability. Each function should possess a well-defined interface, characterized by explicit input parameters and clearly outlined return values. In such a formulation, the function behaves as an independent computational unit, facilitating its repeated use in varying contexts. Emphasis is placed on minimizing side effects and maintaining immutability of internal states wherever possible, thereby ensuring that the function's behavior remains consistent regardless of external state variations. Detailed in-code documentation that describes the function's purpose, expected input types, and resultant output is essential for verifying correctness and aiding future maintenance efforts. This methodical approach to function design lays the groundwork for constructing an ecosystem of reliable, self-contained modules that can be assembled to address increasingly complex computational tasks.

Organizational Strategies for Reusable Scripts

The overarching structure of a software system significantly benefits from the deliberate organization of scripts into logically segmented files. This strategy involves a hierarchical arrangement whereby each file is dedicated to a specific subset of the system's functionality, thus enhancing clarity and facilitating targeted modifications. Standardized naming conventions and rigorous documentation protocols are incorporated to ensure that every script is identifiable and its purpose readily understood. This systematic division allows developers to navigate the codebase with efficiency, reduce cognitive load when performing updates, and promote consistency across the entire project. By structuring code into modular and reusable scripts, the software environment becomes inherently scalable and maintainable, laying a sound foundation for both immediate utility and future adaptability in the face of evolving computational demands.

R Code Snippet

```r
# Custom function f: D -> R
# This function maps a numeric vector (D: domain) to a list (R:
↪   range) containing:
#   - The original input vector,
#   - Its element-wise squared values,
#   - An informative message about the computation.
# This encapsulates the idea of a deterministic and predictable
↪   mapping f: D -> R.

f <- function(x) {
  # Validate that the input is numeric; if not, halt execution with
  ↪   an error message.
  if (!is.numeric(x)) {
    stop("Input must be numeric.")
  }

  # Optionally remove NA values to prevent propagation of missing
  ↪   data.
  x <- na.omit(x)

  # Compute the squared values for each element in the vector.
  squared <- x^2

  # Compose the result as a list with a clear structure.
```

```r
  result <- list(
    original = x,
    squared = squared,
    message = sprintf("Successfully computed squared values for %d
    ↪  element(s).", length(x))
  )

  return(result)
}

# Example usage:
# Define a sample domain vector (D) from 1 to 10.
domain_vector <- 1:10

# Apply the custom function f to the domain vector.
result <- f(domain_vector)

# Display the computed result.
print(result)

# Demonstration of modularity and code reusability:
# A higher-order function that applies f to every element in a list
↪  of numeric vectors.
apply_f_to_list <- function(list_of_vectors) {
  # Use lapply to iterate over the list components and apply the
  ↪  custom function f.
  results_list <- lapply(list_of_vectors, f)
  return(results_list)
}

# Create a sample list containing various numeric vectors (some with
↪  NA values).
vector_list <- list(
  vec1 = 1:5,
  vec2 = c(2, NA, 4, 6),
  vec3 = c(10, 20, 30)
)

# Apply the function to each vector in the list.
list_results <- apply_f_to_list(vector_list)

# Print the list of results.
print(list_results)

# Additional demonstration: integrating function calls in a modular
↪  script.
# Here, define a workflow function that organizes the process of
↪  validating, computing,
# and reporting the transformation of input data.
workflow <- function(input_vector) {
  cat("Starting workflow for processing input vector...\n")

  # Log the input data.
```

```
cat("Input Data:", toString(input_vector), "\n")

# Apply the custom transformation using function f.
output <- f(input_vector)

# Report the computed squared values and message.
cat("Squared Data:", toString(output$squared), "\n")
cat("Message:", output$message, "\n")

  return(output)
}

# Execute the workflow with a test input.
test_vector <- c(3, 5, NA, 7, 9)
workflow_result <- workflow(test_vector)

# End of R code snippet demonstrating principles of code
↪   reusability,
# modular function design, and practical application of formal
↪   mappings.
```

Chapter 51

Organizing Code: Sourcing and Scripting

Conceptual Foundations of External Script Sourcing

The systematic separation of computational functionalities into discrete script files constitutes a core tenet of modular software engineering. This approach formalizes the decomposition of monolithic codebases into independent units whose behaviors can be viewed as mappings from well-defined input domains to predictable output ranges, denoted by $f : \mathcal{D} \to \mathcal{R}$. Through the abstraction provided by external script sourcing, each file encapsulates a segment of computational logic that can be verified in isolation and later integrated into a larger architecture. The resultant benefits include enhanced maintainability, reduced redundancy, and an overall increase in the clarity of the codebase. This methodology rises from the theoretical foundations of modular design and separation of concerns, both of which are pillars supporting scalable and robust software systems.

Methodologies for Integrating External Scripts

The act of incorporating external script files into an active coding environment demands a refined strategy that balances flexibility with structural rigidity. The process involves determining appropriate boundaries between distinct functionalities and establishing clear interfaces for interaction. A well-structured sourcing mechanism facilitates the dynamic inclusion of external code while preserving the integrity of the computational environment. The integration is achieved by invoking designated procedures that import the contents of external files, thereby merging multiple isolated modules into a cohesive execution framework. This technique minimizes the risk of unintended side effects and ensures that each sourced component adheres to its predefined operational contract.

Structural Organization and Dependency Management

An effective organization of external scripts requires careful planning of directory hierarchies and file naming conventions. In a modular framework, interscript dependencies must be explicitly documented and managed to prevent inconsistencies and cyclic dependencies. A rigorous structural arrangement supports the automatic resolution of component linkages, where the relationship between various code modules is depicted as a directed graph. In this context, nodes represent individual scripts while edges symbolize dependency links. By formalizing these relationships, the organization of the codebase can be quantified and controlled, employing strategies analogous to those used in the design of complex systems. The precision in specifying dependency chains not only enhances the reliability of script sourcing but also serves as a critical factor in the scalability of the entire software system.

Maintaining Reproducibility and Code Longevity through Sourcing

The practice of sourcing external scripts inherently provides a robust mechanism for ensuring reproducibility across diverse computational environments. By isolating and encapsulating functionalities into dedicated files, the codebase attains a high degree of transparency and traceability. This arrangement allows for systematic updates and iterative refinements without introducing regressions into previously validated code segments. The sustained reusability of externally maintained modules contributes substantially to the longevity of the software, as individual scripts can evolve independently while their interfaces remain unchanged. The preservation of this stability across successive iterations of software development aligns with the overarching objective of creating reliable, long-term computational infrastructures.

R Code Snippet

```
# -------------------------------------------------------------------
# R Code Example: Modular Sourcing and Dependency Management
#
# This script demonstrates:
# 1. Defining a mapping function f_mapping that represents the
↪    theoretical
#    mapping f: D -> R, where f(x) = x^2 + 3*x + 2.
# 2. Creating external modules (module1.R and module2.R) that
↪    encapsulate
#    specific functionalities.
# 3. Sourcing external R scripts to integrate individual modules
↪    into a cohesive
#    execution framework.
# 4. Ensuring reproducibility through the use of set.seed and
↪    simulation.
# -------------------------------------------------------------------

# ---------- Module 1: Mapping Function Definition (module1.R)
↪    ----------

module1_code <- "
# module1.R: Mapping Function Module
# This module defines the function f_mapping which computes the
↪    mapping:
#    f(x) = x^2 + 3*x + 2
#
# The function serves as a concrete example of transforming an input
↪    from the
# domain (numeric values) to a predictable output range based on a
↪    well-defined
# mathematical formula.

f_mapping <- function(x) {
  # Validate that the input is numeric
  if (!is.numeric(x)) {
    stop('f_mapping error: Input must be numeric.')
  }
  # Compute the mapping based on the formula: f(x) = x^2 + 3*x + 2
  return(x^2 + 3*x + 2)
}
```

```
# Test utility for f_mapping: Applies f_mapping over a set of sample
↪   inputs
test_f_mapping <- function() {
  test_values <- c(-2, -1, 0, 1, 2)
  outputs <- sapply(test_values, f_mapping)
  data.frame(Input = test_values, Output = outputs)
}
"

# Write the contents of module1_code to an external file named
↪   "module1.R"
writeLines(module1_code, con = "module1.R")

# ---------- Module 2: Integration and Simulation (module2.R)
↪   ----------

module2_code <- "
# module2.R: Integration and Simulation Module
#
# This module demonstrates how external functionalities can be
↪   integrated.
# It defines a function integrate_module that applies f_mapping to
↪   an input
# vector and summarizes the results. It also provides
↪   simulate_and_integrate,
# which generates reproducible random input data and applies the
↪   integration.

integrate_module <- function(input_vector) {
  # Ensure that f_mapping is available; if not, source module1.R
  if (!exists('f_mapping')) {
    source('module1.R')
  }

  # Apply f_mapping to each value in the input vector
  results <- sapply(input_vector, f_mapping)

  # Compute summary statistics from the transformed results
  summary_stats <- list(
    Mean = mean(results),
    StdDev = sd(results),
    Min = min(results),
    Max = max(results)
  )

  return(list(MappingResults = results, Summary = summary_stats))
}

# simulate_and_integrate:
# Generates a vector of random numbers, applies integrate_module to
↪   perform
# the mapping, and returns both the input and computed results.
simulate_and_integrate <- function(n = 10, seed = 123) {
```

```r
  # Set seed for reproducibility
  set.seed(seed)

  # Generate random input data from a uniform distribution between
  ↪   -5 and 5
  input_vector <- runif(n, min = -5, max = 5)

  # Integrate module functionality using the provided input_vector
  integration_result <- integrate_module(input_vector)

  return(list(Input = input_vector, Result = integration_result))
}
"

# Write the contents of module2_code to an external file named
↪   "module2.R"
writeLines(module2_code, con = "module2.R")

# ---------- Main Script: Sourcing and Executing External Modules
↪   ----------

# Source external module files in the order of dependency
source("module1.R")
source("module2.R")

# Test the mapping function f_mapping using predefined sample inputs
cat("Testing f_mapping with sample inputs:\n")
print(test_f_mapping())

# Demonstrate the integration by simulating random input data and
↪   processing it
cat("\nSimulating integration with random input data:\n")
simulation_result <- simulate_and_integrate(n = 5, seed = 42)
print(simulation_result)

# End of R Code Example
```

Chapter 52

Parsing and Evaluating R Expressions

Structural Composition of Parsed Expressions

The parse() function is responsible for transforming textual representations of R code into an internal expression structure that mirrors the syntactic and semantic rules of the language. This process begins with tokenization, wherein the input string is segmented into atomic symbols and keywords, followed by syntax analysis that arranges these tokens into an abstract syntax tree. The resulting tree is a hierarchical structure that encapsulates the operational dependencies and relationships inherent in the input. One may formalize this transformation as a mapping

$$P : S \to A,$$

where S denotes the set of syntactically valid string sequences, and A represents the corresponding space of abstract syntax trees. This abstraction provides a clear delineation between raw input and executable constructs, ensuring that subsequent evaluation proceeds on a foundation that respects the formal grammar of the language.

Operational Semantics of Dynamic Evaluation

The evaluation of parsed expressions is accomplished via the eval() function, which interprets the abstract syntax tree in the context of a defined environment. This evaluation process adheres to the principles of operational semantics, recursively resolving subexpressions and applying function closures and operators according to predefined rules. In formal terms, eval() may be characterized as a higher-order function

$$E : A \times \Gamma \to V,$$

where A is the set of abstract syntax trees produced by parse(), Γ symbolizes the environment that maps identifiers to their respective values, and V represents the set of computed outcomes. The evaluation mechanism traverses the tree structure, ensuring that each node is processed in accordance with the dynamic bindings present in the environment. This recursive descent and resolution lead to a precise determination of output values while accommodating constructs such as conditional execution and iterative control flows intrinsic to R.

Contextual Interactions and Environmental Dependencies

The dynamic evaluation process is intrinsically linked to the environmental context in which expressions are executed. The environment supplied to eval() encapsulates all variable bindings, function definitions, and operator overloads that influence the outcome of the evaluation. This interaction forms a bidirectional dependency between static parsed structures and the dynamic state of the computation. Conceptually, the evaluation of an expression can be seen as the interplay between its syntactic decomposition and the semantic interpretation provided by the environment, yielding a composite function

$$E(a, \gamma),$$

where $a \in A$ is an abstract syntax tree and $\gamma \in \Gamma$ is the corresponding environment. The careful management of this interface is vital for ensuring that variable scopes are maintained and that side effects are controlled. Such rigorous handling of contextual dependencies underscores the importance of isolating evaluation contexts to achieve deterministic and reproducible computational behavior within the R programming environment.

R Code Snippet

```r
# Comprehensive R Code Demonstrating Parsing and Evaluating R
↪   Expressions

# Function: evaluate_expression
# This function accepts a string representation of an R expression,
# parses it into an abstract syntax tree (AST), and then evaluates
↪   it
# within a specified environment.
evaluate_expression <- function(expr_str, env = parent.frame()) {
    # Parse the input string into an R expression (AST)
    ast <- parse(text = expr_str)
    # Evaluate the parsed expression within the given environment
    result <- eval(ast, envir = env)
    return(result)
}


# Example 1: Basic Arithmetic Expression Demonstrating S -> A
↪   Mapping
expr1 <- "3 + 5 * (10 - 2)"  # raw string representation, S
# The parse() function maps S to A (abstract syntax tree), and
↪   eval() computes the value V.
result1 <- evaluate_expression(expr1)
cat("Result of expression '", expr1, "' is: ", result1, "\n")


# Example 2: Defining and Evaluating an Anonymous Function
# Here the expression defines a function structural rule.
expr_func <- "function(x) { x^2 + 2*x + 1 }"
# Evaluate to obtain a function object.
square_plus <- evaluate_expression(expr_func)
cat("square_plus(5): ", square_plus(5), "\n")


# Example 3: Using a Custom Environment (Gamma) for Evaluation
# Create a custom environment with specific variable bindings.
custom_env <- new.env()
custom_env$a <- 10
custom_env$b <- 20
custom_env$c <- 5


# Expression refers to variables a, b, and c in the custom
↪   environment.
expr2 <- "a * b + c"
# Map S -> A and then E: A x Gamma -> V
result2 <- evaluate_expression(expr2, env = custom_env)
```

```
cat("Result of expression '", expr2, "' with custom environment: ",
↪  result2, "\n")

# Example 4: Conditional Execution Using if-else Structure
# This demonstrates dynamic control flow evaluation.
expr_conditional <- "
if (a > b) {
  a - b
} else {
  b - a
}
"
# Evaluate in the context of custom_env (where a and b are defined)
result_cond <- evaluate_expression(expr_conditional, env =
↪  custom_env)
cat("Result of conditional expression: ", result_cond, "\n")

# Example 5: Loop Structure for Summing a Sequence
# Evaluate a block of code that includes loop-based iterative
↪  computation.
expr_loop <- "
total <- 0
for (i in 1:5) {
  total <- total + i
}
total
"
result_loop <- evaluate_expression(expr_loop)
cat("Result of loop summation (1 to 5): ", result_loop, "\n")

# Example 6: Nested Environments and Variable Scoping
# Create an outer and inner environment to demonstrate environmental
↪  dependencies.
outer_env <- new.env()
outer_env$value <- 100
inner_env <- new.env(parent = outer_env)
inner_env$value <- 50   # Overrides the outer environment's value

# Expression uses the variable 'value' to illustrate dynamic
↪  evaluation.
expr_nested <- "value + 10"
result_nested <- evaluate_expression(expr_nested, env = inner_env)
cat("Result of nested environment evaluation: ", result_nested,
↪  "\n")
```

Chapter 53

Functional Programming: First-Class Functions

Conceptual Foundations of First-Class Functions

Within the realm of functional programming, the property of first-class status for functions signifies that functions are not merely subroutines but are treated as intrinsic data objects. This treatment permits the assignment of functions to variables, the transmission of functions as parameters to other functions, and the return of functions as outcomes from computations. In the R programming language, the function object embodies a dual nature, serving both as an executable procedure and as a structured data entity. Such a duality is fundamental to the design of flexible programming techniques that enable modularity and high degrees of abstraction. In this context, the function becomes an autonomous computational unit that can be manipulated, analyzed, and composed in a manner analogous to other data types.

Mathematical Formalism and Operational Characteristics

From an abstract mathematical perspective, the notion of first-class functions is encapsulated by principles derived from lambda calculus. A function may be formally represented as $\lambda x.E$, where x is a variable and E is an expression that defines the computation. Let F denote the collection of all admissible function objects; then the assignment of a function to a variable may be succinctly expressed as $v = f$, where $f \in F$ and v belongs to a set of entities that includes all possible function objects. Such a formal mapping underlies the semantics of higher-order operations and function composition. Moreover, the operational evaluation of function objects, when applied to arguments, is resolved in accordance with well-defined evaluation strategies. These strategies reflect the inherent characteristics of the R language, such as the preservation of referential transparency and the management of side effects. The interplay between abstraction and application in this setting exemplifies the rigorous mathematical structure that supports dynamic and flexible programmatic transformations.

Lexical Scoping, Closures, and Flexible Programming Techniques

A distinguishing feature that amplifies the efficacy of first-class functions is the mechanism of lexical scoping, which produces closures. A closure in R is a function bundled together with its referencing environment, thus maintaining associations between formal parameters and the variables that lie outside the function's immediate scope. This encapsulation enables a function to access variables that were present at the time of its definition, ensuring consistency and predictability in the behavior of dynamically generated function objects. The environment attached to each function enables complex compositions and the creation of higher-order functions that rely on contextual information. Consequently, the formation of closures facilitates a paradigm in which computational routines can be dynamically constructed and reconfigured, leading to programming techniques characterized by increased modularity and expressive power. The capacity to generate, pass, and return functions as first-class objects engenders a flexible infrastructure that

underpins advanced software design and promotes the development
of adaptive algorithmic solutions.

R Code Snippet

```r
# Demonstration of Functional Programming Concepts in R

# 1. FIRST-CLASS FUNCTIONS
# In R, functions are treated as first-class objects: they can be
↪   assigned to variables,
# passed as arguments, and returned from other functions. This is
↪   analogous to the
# lambda calculus representation: x. E, where a function is defined
↪   as an anonymous expression.

# Basic function definition (x. (x + 1))
f <- function(x) {
  return(x + 1)
}

# Assigning function f to a new variable 'increment'
increment <- f
cat("Increment 5:", increment(5), "\n")   # Expected output: 6

# 2. HIGHER-ORDER FUNCTION: Accepting a function as an argument
apply_function <- function(func, value) {
  # This function demonstrates that functions can be passed as
  ↪   parameters.
  # It applies the passed function 'func' to 'value'.
  return(func(value))
}

result_apply <- apply_function(increment, 10)
cat("Apply increment to 10:", result_apply, "\n")   # Expected
↪   output: 11

# 3. FUNCTION FACTORY AND CLOSURES
# Function to create a multiplier function. The inner function makes
↪   use of the variable
# 'factor' from its enclosing environment, demonstrating lexical
↪   scoping and closure.
create_multiplier <- function(factor) {
  multiplier <- function(x) {
    return(x * factor)
  }
  return(multiplier)
}

# Create a new function that multiplies its input by 3.
times_three <- create_multiplier(3)
```

```r
cat("Multiply 4 by 3:", times_three(4), "\n")  # Expected output: 12

# 4. FUNCTION COMPOSITION
# Define a function 'compose' that takes two functions f and g, and
#   returns a new function
# representing the composition f(g(x)). This is an operational
#   interpretation of mathematical
# function composition.
compose <- function(f, g) {
  composed_function <- function(x) {
    return(f(g(x)))
  }
  return(composed_function)
}


# Define example functions for composition.
square <- function(x) {
  # Represents: square(x) = x^2
  return(x^2)
}
add_two <- function(x) {
  # Represents: add_two(x) = x + 2
  return(x + 2)
}


# Create a composite function: square(add_two(x)) i.e., (x + 2)^2
composite <- compose(square, add_two)
cat("Composite function on 3: (3 + 2)^2 =", composite(3), "\n")  #
#   Expected: 25

# 5. LEXICAL SCOPING & CLOSURES FOR STATE MANAGEMENT
# Create a counter function that maintains state across calls using
#   lexical scoping.
create_counter <- function() {
  count <- 0  # This variable is captured by the inner function.
  counter <- function(increment = 1) {
    # Using the <<- operator to modify 'count' in the parent
    #   environment.
    count <<- count + increment
    return(count)
  }
  return(counter)
}


# Initialize a counter and demonstrate its stateful behavior.
counter <- create_counter()
cat("Counter first call (increment 1):", counter(), "\n")   #
#   Expected: 1
cat("Counter second call (increment 1):", counter(), "\n")  #
#   Expected: 2
cat("Counter third call (increment 5):", counter(5), "\n")    #
#   Expected: 7
```

```r
# 6. ANONYMOUS FUNCTIONS AND LAMBDA EXPRESSIONS
# Directly using an anonymous function (lambda) to add two numbers.
anonymous_result <- (function(x, y) {
  # Represents the lambda expression: x.y. x + y
  return(x + y)
})(5, 7)
cat("Anonymous function result (5 + 7):", anonymous_result, "\n")  #
↪ Expected: 12


# 7. EVALUATION STRATEGIES AND FUNCTIONAL COMPOSITION
# The following demonstrates dynamic function creation and
↪ composition, integrating
# mathematical formalism with programmatic implementation. The usage
↪ of higher-order functions
# ensures referential transparency where functions have no side
↪ effects unless explicitly defined.

# A composite function that uses multiple concepts above for
↪ computation.
# For example, define a function that increments a number, squares
↪ the result, and finally multiplies by a factor.
complex_operation <- function(x, factor) {
  # Compose functions: first increment, then square, then multiply.
  op <- compose(times_three, compose(square, increment))
  # Here, 'increment' adds 1, 'square' squares the result,
  # and 'times_three' multiplies by 3 (but we adjust it to the given
  ↪ factor for flexibility).
  temp_multiplier <- create_multiplier(factor)
  result <- temp_multiplier(op(x))
  return(result)
}

cat("Complex operation on 2 with factor 4:", complex_operation(2,
↪ 4), "\n")
# Explanation:
# Step 1: increment(2) = 3
# Step 2: square(3) = 9
# Step 3: times_three(9) = 27
# Step 4: create_multiplier(4)(27) = 108, so expected output: 108

# End of R code snippet demonstrating key aspects of functional
↪ programming in R,
# including first-class functions, closures, higher-order functions,
↪ and function composition.
```

Chapter 54

Memory Management and Object Lifecycles

Memory Allocation Mechanisms in R

R employs a rigorous and systematic approach to memory allocation that is essential for supporting its dynamic and statistical computing capabilities. The memory manager in R is responsible for allocating contiguous blocks of memory to newly created objects from a predesignated system pool. Upon the instantiation of an object, the memory allocator examines the size requirements dictated by the object's structure and type, subsequently mapping these requirements to a specific memory region. This process can be mathematically conceptualized by a function

$$A : S \to M,$$

where each object size specification $s \in S$ is associated with a memory block $m \in M$. Metadata pertaining to object type, size, and identification is embedded during allocation, ensuring that each object is uniquely traceable and that its memory footprint is accounted for. The allocation strategy is refined to handle a diverse range of object sizes and complexities, thereby optimizing the usage of the underlying memory resources and mitigating issues related to over-allocation or fragmentation.

Object Lifecycle and Management

The lifecycle of an object in R is governed by a combination of lexical scoping rules and reference management strategies that dictate its persistence within the runtime environment. Upon creation, every object is endowed with a reference count that quantifies the number of active bindings to that object. This mechanism, often internalized as the NAMED count, is pivotal in managing object longevity. Bearing in mind an object set O, the function

$$\rho : O \to \mathbb{N},$$

assigns to each object $o \in O$ a reference count $\rho(o)$, with the relation $\rho(o) > 0$ characterizing objects that are actively in use. As objects are manipulated through various operations, their references are updated in accordance with the scoping rules, thereby tracking the reachability of each object. The transition of an object from an active state to one that is eligible for deallocation is marked by a decrease of its reference count to zero, signifying that no active binding persists. This precise control of object state ensures that memory is reserved only as long as the object is needed, which is critical for maintaining system efficiency in long-running computational processes.

Garbage Collection and Memory Reclamation

Garbage collection in R is an automated process designed to reclaim memory by identifying and eliminating objects that have become unreachable. When the aggregate memory usage surpasses established thresholds or when fragmentation metrics indicate inefficiencies, the garbage collector is triggered. It performs a thorough analysis across various scopes and environments to isolate objects whose reference counts have fallen to zero. Let

$$U = \{o \in O \mid \rho(o) = 0\},$$

denote the set of unreachable objects within the total object space O. The garbage collector systematically deallocates the memory associated with each $o \in U$, thereby returning this memory to the free pool and mitigating potential fragmentation issues. Advanced strategies in garbage collection, such as generational collection techniques, are employed to differentiate between frequently and infrequently used objects. This stratification ensures that the majority of transient objects are collected swiftly, while stable objects remain untouched, enhancing the overall efficiency of the memory management system.

R Code Snippet

```
# R Code for simulating Memory Management and Object Lifecycles in R
# This snippet demonstrates the core equations and algorithms
↪   discussed in the chapter:
# 1. Memory allocation function: A : S -> M
# 2. Object reference count mapping:  : O ->
# 3. Identification of unreachable objects: U = { o in O | (o) = 0 }
#
# Note: In this simulation, objects are represented as lists
↪   containing their value,
# allocated memory (simulated by a generated address and size), and
↪   a reference count.

# Function to simulate memory allocation based on object size.
allocate_memory <- function(size) {
  # For simulation purposes, the memory block is represented with an
  ↪   address (hexadecimal string)
  # and the size of the allocation. In a real system, low-level
  ↪   allocation details are handled internally.
  memory_block <- list(
    address = paste0("0x", toupper(format(as.hexmode(sample(1e6:1e7,
    ↪   1)), width = 8))),
    size = size
  )
  return(memory_block)
}

# Function to create a new object.
# It assigns a memory block using the allocate_memory() function and
↪   initializes the reference count.
create_object <- function(value) {
  # Determine object size using object.size() to simulate size
  ↪   specification s  S.
  size <- object.size(value)
  memory_block <- allocate_memory(size)

  # Each new object is assigned an initial reference count of 1.
  # This mimics the mapping : O ->  with (o) = 1
  object <- list(
    value = value,
    memory_block = memory_block,
    refCount = 1
  )
  return(object)
```

```r
}

# Function to simulate updating the reference count when an object
#  is referenced.
update_refCount <- function(obj, increment = 1) {
  # Increase the reference count (modeling assignment or new binding
  #  of the object)
  obj$refCount <- obj$refCount + increment
  return(obj)
}

# Function to simulate dereferencing (removing a binding to an
#  object).
# This decreases the reference count, and if it reaches 0, the
#  object becomes eligible for garbage collection.
dereference_object <- function(obj) {
  obj$refCount <- obj$refCount - 1
  return(obj)
}

# Function to simulate garbage collection.
# It identifies unreachable objects U = { o in O | (o) = 0 } and
#  "frees" them from memory.
garbage_collection <- function(objects) {
  cat("Running Garbage Collector...\n")
  # Identify objects with reference count equal to 0.
  unreachable_indices <- which(sapply(objects, function(o)
    o$refCount) == 0)

  if (length(unreachable_indices) > 0) {
    cat("Collecting unreachable objects at positions:",
      unreachable_indices, "\n")
    objects <- objects[-unreachable_indices]
  } else {
    cat("No unreachable objects to collect.\n")
  }

  return(objects)
}

# Main simulation function to demonstrate the memory management and
#  object lifecycle process.
simulate_memory_management <- function() {
  # Create a list to store objects (simulating the object set O).
  objects <- list()

  # Create several objects using create_object(), simulating
  #  different types and sizes.
  objects[[1]] <- create_object(42)          # Numeric object
  objects[[2]] <- create_object("Hello, R!")   # Character object
  objects[[3]] <- create_object(rnorm(100))    # Numeric vector
  #  object
```

```r
cat("Initial Objects and Reference Counts:\n")
print(sapply(objects, function(o) o$refCount))

# Simulate operations that increase references:
# For example, assigning object 1 to another variable increases
↪  its reference count.
objects[[1]] <- update_refCount(objects[[1]], increment = 1)  #
↪  Now refCount becomes 2

# Simulate dereferencing objects:
# In this simulation, we dereference object 2 twice to bring its
↪  reference count to 0.
objects[[2]] <- dereference_object(objects[[2]])
objects[[2]] <- dereference_object(objects[[2]])

cat("Updated Objects Reference Counts after Assignment and
↪  Dereferencing:\n")
print(sapply(objects, function(o) o$refCount))

# Invoke garbage collection to remove unreachable objects
↪  (refCount == 0).
objects <- garbage_collection(objects)

cat("Remaining Objects after Garbage Collection:\n")
print(sapply(objects, function(o) o$refCount))

return(objects)
}

# Run the simulation of memory management.
simulate_memory_management()
```

Chapter 55

Vector Recycling Rules

Mechanism of Recycling

In the R computational environment, element-wise operations on vectors with differing lengths are facilitated by an implicit recycling process. Consider two vectors, $v \in \mathbb{R}^n$ and $w \in \mathbb{R}^m$, where $n \geq m$. When an operation is applied element-wise between these vectors, the shorter vector w is conceptually extended by reusing its elements cyclically until its length effectively matches that of v. In formal terms, for an operator $\oplus$, the operation at index i, with $1 \leq i \leq n$, is defined as

$$(v \oplus w)_i = v_i \oplus w_{((i-1) \bmod m)+1}.$$

This mapping guarantees that the sequence of elements in w is repeated in a periodic manner, thereby aligning the operands for the execution of vectorized operations.

Mathematical Formalism of the Recycling Process

The recycling rule can be expressed rigorously by introducing a function $r : \{1, 2, \ldots, n\} \to \{1, 2, \ldots, m\}$ defined by

$$r(i) = ((i - 1) \bmod m) + 1.$$

This function assigns to each index i in the longer vector v an index $r(i)$ corresponding to an element in the shorter vector w. Consequently, an element-wise operation involving the recycled vector is expressed as

$$(v \oplus w)_i = v_i \oplus w_{r(i)}.$$

When n is an integer multiple of m, that is, $n = km$ for some $k \in \mathbb{N}$, the recycling produces a complete and regular tiling of w. In cases where n is not an integer multiple of m, a partial repetition occurs in the final cycle, a situation that is typically accompanied by an informative warning in the R runtime environment.

Implications for Computational Operations

The recycling mechanism is central to the efficiency of vectorized computations in R, enabling operations without requiring explicit replication of shorter vectors. For a binary operator $\oplus$, the computing process is characterized by the composition of the operation with the recycling function, yielding

$$v \oplus w' = \big(v_1 \oplus w_{r(1)}, \; v_2 \oplus w_{r(2)}, \; \ldots, \; v_n \oplus w_{r(n)}\big),$$

where w' denotes the effective extension of w via the recycling rule. This mechanism relies on principles of modular arithmetic to ensure that the periodic structure of w is preserved throughout the computation. The periodic reuse of elements inherent to the recycling process introduces subtle intricacies in computations, particularly when the length of the longer vector is not an exact multiple of the shorter vector's length. In such scenarios, the partial final cycle may lead to misalignments that affect the outcome of aggregate computations. The interplay between the recycling rule and element-wise operations thus reflects a blend of theoretical mathematical rigor and practical computational strategy that is fundamental to R's design for handling heterogeneous data structures.

R Code Snippet

```
# This R script demonstrates the vector recycling mechanism as
↪   described in the chapter.
# It implements the recycling function r(i) = ((i-1) %% m) + 1 and
↪   applies a binary operator
# in an element-wise fashion between two vectors using recycling.

# Function to compute the recycled index for a given position i and
↪   the length m of the shorter vector
```

```
recycle_index <- function(i, m) {
  # Using the formal definition:
  # r(i) = ((i - 1) mod m) + 1
  return (((i - 1) %% m) + 1)
}


# Function that applies a binary operation using the recycling
↪  mechanism.
# v: longer vector (of length n)
# w: shorter vector (of length m)
# binary_op: a function representing the binary operation (e.g.,
↪  addition, multiplication)
recycled_operation <- function(v, w, binary_op) {
  n <- length(v)
  m <- length(w)
  result <- numeric(n)  # Initialize a numeric vector to store
  ↪  result
  for (i in 1:n) {
    # Determine the corresponding index in w using the recycling
    ↪  rule.
    j <- recycle_index(i, m)
    result[i] <- binary_op(v[i], w[j])
  }
  return(result)
}


# Example vectors:
# v is the longer vector and w is the shorter vector to be recycled.
v <- c(10, 20, 30, 40, 50, 60, 70, 80)
w <- c(1, 2, 3)

# Demonstrate element-wise addition using the custom
↪  recycled_operation function.
added_result <- recycled_operation(v, w, `+`)
print("Recycled addition result:")
print(added_result)
# Expected computation:
# 10+1, 20+2, 30+3, 40+1, 50+2, 60+3, 70+1, 80+2

# Compare with R's native recycling mechanism.
native_added <- v + w
print("Native R addition (using implicit recycling):")
print(native_added)

# Demonstrate element-wise multiplication using recycling.
multiplied_result <- recycled_operation(v, w, `*`)
print("Recycled multiplication result:")
print(multiplied_result)
# Expected computation following the recycling pattern.

native_multiplied <- v * w
print("Native R multiplication (using implicit recycling):")
print(native_multiplied)
```

274

```r
# Show the mapping of indices from v to w via the recycling
↪   function.
indices_mapping <- sapply(1:length(v), function(i) recycle_index(i,
↪   length(w)))
print("Recycled indices mapping for vector w:")
print(indices_mapping)
# Expected mapping: 1, 2, 3, 1, 2, 3, 1, 2

# Test the recycling mechanism when the vector lengths are not an
↪   exact multiple.
v2 <- c(5, 10, 15, 20, 25, 30, 35)  # Length of 7, while length(w)
↪   is 3.
print("Recycled addition for non-multiple vector lengths:")
print("Result using custom recycled_operation:")
print(recycled_operation(v2, w, `+`))
print("Result using native R operation (may emit a warning):")
print(v2 + w)  # In some versions of R, this may generate a warning
↪   if lengths are mismatched.

# End of R code snippet demonstrating the vector recycling
↪   mechanism.
```

Chapter 56

Efficient Vectorized Computation

Fundamentals of Vectorization in R

Vectorization in R is predicated upon the execution of operations on entire collections of data elements simultaneously, rather than through iterative constructs that process individual elements sequentially. Given two vectors, $A = (a_1, a_2, \ldots, a_n)$ and $B = (b_1, b_2, \ldots, b_n)$, an operation such as addition is performed in a single, cohesive step resulting in a vector $C = (a_1 + b_1, a_2 + b_2, \ldots, a_n + b_n)$. The capacity to apply such element-wise operations en masse is undergirded by implementations in low-level languages, which exploit hardware-specific optimizations and memory management techniques. This methodology obviates the latency inherent in interpreting explicit loops, thereby facilitating a more direct mapping of computation to the underlying system architecture and achieving significant enhancements in performance.

Memory and Data Alignment Considerations

Efficient vectorized computation requires a rigorous understanding of memory allocation and data alignment. Vectors stored in contiguous memory blocks enhance data locality, thereby reducing the frequency of cache misses—a critical determinant of computational speed. Memory alignment ensures that data is accessed in a manner that coincides with the architecture's cache line boundaries, optimizing both read and write operations. The performance impact can be abstracted in terms of the effective data processing rate, where the rate R is a function of the memory bandwidth B and the access latency L, expressible as

$$R = \frac{B}{L}.$$

When vectors are aligned and processed vectorially, the aggregated benefit is reflected in minimized overhead and maximized throughput, particularly on modern hardware where memory hierarchies are finely tuned to accommodate such patterns.

Algorithmic Manipulation and Operation Fusion

Strategy for efficient computation extends beyond mere exploitation of vectorized operations; it encompasses the synthesis of multiple operations into single computational kernels. Operation fusion, which amalgamates a sequence of transformations into a composite operation, mitigates the overhead associated with intermediate data structures and redundant memory allocation. Consider two functions f and g applied to a data vector X, where the sequential application $g(f(X))$ can be fused into a singular operation. This consolidation decreases temporary memory requirements and improves cache performance, as the data passes through fewer stages of repackaging. Through rigorous algorithmic restructuring, the composite function effectively reduces extraneous computational complexity and enhances overall efficiency.

Analytical Perspectives on Scalability and Performance Metrics

A quantitative evaluation of efficient vectorized computation necessitates a detailed analysis of performance metrics across varying scales of data. Let $T_{vector}(n)$ denote the execution time required for a vectorized implementation operating on a vector of length n, and let $T_{loop}(n)$ represent that required for an equivalent loop-based process. The relative performance gain is encapsulated by the speedup factor

$$S(n) = \frac{T_{loop}(n)}{T_{vector}(n)}.$$

Under conditions of optimal vectorization, $S(n)$ exhibits an upward trajectory as n increases, thereby verifying superior scalability. Attention to factors such as memory allocation overhead, cache line utilization, and processor-specific instruction sets provides additional layers of insight. Such analytical frameworks foster a comprehensive understanding of how vectorization can be methodically optimized to achieve not only lower computational latency but also a more efficient utilization of available system resources.

R Code Snippet

```
# Efficient Vectorized Computation: Comprehensive Code Example
# This code snippet demonstrates the following:
# 1. Simulation of memory performance using the equation R = B / L.
# 2. Comparison of vectorized operations versus loop-based
↪ computations.
# 3. Calculation of the speedup factor S(n) = T_loop(n) /
↪ T_vector(n).
# 4. Illustration of operation fusion by combining sequential
↪ function applications.

# Clear the current workspace
rm(list = ls())


# ---------------------------
# Part 1: Memory Performance Simulation
# ---------------------------
# Define memory bandwidth (B in bytes per second) and latency (L in
↪ seconds per byte)
B <- 1e9        # Example: 1 gigabyte per second
L <- 1e-9       # Example: 1 nanosecond per byte
R <- B / L      # Effective Data Processing Rate (R = B / L)
cat("Effective Data Processing Rate (R = B / L):", R,
↪ "bytes/sec\n\n")


# ---------------------------
# Part 2: Vectorized vs Loop-Based Computation Performance
# ---------------------------
# For precise timing, load the microbenchmark package.
# Install it if necessary: install.packages("microbenchmark")
if (!require("microbenchmark")) {
  install.packages("microbenchmark")
  library(microbenchmark)
}
```

```r
# Define functions for vectorized and loop-based addition.
# These functions will add two randomly generated vectors of length
↪  n.

vectorized_add <- function(n) {
  A <- runif(n)
  B <- runif(n)
  C <- A + B
  return(C)
}

loop_add <- function(n) {
  A <- runif(n)
  B <- runif(n)
  C <- numeric(n)
  for (i in 1:n) {
    C[i] <- A[i] + B[i]
  }
  return(C)
}

# Define vector sizes for performance evaluation
sizes <- c(1e4, 1e5, 1e6)

# Create a data frame to store benchmark results
results <- data.frame(Size = sizes, VectorizedTime = NA, LoopTime =
↪  NA, Speedup = NA)

# Loop over different vector sizes, measure execution times and
↪  compute speedup factor S(n)
for (i in seq_along(sizes)) {
  n <- sizes[i]

  # Measure vectorized addition time, using median to reduce noise
  ↪  (time in seconds)
  time_vector <- median(microbenchmark(vectorized_add(n), times =
  ↪  10)$time) / 1e9

  # Measure loop-based addition time (time in seconds)
  time_loop <- median(microbenchmark(loop_add(n), times = 10)$time)
  ↪  / 1e9

  results$VectorizedTime[i] <- time_vector
  results$LoopTime[i] <- time_loop
  # Speedup factor: S(n) = T_loop(n) / T_vector(n)
  results$Speedup[i] <- time_loop / time_vector
}

cat("Performance Comparison for Vectorized vs Loop-Based
↪  Addition:\n")
print(results)
```

279

```r
# ----------------------------
# Part 3: Operation Fusion in Functional Composition
# ----------------------------
# Demonstrate how two functions can be fused to avoid extra data
#   passes.
# Define function f: squares its input.
# Define function g: adds 1 to its input.

f <- function(x) {
  x^2
}

g <- function(x) {
  x + 1
}

# Sequential application: first apply f, then g
sequential_application <- function(X) {
  return(g(f(X)))
}

# Fused application: combine the two operations into a single step.
fused_application <- function(X) {
  return(X^2 + 1)
}

# Validate that both approaches yield the same result using a test
#   vector.
set.seed(123)  # For reproducibility
test_vector <- runif(10)
seq_result <- sequential_application(test_vector)
fus_result <- fused_application(test_vector)
equivalence <- all.equal(seq_result, fus_result)

cat("\nOperation Fusion Check:\n")
cat("Are sequential and fused applications equivalent? ",
    equivalence, "\n")

# End of Comprehensive R Code Snippet
```

Chapter 57

Conditional Vector Assignment using ifelse()

Fundamental Concepts of Vectorized Conditional Evaluation

The ifelse() construct embodies a vectorized conditional paradigm that enables element-wise assignment based on a corresponding logical predicate. In the context of large-scale data processing, ifelse() operates under the principle of applying a condition simultaneously to all elements of a data vector. Given an input vector $X = (x_1, x_2, \ldots, x_n)$ together with an associated Boolean vector $B = (b_1, b_2, \ldots, b_n)$, the ifelse() function produces an output vector $Y = (y_1, y_2, \ldots, y_n)$ such that each element is determined by a predefined condition:

$$y_i = \begin{cases} \phi(x_i), & \text{if } b_i \text{ is true,} \\ \psi(x_i), & \text{otherwise.} \end{cases}$$

In this formulation, $\phi(x_i)$ and $\psi(x_i)$ denote the candidate assignments that are contingent upon the truth value of b_i. This vectorized approach supersedes the iterative evaluation of scalar conditions by leveraging low-level, highly optimized computational routines.

Mathematical Formalism and Underlying Mechanics

The working semantics of ifelse() can be rigorously formalized through the examination of its mapping properties. Consider a mapping $f : \{0, 1\} \times \mathbb{R} \times \mathbb{R} \to \mathbb{R}$ defined by:

$$f(b, a, c) = \begin{cases} a, & \text{if } b = 1, \\ c, & \text{if } b = 0. \end{cases}$$

When extended over a vectorized domain, ifelse() acts as a function F that transforms a triple of vectors (B, A, C) into an output vector Y, where for every index i,

$$y_i = f(b_i, a_i, c_i).$$

This mathematical abstraction underscores the dichotomous evaluation that ifelse() enacts on each element. The critical efficiency stems from the inherent parallelism when the guard condition b_i is computed over overlapping memory regions, thereby reducing computational overhead relative to traditional scalar conditional statements.

Performance Analysis and Memory Access Considerations

The vectorized nature of ifelse() contributes significantly to performance gains in modern computational environments. With data stored in contiguous memory locations, the parallel evaluation of conditions maximizes cache utilization and minimizes memory access latency. When processing vectors of length n, the computational complexity associated with ifelse() is primarily linear, often denoted as $O(n)$.

Furthermore, the elimination of explicit loop constructs enables the underlying system to employ low-level memory prefetching and instruction-level parallelism. This results in a marked reduction in overhead. The effective throughput, when measured in terms of data elements processed per unit time, is directly enhanced by optimizations catered to modern memory architectures. As a consequence, large-scale conditional vector assignments become feasible with minimal performance penalties, even when applied to extensive datasets.

Robustness in Heterogeneous Data Contexts and Edge Cases

In scenarios involving non-uniform input structures or heterogeneous data types, the application of ifelse() necessitates rigorous attention to type coercion and input consistency. The function accommodates vectors A and C that may differ in type, relying on intrinsic coercion rules to produce a coherent output vector. When the conditional vector B contains indeterminate values, such as missing or undefined logical entries, the evaluation semantics ensure that the fallback mechanism is clearly defined.

Edge cases, including mismatches in vector lengths and atypical data structures, are addressed through implicit validation and standardization phases within the computational pipeline. These mechanisms guarantee that the element-wise execution of ifelse() conforms to expected behaviors, thus preserving the integrity of the resultant assignments. The robustness of these procedures is critical in environments where data irregularities are prevalent and where the cost of misassignment can substantially impact downstream analytical processes.

R Code Snippet

```
#
↪   -----------------------------------------------------------------------
# Vectorized Conditional Assignment in R using ifelse()
#
↪   -----------------------------------------------------------------------
# This code demonstrates the vectorized conditional evaluation where
↪   for each
# element x[i] we assign:
#   y[i] = phi(x[i])    if the condition b[i] is TRUE,
#   y[i] = psi(x[i])    otherwise.
#
# The mapping being implemented is defined as:
#   f(b, a, c) = a if b is TRUE, or c if b is FALSE,
# and when applied to vectors:
#   y = ifelse(b, phi(x), psi(x))
#
# Example 1: Basic Usage with a Small Vector
#
↪   -----------------------------------------------------------------------

# Define an input vector of numeric values
x <- 1:20
```

```r
# Define a logical condition: TRUE if the element is even, FALSE
↪   otherwise.
b <- (x %% 2 == 0)

# Define candidate assignment functions:
phi <- function(x) {
  # For elements satisfying the condition (even numbers), compute
  ↪   the square.
  x^2
}

psi <- function(x) {
  # For elements not satisfying the condition (odd numbers), compute
  ↪   the cube root.
  x^(1/3)
}

# Apply ifelse() to perform element-wise conditional assignment:
# For each index i, y[i] = phi(x[i]) if b[i] is TRUE, else
↪   psi(x[i]).
y <- ifelse(b, phi(x), psi(x))

# Output the input, condition, and resultant vectors
cat("Input vector x:\n")
print(x)
cat("Condition vector b (TRUE for even numbers):\n")
print(b)
cat("Result vector y computed using ifelse() with phi(x) and
↪   psi(x):\n")
print(y)

#
↪   -----------------------------------------------------------------------
# Example 2: Performance Comparison on a Large Dataset
#
↪   -----------------------------------------------------------------------

# Generate a large vector to demonstrate performance benefits of
↪   vectorization
n <- 1e6
x_large <- runif(n, 1, 100)     # 1,000,000 random numbers uniformly
↪   distributed between 1 and 100

# Define a logical condition: TRUE if the number is greater than 50
b_large <- (x_large > 50)

# Define new candidate functions for the large dataset:
phi_large <- function(x) { sin(x) }   # Compute sine when condition
↪   is met
psi_large <- function(x) { cos(x) }   # Compute cosine when condition
↪   is not met
```

```r
# Measure computation time using the vectorized ifelse()
time_ifelse <- system.time({
  y_large <- ifelse(b_large, phi_large(x_large), psi_large(x_large))
})
cat("Time taken using vectorized ifelse():\n")
print(time_ifelse)

# For comparison purposes, implement the same logic using an
↪  explicit for-loop
y_loop <- numeric(n)  # Initialize the result vector
time_loop <- system.time({
  for (i in 1:n) {
    if (b_large[i]) {
      y_loop[i] <- phi_large(x_large[i])
    } else {
      y_loop[i] <- psi_large(x_large[i])
    }
  }
})
cat("Time taken using a for-loop:\n")
print(time_loop)

# Validate that both methods yield nearly identical results by
↪  computing the mean absolute difference
cat("Mean absolute difference between ifelse() and loop results:\n")
print(mean(abs(y_large - y_loop)))

#
↪  ------------------------------------------------------------------
# Example 3: Handling Missing Values (NA) in Conditional Evaluation
#
↪  ------------------------------------------------------------------

# Create a sample vector containing NA values
x_na <- c(5, 15, NA, 25)

# Define a condition: TRUE if element is greater than 10 (NA
↪  comparisons yield NA)
b_na <- x_na > 10

# Apply ifelse() where:
#  - For TRUE, double the element: phi(x) = x * 2
#  - For FALSE, halve the element: psi(x) = x / 2
result_na <- ifelse(b_na, x_na * 2, x_na / 2)

cat("Result when handling NA in the condition vector:\n")
print(result_na)
```

Chapter 58

Using Logical Operators in Data Filtering

Fundamental Principles of Boolean Filtering

The process of filtering data based on logical conditions is rooted in the formalism of Boolean algebra. In a typical data set $D = d_1, d_2, ldots, d_n$, each element is associated with a predicate function $P : D$

rightarrow

$0, 1$, which determines membership in a subset based on the truth value returned. Logical operators, namely conjunction (

land), disjunction (

lor), and negation (

lnot), are used to construct complex predicates from basic relational and equality conditions. A filtering operation can be understood as the extraction of a subset

$$D' = d in D : P(d) = 1,$$

where the function P is formed by the composition of such operators. The sound application of these operators is essential for ensuring that data elements satisfying compound criteria are reliably and efficiently isolated.

Computational Considerations in Data Filtering

The implementation of logical operators in data filtering leverages vectorized evaluation to perform simultaneous computations across large-scale datasets. When applying the composite predicate function E to a data vector, the evaluation is carried out in an element-wise fashion, thus enabling concurrency and efficient utilization of processor architectures. The operation inherently exhibits linear complexity, denoted by $O(n)$ for a dataset of size n, which is a substantial improvement over iterative, scalar-based evaluation methodologies.

Memory access patterns also benefit from the contiguous storage of data, ensuring that filtering operations maximize cache performance and reduce latency. The interplay between high-level logical operations and low-level hardware optimizations, including the use of Single Instruction, Multiple Data ($SIMD$) paradigms, constitutes an essential aspect of modern data processing systems. In this context, the systematic application of logical operators ensures that data extraction is both robust and computationally efficient.

Logical Operator Compositions and Case Analysis

Complex data filtering scenarios often require the formulation of nested logical expressions. Consider a data element d $in D$ subject to the constraint

$$E(d) = left[P_1(d) land left(P_2(d) lor lnot P_3(d) right) right] lor lnot P_4(d).$$

Such an expression necessitates deliberate structuring to guarantee unambiguous evaluation, particularly when predicates are derived from heterogeneous data sources. The explicit use of parentheses ensures that each component of the logical expression is evaluated in the prescribed order, thereby preserving the semantic integrity of the filter.

In many instances, logical operators are integrated with relational comparisons, yielding expressions of the form

$$bigl(d > alpha bigr) land bigl(d leq beta bigr),$$

where
alpha and
beta represent threshold values. The resulting boolean mask determines the indices corresponding to data elements that satisfy the condition within a closed or open numerical interval. Rigorous analysis of these cases involves addressing issues such as type consistency, ensuring that operands can be concomitantly compared, and managing precision in floating-point comparisons. The concomitant application of logical and relational operators thereby facilitates the precise extraction of data subsets tailored to specific analytical requirements.

R Code Snippet

```
# R Code Snippet: Demonstrating Logical Operators in Data Filtering

# Create a dataset vector D containing integers from 1 to 100
D <- 1:100

# Define threshold values for relational comparisons
alpha <- 30
beta <- 70

# Define basic predicate functions
# P1: Returns TRUE if an element is greater than alpha
P1 <- function(x) {
  return(x > alpha)
}

# P2: Returns TRUE if an element is even
P2 <- function(x) {
  return(x %% 2 == 0)
}

# P3: Returns TRUE if an element is less than or equal to beta
P3 <- function(x) {
  return(x <= beta)
}

# P4: Returns TRUE if an element is divisible by 3
P4 <- function(x) {
  return(x %% 3 == 0)
}

#------------------------------------------------------------------
# Composite Predicate 1
# Evaluate the logical expression:
# E(x) = (P1(x) AND NOT P2(x)) OR P3(x)
```

288

```r
# This follows the formulation:
#    D' = { d in D : [P1(d) & !P2(d)] | P3(d) is TRUE }
E <- (P1(D) & (!P2(D))) | P3(D)

# Filter the dataset D based on the composite predicate E
subset_D <- D[E]
cat("Subset of D satisfying (P1 and not P2) or P3:\n")
print(subset_D)


#---------------------------------------------------------------------
# Composite Predicate 2
# Evaluate a more complex expression:
# E2(x) = [P1(x) AND (P2(x) OR NOT P3(x))] OR NOT P4(x)
# This demonstrates nested logical operators with explicit grouping.
E2 <- (P1(D) & (P2(D) | (!P3(D)))) | (!P4(D))
subset_D2 <- D[E2]
cat("\nSubset of D satisfying [P1 and (P2 or not P3)] or not P4:\n")
print(subset_D2)


#---------------------------------------------------------------------
# Using ifelse() for Conditional Vector Assignment
# Assign "High" to elements in D that are above beta and "Low"
# ↪  otherwise.
result_label <- ifelse(D > beta, "High", "Low")
cat("\nConditional labeling of D (High if > beta, else Low):\n")
print(result_label)


#---------------------------------------------------------------------
# Data Frame Example: Logical Filtering with Multiple Conditions
# Create a data frame with an identifier and a randomly generated
# ↪  value
set.seed(123)   # Ensure reproducibility of random numbers
df <- data.frame(id = 1:100, value = runif(100, min = 0, max = 100))

# Apply filtering on the data frame:
#    Select rows where 'value' is between 25 and 75 (inclusive)
#    AND where the id is odd (to demonstrate combined relational and
# ↪  modulus conditions)
filtered_df <- df[(df$value >= 25) & (df$value <= 75) & (df$id %% 2
# ↪  == 1), ]
cat("\nFiltered data frame rows (value between 25 and 75 and odd
# ↪  id):\n")
print(filtered_df)

# End of R code snippet demonstrating logical operators in data
# ↪  filtering.
```

Chapter 59

Basic Data Transformation with the transform() Function

Foundational Principles of Data Frame Transformation

Data frames represent a structured collection of variables, each maintained as a column with an equal number of observations. Within this framework, data transformation refers to the process of modifying existing variables or generating new ones through the evaluation of arithmetic, logical, or functional expressions. The function transform() in R is designed to encapsulate these operations in a succinct manner by evaluating expressions in an environment where every column of the input data frame is directly accessible. This process can be formally represented by considering a data frame D composed of columns $x_1, x_2, \ldots, x_k$. A transformation applies an evaluative function f, yielding a new variable y defined as

$$y = f(x_1, x_2, \ldots, x_k),$$

with the resulting data frame denoted by

$$D' = D \cup \{y\}.$$

In this context, transform() abstracts the procedural details of variable extraction, modification, and subsequent binding within the original data frame structure.

Mechanisms of the transform() Function

The core functionality of transform() is rooted in its capacity to evaluate supplied expressions within the environment of the data frame. Each expression, whether it represents a transformation of an existing variable or the creation of a new one, is processed in a vectorized fashion. This implies that for a data frame containing n rows, the operation executes over vectors of length n, ensuring that the computational overhead is linear, i.e., of complexity $O(n)$. The evaluation is performed atomically, thereby guaranteeing that modifications are internally consistent and that column attributes—such as class definitions and metadata—are preserved unless explicitly redefined. Such design promotes both conciseness in code and clarity in the operational semantics, as the transformation can be regarded as a mapping from a set of original variables to an augmented set through the function

$$f : \mathbb{R}^k \to \mathbb{V},$$

where $\mathbb{V}$ signifies the collection of valid variable types within the R environment.

Structural and Computational Considerations

The transform() function embodies a declarative paradigm, enabling modifications to the data frame without the need for iterative procedures or temporary constructs. Its internal mechanism leverages the contiguous storage model of data frames, thereby optimizing memory access patterns and capitalizing on vectorized instruction sets. The function evaluates expressions in an environment in which every column is available as a variable, thereby obviating the manual indexing and explicit assignment that might otherwise be required. In a formal sense, given a data frame D and a set of transformation expressions $\{E_1, E_2, \ldots, E_l\}$, each expression E_i is interpreted as a mapping

$$E_i : D \to \mathbb{V},$$

291

with the aggregate result constituting a modified data frame D' that reflects the cumulative effects of the individual transformations. This process, driven by an underlying vectorized and lazy evaluation model, ensures that the operational semantics are both robust and efficient, maintaining data integrity while facilitating rapid analytical progression.

R Code Snippet

```
# Set seed for reproducibility
set.seed(123)

# Create an initial data frame with multiple columns
# This data frame (D) contains:
#   - value1: a sequence of integers (x1)
#   - value2: normally distributed values (x2)
#   - value3: uniformly distributed values (x3)
df <- data.frame(
  value1 = 1:10,
  value2 = rnorm(10, mean = 50, sd = 10),
  value3 = runif(10, min = 1, max = 100)
)

# Display the original data frame
cat("Original Data Frame:\n")
print(df)

#
↪ ---------------------------------------------------------------------
# Transformation using transform():
#
# We want to compute a new variable 'new_value' as a function of the
↪ existing
# columns, following the formula:
#
#   y = f(value1, value2, value3) = value1 + 0.5 * value2 -
↪ log(value3 + 1)
#
# This operation represents:
#   - Extraction of columns (value1, value2, value3) from D
#   - Application of the function f to compute y
#   - Binding the new variable 'new_value' into the original data
↪ frame,
#     i.e., D' = D  {y}
#
# Additionally, we create a categorical column 'status' using
↪ ifelse(), where:
#   status = "High" if value2 > 50, otherwise "Low"
```

```
#
↪  -------------------------------------------------------------------
df_transformed <- transform(df,
  new_value = value1 + 0.5 * value2 - log(value3 + 1),
  status    = ifelse(value2 > 50, "High", "Low")
)

# Display the transformed data frame
cat("\nTransformed Data Frame (after adding new_value and
↪  status):\n")
print(df_transformed)

#
↪  -------------------------------------------------------------------
# Additional Transformation to Illustrate Further Data Manipulation:
#
# Here we apply an extra transformation that scales 'value3' via a
↪  simple linear
# operation:
#
#   scaled_value3 = value3 * 100 + 10
#
# This demonstrates another example of a vectorized arithmetic
↪  operation applied
# to all rows simultaneously.
#
↪  -------------------------------------------------------------------
df_transformed <- transform(df_transformed,
  scaled_value3 = value3 * 100 + 10
)

cat("\nData Frame after additional transformation (scaled_value3
↪  added):\n")
print(df_transformed)

#
↪  -------------------------------------------------------------------
# Performance and Vectorized Computation Demonstration:
#
# To showcase the linear (O(n)) complexity of vectorized operations
↪  in R,
# we generate a larger data frame 'large_df' with 1000 rows and
↪  perform a cumulative
# sum on the 'y' variable.
#
↪  -------------------------------------------------------------------
large_df <- data.frame(
  x = 1:1000,
  y = rnorm(1000)
)

# Apply transform() to calculate cumulative sum of 'y'
large_df <- transform(large_df,
```

```
  cumsum_y = cumsum(y)
)

# Display a summary of the cumulative sum to verify the outcome
cat("\nSummary of cumulative sum transformation on large data
↪  frame:\n")
print(summary(large_df$cumsum_y))
```

Chapter 60

Understanding Internal Structure of Data Objects

Architectural Foundations of R Objects

R data objects are encapsulated within an internal framework that abstracts low-level memory representations and provides a uniform interface through which diverse types of data are manipulated. At the core of this abstraction lies a dynamic type system in which every data object is constructed as a container coupled with a set of metadata elements. The intrinsic design is grounded in the concept of a symbolic expression, or S-expression, which is a pointer to a structured memory block. This memory block inherently comprises a header, encoding both the object's type and its reference count, and a payload where the substantive data reside. Formally, an object can be envisaged as a tuple

$$(\tau, \rho, \mu, d),$$

where τ denotes the type tag, ρ is the reference counter, μ embodies the collection of attributes, and d represents the actual data content stored contiguously.

The Role of Attributes and Metadata

Attributes serve as a pivotal mechanism for imbuing data objects with additional semantic context. These attributes are stored as a named list that is intrinsic to every object and facilitate flexible metadata representation including descriptors such as names, dimensions, and class labels. The metadata encapsulates supplementary information that enables higher-level abstraction and customization. For instance, a matrix not only holds numeric values but also contains attributes specifying its dimensions and, optionally, dimension names. This separation between raw data and its descriptive attributes allows the computational engine to efficiently perform vectorized operations while preserving the contextual information required for accurate interpretation and manipulation. Let the attribute collection be denoted as

$$\mu = \{\texttt{name} : v_{\texttt{name}}, \texttt{dim} : v_{\texttt{dim}}, \texttt{class} : v_{\texttt{class}}, \ldots\},$$

where each v_i is itself an R object representing the corresponding metadata element.

Internal Representation and Memory Management

The memory layout underlying an R object adheres to principles that optimize for both performance and flexibility. Each object is instantiated as a contiguous block in memory, with the header preamble containing essential information such as the type identifier τ and reference count ρ. This design facilitates garbage collection through reference counting and ensures that objects can be shared across different contexts without superfluous copying. The payload d, representing the actual data, is organized in a manner that permits vectorized operations, which are central to R's performance characteristics. The alignment and storage strategies are engineered to exploit hardware-level optimizations, and the overall representation supports constant-time attribute retrieval and linear-time data traversal for operations spanning n elements, i.e., a computational complexity of $O(n)$.

Formalization of Object Structures in R

The internal formalism that underpins R objects can be characterized by a mapping from the abstract notion of a data object to its concrete memory representation. Consider an object O defined by the mapping

$$O : \mathcal{D} \to (\tau, \rho, \mu, d),$$

where $\mathcal{D}$ is the set of potential data domains. Within this formulation, the attribute set μ plays a dual role: it serves as both an identifier of the object's contextual semantics and as a facilitator for method dispatch in the object-oriented systems native to R. The integration of metadata into the object's structure enables a consistent and robust mechanism for method overloading and inheritance. Moreover, the encapsulation of such metadata ensures that the operations performed on the data (e.g., subsetting, transformation, and aggregation) are contextually aware, thereby preserving both data integrity and the logical relationships that the attributes are designed to represent.

R Code Snippet

```r
# Define a constructor for simulating an R object using the tuple
↪    representation (, , , d)
createRObject <- function(tau, d, mu = list(), rho = 1) {
  structure(
    list(
      type = tau,         # : Type tag of the object
      refCount = rho,     # : Reference counter for memory management
      attributes = mu,    # : Collection of metadata (e.g., name,
      ↪    dimensions, class)
      data = d            # d: The actual data payload
    ),
    class = "R_Object"
  )
}


# Custom print method for objects of class "R_Object"
print.R_Object <- function(x, ...) {
  cat("R_Object of type:", x$type, "\n")
  cat("Reference Count:", x$refCount, "\n")
  if (length(x$attributes) > 0) {
    cat("Attributes:\n")
    print(x$attributes)
  }
  cat("Data:\n")
```

```r
  print(x$data)
}

# Function to increment the reference count, simulating shared
↪  object usage
incrementRefCount <- function(obj) {
  obj$refCount <- obj$refCount + 1
  return(obj)
}

# Function to perform a vectorized operation on the data payload:
# Adds a constant value to each element in the data (assuming
↪  numeric data)
vecAdd <- function(obj, value) {
  if (!is.numeric(obj$data)) {
    stop("Data must be numeric for vectorized addition!")
  }
  obj$data <- obj$data + value
  return(obj)
}

# Function to update a specific attribute in the object
updateAttribute <- function(obj, attr_name, attr_value) {
  obj$attributes[[attr_name]] <- attr_value
  return(obj)
}

# Dispatch function to simulate method selection based on the
↪  object's class attribute
dispatchFunction <- function(obj) {
  cls <- obj$attributes$class
  if (cls == "matrix") {
    cat("Performing matrix-specific operations.\n")
    cat("Dimensions: ", paste(obj$attributes$dim, collapse = " x "),
    ↪  "\n")
  } else {
    cat("No specific operations available for class:", cls, "\n")
  }
}

#
↪  -------------------------------------------------------------------------
# Simulation of the internal structure of an R object as described:
#   Object O is defined as a mapping from the data domain   to its
↪  tuple (, , , d)
#   Here the tuple represents:
#           - Type tag (e.g., "matrix", "vector")
#           - Reference count (for memory sharing and garbage
↪  collection)
#           - Attributes (metadata such as names, dimensions, class
↪  labels)
#       d       - The actual data in a contiguous block of memory
```

298

```
#
↪   ----------------------------------------------------------------------

# Example: Create an R object representing a 2x2 numeric matrix
mu_matrix <- list(
  name = "exampleMatrix",
  dim = c(2, 2),    # dimensions of the matrix
  class = "matrix" # class attribute indicating a matrix object
)
m <- matrix(1:4, nrow = 2)   # The data payload: a simple 2x2 matrix

# Create the R object using the tuple representation
robj <- createRObject("matrix", m, mu_matrix)

# Print the initial state of the object
print(robj)

# Simulate sharing of the object by incrementing the reference count
robj <- incrementRefCount(robj)

# Perform a vectorized addition: add 10 to each element of the data
↪   payload
robj <- vecAdd(robj, 10)

cat("After vectorized addition:\n")
print(robj)

# Update an attribute (e.g., renaming the object)
robj <- updateAttribute(robj, "name", "updatedMatrix")

# Demonstrate method dispatch based on the 'class' attribute of the
↪   object
dispatchFunction(robj)
```

Chapter 61

Working with Named Vectors and Lists

Fundamental Concepts of Naming in Vectors

The assignment of names to the individual elements of a vector constitutes an intrinsic method for embedding semantic information directly within the data structure. In formal terms, a vector may be represented as an ordered tuple

$$(v_1, v_2, \ldots, v_n)$$

accompanied by an associated set of keys

$$(k_1, k_2, \ldots, k_n)$$

such that a bijective mapping

$$f : \{1, 2, \ldots, n\} \to \{k_1, k_2, \ldots, k_n\}$$

is established. This mapping enables each data element v_i to be referenced by its corresponding name k_i rather than solely by its numerical index. The embedded naming convention facilitates not only clarity in data manipulation but also enhances the interpretability of the underlying datasets when subject to complex computational transformations. Naming elements in vectors serves as a mechanism for encoding metadata, thereby reducing ambiguity and supporting semantic consistency during both iterative computation and analytical review.

Structural Characteristics of Named Lists

Named lists extend the paradigm of semantic labeling by permitting heterogeneous elements to be stored alongside descriptive keys. Each element in a list is paired with a name that expresses its intended role or identity, generating a compound data structure in which different data types are coherently organized. The arrangement of a named list may be considered in abstract terms as a finite set of pairs

$$\{(k_i, l_i) \mid i = 1, 2, \ldots, m\},$$

where each key k_i enables direct access to the list element l_i. This structure obviates the reliance on positional indices, often prone to error in extensive data manipulations, and instead propagates an environment in which each component is self-descriptive. The clear delineation provided by named elements within lists supports advanced operations such as dynamic attribute resolution and context-aware indexing. The inherent design ensures that modifications to one part of the data structure preserve the logical associations established by the naming, a property imperative for maintaining data integrity during transformations and aggregations.

Semantic Advantages in Data Manipulation

The incorporation of explicit names into vectors and lists engenders a framework wherein data elements are immediately identifiable and their relationships are explicitly defined. When considering complex data manipulation, the semantic clarity afforded by element naming serves to streamline operations such as filtering, reshaping, and merging. With named elements, the processing algorithm can reference keys directly, thus bypassing the uncertainty of positional ambiguities. In analytical environments, this leads to reduced cognitive overhead during algorithm design and a lowered incidence of errors in function interfacing. The semantic network emerging from such naming conventions is analogous to the role played by keys in associative arrays or dictionaries, where each key guarantees a unique correspondence with its respective value. This guarantees that during iterative transformations, the integrity of data associations is maintained, ensuring that downstream computations reflect the original logical structure of the dataset.

The explicit naming convention further supports modularity in algorithm design by decoupling data reference from memory location. By abstracting the access mechanism through named keys, data manipulation functions can be designed with heightened robustness and adaptability, thereby fostering a development environment where code clarity and maintainability are prioritized. The resulting benefits in code interpretability and streamlined data operations underscore the significance of naming elements in sophisticated data-driven applications.

R Code Snippet

```r
# Example R Code demonstrating Named Vectors and Named Lists

# --------------------------------
# Named Vectors: Mapping Index to Keys
# --------------------------------

# Create a numeric vector of sample data
values <- c(25, 30, 22, 28, 35)
# Define corresponding names for each element
names(values) <- c("Alice", "Bob", "Charlie", "David", "Eva")

# Display the named vector
print("Named Vector (ages):")
print(values)

# Access an element by its name
alice_age <- values["Alice"]
cat("Alice's age is:", alice_age, "\n")

# Perform vectorized operations using named elements
# Filter ages greater than 25 using names
filtered_ages <- values[values > 25]
cat("Ages greater than 25:\n")
print(filtered_ages)

# Update an element using its name
values["Charlie"] <- 23   # updating Charlie's age
cat("Updated ages:\n")
print(values)


# --------------------------------
# Mapping indices to names (explicitly)
# --------------------------------
```

302

```r
# Create a mapping function from index to name
map_index_to_name <- function(idx, vec) {
    if (idx >= 1 && idx <= length(vec)) {
        return(names(vec)[idx])
    } else {
        return(NA)
    }
}

# Demonstrate the mapping function
for (i in 1:length(values)) {
    cat("Index", i, "maps to name:", map_index_to_name(i, values),
    ↪  "\n")
}

# --------------------------------
# Named Lists: Heterogeneous Structures
# --------------------------------

# Create a named list containing diverse elements: a title, a
↪  numeric vector,
# another numeric vector for scores, and a nested list with
↪  additional details.
my_list <- list(
    title = "Employee Data",
    ages = values,
    scores = c(88, 92, 79, 95, 85),
    details = list(
        department = c("HR", "Finance", "IT", "Marketing", "Sales"),
        bonus = c(500, 700, 450, 800, 650)
    )
).
# Assign explicit names to the list components (optional as they are
↪  already named)
names(my_list) <- c("Title", "Ages", "Scores", "Details")

# Display the complete named list
print("Named List:")
print(my_list)

# Access elements in the list by processing the names
cat("Employee Title:", my_list$Title, "\n")
cat("Employee Ages Vector:\n")
print(my_list$Ages)

# Access a nested list element: department names
cat("Departments:\n")
print(my_list$Details$department)

# Modify a nested list element: update the bonus for the second
↪  employee
my_list$Details$bonus[2] <- 750
cat("Updated Bonuses:\n")
```

```r
print(my_list$Details$bonus)

# -------------------------------
# Algorithm: Compute Average Age of Employees With Score Above
↪   Threshold
# -------------------------------

compute_average_age <- function(age_vec, score_vec, threshold = 85)
↪  {
    # Verify the length of vectors match
    if (length(age_vec) != length(score_vec)) {
        stop("Vectors must be of the same length")
    }
    # Filter employees with scores above the threshold using their
    ↪   names
    high_score_indices <- score_vec > threshold
    high_score_ages <- age_vec[high_score_indices]
    # Compute the average age among the filtered results
    avg_age <- mean(high_score_ages)
    return(avg_age)
}

# Apply the algorithm: Compute average age for employees with scores
↪   above 85
average_age <- compute_average_age(my_list$Ages, my_list$Scores,
↪   threshold = 85)
cat("Average age of employees with score above 85 is:", average_age,
↪   "\n")
```

Chapter 62

Manipulating Dimensions and Attributes

Fundamental Aspects of Dimensional Attributes

The intrinsic organization of multidimensional data within R is governed by a set of attributes that define its shape and structure. In many instances, an object such as a matrix or an array is characterized by a dimension vector

$$\mathbf{d} = (d_1, d_2, \ldots, d_k),$$

where each component d_i represents the extent along the corresponding axis. This attribute not only determines how data are laid out in memory but also plays a crucial role in enabling operations that require an understanding of the data's structural context. The extraction and utilization of the dimension attribute facilitate numerous mathematical and computational operations, ranging from fundamental indexing procedures to sophisticated linear algebra computations. In this formal framework, the property that stipulates the dimensions is indispensable for aligning the data's physical representation with its abstract, multidimensional interpretation.

Modifying Names and Dimensional Identifiers

In R, the ability to ascribe and alter names within data objects introduces a layer of semantic annotation that bridges numerical indices with contextual meaning. A vector, for example, can be conceived as an ordered tuple

$$V = (v_1, v_2, \ldots, v_n)$$

accompanied by a corresponding set of names

$$N = (n_1, n_2, \ldots, n_n),$$

which defines a bijective mapping

$$f : \{1, 2, \ldots, n\} \to \{n_1, n_2, \ldots, n_n\}.$$

This mapping provides a formal mechanism for associating each element v_i of the vector with a distinctive identifier n_i, thereby enhancing the clarity of data operations by mitigating reliance on implicit positional references. The concept extends naturally to higher-dimensional objects, where each axis may be annotated with labels that delineate row names, column names, or more complex identifiers. The deliberate modification of these names and identifiers is a critical step in ensuring that the logical structure of the dataset transparently reflects the semantic roles of its constituents.

Accessing and Adjusting Auxiliary Object Attributes

Beyond dimensions and nomenclature, R objects frequently incorporate an array of additional attributes that encapsulate metadata essential to their identity and functionality. Among these are attributes such as the class, storage mode, and user-defined annotations, each of which informs method dispatch and influences the behavior of generic operations. Altering these attributes demands a rigorous approach to ensure consistency; for instance, modifying the class attribute of an object may alter the default operational semantics by invoking alternative methods under the generic function paradigm. In the abstract, an object may be viewed as a composite structure endowed with a suite of attributes

$$\mathcal{A} = \{a_1, a_2, \ldots, a_p\},$$

each element of which contributes to the overall descriptive and operational profile of the object. The systematic access to and modification of these attributes not only preserve the data integrity of the object but also enhance the modularity and adaptability of computational processes within the R environment.

R Code Snippet

```
#----------------------------------------------------------------
# 1. Creating and Exploring a Matrix (Dimension Attributes)
#----------------------------------------------------------------
# Create a matrix with 3 rows and 4 columns
mat <- matrix(1:12, nrow = 3, ncol = 4)
cat("Initial Matrix:\n")
print(mat)

# Extract the dimension vector: d = (d1, d2)
dims <- dim(mat)
cat("\nDimension vector of the matrix (d1 = number of rows, d2 =
↳  number of columns):\n")
print(dims)


#-------------------------------------------------------------------
# 2. Modifying Row and Column Names (Mapping Indices to Names)
#-------------------------------------------------------------------
# Assign row names and column names to the matrix
rownames(mat) <- c("row1", "row2", "row3")
colnames(mat) <- c("col1", "col2", "col3", "col4")
cat("\nMatrix after assigning row and column names:\n")
print(mat)

# Create a named vector representing an ordered tuple V = (v1, v2,
↳  ..., vn)
vec <- c(10, 20, 30, 40)
# Define a mapping f: {1,2,...,n} -> {n1, n2, ..., nn} by assigning
↳  names
names(vec) <- c("A", "B", "C", "D")
cat("\nNamed Vector (with bijective mapping f):\n")
print(vec)

# Access an element using its name instead of its position
cat("\nAccessing element with name 'B':\n")
print(vec["B"])


#-------------------------------------------------------------------
# 3. Accessing and Adjusting Auxiliary Object Attributes (Metadata)
#-------------------------------------------------------------------
# Create a simple vector and assign additional attributes
obj <- 1:5
```

```r
attr(obj, "description") <- "A simple integer vector representing V"
attr(obj, "version") <- 1.0
cat("\nAttributes of obj before class modification:\n")
print(attributes(obj))

# Modify the class attribute to simulate a custom object structure
class(obj) <- "custom"
cat("\nObject after changing class to 'custom':\n")
print(obj)
cat("Class of obj:\n")
print(class(obj))

# Define a custom print method for objects of class 'custom'
print.custom <- function(x, ...) {
    cat("Custom object with values:\n")
    print(unclass(x))
    cat("\nAssociated Attributes:\n")
    print(attributes(x))
}
# Invoke the custom print method
cat("\nInvoking custom print method on obj:\n")
print.custom(obj)


#----------------------------------------------------------------------
# 4. Reshaping a Vector into a Matrix and Modifying Its Attributes
#----------------------------------------------------------------------
# Create a vector and assign it a dimension to become a 3x3 matrix
vec2 <- 1:9
dim(vec2) <- c(3, 3)
cat("\nReshaped vector (vec2) into a 3x3 matrix:\n")
print(vec2)
cat("\nDimensions of vec2:\n")
print(dim(vec2))

# Assign semantic row and column names to vec2
rownames(vec2) <- paste("R", 1:3, sep = "_")
colnames(vec2) <- paste("C", 1:3, sep = "_")
cat("\nvec2 after assigning row and column names:\n")
print(vec2)

# Use indexing with the new names to extract a specific row and
# ↪ column
row_extracted <- vec2[1, ]
col_extracted <- vec2[, 2]
cat("\nExtracted first row of vec2:\n")
print(row_extracted)
cat("\nExtracted second column of vec2:\n")
print(col_extracted)

# Display all attributes of vec2, including dimensions and names
cat("\nAttributes of vec2:\n")
print(attributes(vec2))
```

Chapter 63

Using the with() and within() Functions

Conceptual Foundation of Environment Evaluation

Within the realm of data manipulation in R, the execution of expressions within a specified data frame environment represents a formal abstraction that greatly reduces syntactic verbosity. In this context, the data frame is regarded not merely as an aggregate of variables but as a compositional environment, wherein each element is bound to an identifier. By constructing a temporary evaluation environment, it becomes possible to resolve identifiers directly against the data frame's embedded namespace. In formal terms, let D denote the set of all variables contained within a data frame. The evaluation mechanism functionally defines an environment E such that $E \supseteq D$. When an expression is processed within E, the search for any identifier commences with the local scope defined by D, thereby obviating the repeated specification of the data frame's name. This reduction in notational overhead streamlines the expression of operations that are intrinsically linked with the individual elements of the data structure.

Mechanics of the with() Function

The with() function embodies the principle of non-intrusive evaluation by establishing a transient environment derived directly from a given data frame. Under its operational semantics, the function temporarily reassigns the data frame's elements as accessible variables within a localized scope. Formally, if $d \in D$ represents an element or a column of the data frame, then, for the duration of the evaluation, an expression referencing d is interpreted as directly accessing the corresponding value within D. This process occurs without altering the original data frame, thereby preserving global state and ensuring that any side effects remain rigorously controlled. The mechanism of the with() function adheres to the rules of lexical scoping, whereby the resolution of identifiers follows a precisely defined search order that privileges the immediate environment over outer scopes. Consequently, the clarity and brevity of code are enhanced by decoupling the reference to the data frame from the intrinsic operations performed on its constituent values.

Mechanics of the within() Function

In contrast to the evaluation-only approach of with(), the within() function extends the paradigm by facilitating both the evaluation and modification of a data frame's attributes within a localized environment. When invoked, within() temporarily establishes an environment that mirrors the data frame's contents, allowing for direct manipulation of its variables. Let the original data frame be denoted by D_0, and let the temporary environment be represented by E', such that $E' \equiv D_0$ initially. As expressions are executed in E', modifications to the corresponding variable values propagate within this ephemeral context. Upon completion of the evaluation, within() recombines any modifications, returning a new data structure that reflects the locally implemented changes. This process preserves the integrity of the original data frame until the transformation is explicitly committed by the function's output. The within() function, therefore, embodies a dual capability: it enables succinct reference to variables in an isolated environment and simultaneously supports principled modifications that are reconciled with the data frame's original structure.

310

Comparative Analysis of with() and within()

Both with() and within() are designed to improve the cogency of operations performed on data frames by leveraging localized evaluation environments. The with() function provides an uncluttered mechanism to execute expressions by temporarily extending the scope in which variables are directly accessible. Its design is particularly suited to scenarios where the evaluation is intended to be read-only, with the explicit aim of extracting results without incurring modifications to the global data structure. Conversely, the within() function not only enables the direct evaluation of expressions but also supports structured modifications within the controlled setting of a temporary environment. Such modifications are systematically aggregated and reintegrated into a modified version of the original data structure. In formal terms, with() yields results based solely on the evaluation within the constrained environment, whereas within() produces an evolved instance of the data frame, formally expressed as D_1, where D_1 is a function of the transformations applied in E'. This distinction underscores a fundamental operational difference: with() adheres to the paradigm of pure functional evaluation, while within() permits procedural bottom-up adjustments that streamline complex data transformations.

R Code Snippet

```
# Create a sample data frame representing a structured environment D
df <- data.frame(
  id    = 1:6,
  a     = c(10, 20, 30, 40, 50, 60),
  b     = c(5, 15, 25, 35, 45, 55),
  group = c("A", "B", "A", "B", "A", "B")
)


# ===================================
# Demonstration of the with() Function
# ===================================
# The with() function establishes a temporary evaluation environment
#     from df, allowing
# direct access to its variables. We use this to compute expressions
#     without prefixing df$.
result_with <- with(df, {
  # Equation: sum of columns a and b
  sum_ab <- a + b
```

```r
  # Basic statistical computation: mean of column a
  mean_a <- mean(a)

  # Conditional evaluation: mark each observation based on a
  ↪   threshold
  # If a > 30, return "High"; otherwise, "Low"
  condition <- ifelse(a > 30, "High", "Low")

  # Return a list of computed results
  list(sum_ab  = sum_ab,
       mean_a  = mean_a,
       status  = condition)
})

cat("Results from with():\n")
print(result_with)

# ================================
# Demonstration of the within() Function
# ================================
# The within() function not only evaluates expressions in a
↪   temporary environment derived
# from df but also allows modification of the data frame. All
↪   changes are merged and a new
# data frame is returned leaving the original untouched.
df_modified <- within(df, {
  # Create a new column 'sum_div2', representing the equation: (a +
  ↪   b) / 2
  sum_div2 <- (a + b) / 2

  # Modify column a: if group is "A", add 10; if "B", subtract 5.
  a <- ifelse(group == "A", a + 10, a - 5)

  # Generate a new variable 'status' based on updated a:
  # If a > 40 then "Pass" else "Fail"
  status <- ifelse(a > 40, "Pass", "Fail")
})

cat("\nModified Data Frame using within():\n")
print(df_modified)

# ================================
# Preservation of Global Environment
# ================================
# Demonstrate that the original data frame remains unaltered after
↪   using within()
cat("\nOriginal Data Frame remains unaltered:\n")
print(df)

# ================================
# Illustrating the Evaluation Mechanism
# ================================
```

```r
# Mimic the formal evaluation in a temporary environment E, where
↪    each identifier in D is
# accessed directly. Here, we evaluate an expression equivalent to
↪    the formula:
#     result = sqrt((a + b)^2)
# This vectorized operation, using with(), resolves variables a and
↪    b within df.
eval_result <- with(df, sqrt((a + b)^2))
cat("\nEvaluated Result Mimicking the E Environment
↪    (sqrt((a+b)^2)):\n")
print(eval_result)
```

Chapter 64

Reading Documentation and Help Files in R

Overview of the R Documentation Ecosystem

The R language is accompanied by an extensive and rigorously structured ecosystem of documentation resources. This multifaceted framework is designed to facilitate the systematic resolution of computational challenges and the precise interpretation of language constructs. At its core, the ecosystem integrates both immediate in-environment help and expansive reference materials. These resources, ranging from succinct help pages to comprehensive manuals, form an interconnected repository wherein syntactic definitions and semantic annotations coexist. The resulting infrastructure embodies an emphasis on clarity and precision that is critical for the explication of statistical methodologies, algorithmic processes, and computational paradigms.

Anatomy of R Help Pages

Help pages in R are architected with a formal structure intended to present multifarious aspects of a function or concept in a coherent and parsimonious manner. Typically, each help page is segmented into distinct portions: an introductory synopsis that briefly conveys the purpose of the construct, a detailed description of its operational semantics, a systematic enumeration of parameters and their types, and an exposition of expected outputs and potential side effects. This modular design is further enhanced through cross-referential annotations that align related functions and concepts. In many cases, the documentation incorporates standard mathematical expressions, such as $\sum_{i=1}^{n} x_i$, to succinctly encapsulate complex algorithmic ideas and performance characteristics.

Mechanisms for Accessing Help Information

Access to the integrated documentation within the R environment is mediated through several well-defined interfaces. A primary method entails the utilization of a special syntactic operator, denoted by a leading symbol ?, which initiates an immediate lookup of the corresponding help page. Alternatively, function-based queries are employed to resolve textual identifiers to their respective documentation entries. This bidirectional interaction between query and response is underpinned by a hierarchically organized index that categorizes documentation by thematic relevance and functional association. Such an arrangement permits a methodical exploration of topics, ensuring that information retrieval is both rapid and contextually pertinent to the computational task at hand.

Structure and Interpretation of Documentation

The formal presentation of documentation in R adheres to a schema that privileges both theoretical exposition and practical utility. Each documentation entry commences with a concise statement of intent, followed by an in-depth treatment of the function's mechanics and its operational parameters. Parameter definitions are articulated with precision, detailing the types of acceptable arguments and outlining the constraints that govern their usage. The documentation further delineates the nature of returned results, often employing standardized notational conventions—such as $O(n)$ for algorithmic complexity—to convey underlying performance metrics. This comprehensive narrative is interleaved with references to related entries, thereby constructing an integrated framework that elucidates the interdependencies between various components of the language.

Utilization of Extended Documentation Resources

Beyond the immediate help pages, R encompasses a suite of extended documentation resources designed to provide a richer and more contextual understanding of its computational model. Comprehensive reference manuals offer exhaustive treatises on the language's constructs, establishing a foundational context that spans both theoretical underpinnings and applied methodologies. In addition, extended narrative documents, commonly distributed as vignettes, exemplify the practical implementation of intricate analytical techniques. These documents are systematically interlinked within the broader documentation ecosystem, thereby enabling a logical traversal from general concepts to highly specialized procedural details. The resulting arrangement ensures that the entire spectrum of documentation—from brief usage notes to elaborate exegeses—remains accessible and conducive to methodical inquiry.

R Code Snippet

```
# Demonstration of accessing R documentation and implementing a
↪   custom algorithm
# that reflects important equations and concepts from the chapter.


# ------------------------------------------------------------
# 1. Accessing Documentation:
# ------------------------------------------------------------
# Use the '?' operator to open the help page for a function, e.g.,
↪   sum
?sum

# Alternatively, the help() function can be used to lookup
↪   documentation.
help("median")


# ------------------------------------------------------------
# 2. Custom Algorithm: Summation Function
# ------------------------------------------------------------
# This custom function computes the arithmetic sum of a numeric
↪   vector,
```

```r
# corresponding to the mathematical formula:
#     i=1 x
# It uses a for-loop to iterate over the vector elements, reflecting
↪  an O(n) algorithm.
customSum <- function(x) {
  # Validate that the input is numeric
  if (!is.numeric(x)) {
    stop("Input must be a numeric vector")
  }

  total <- 0          # Initialize accumulator
  n <- length(x)      # Determine the number of elements (n)

  # Loop through each index to add elements, emulating: i=1 x
  for (i in 1:n) {
    total <- total + x[i]
  }
  return(total)
}


# ---------------------------------------------------------------
# 3. Demonstration of the customSummation:
# ---------------------------------------------------------------
# Create a simple numeric vector and compute its sum using both the
↪  custom function and R's built-in sum.
numbers <- c(1, 2, 3, 4, 5)
cat("Custom Sum:", customSum(numbers), "\n")
cat("Built-in Sum:", sum(numbers), "\n")


# ---------------------------------------------------------------
# 4. Dynamic Evaluation of an Expression:
# ---------------------------------------------------------------
# Use parse() and eval() to dynamically evaluate an expression that
↪  computes the sum.
# Here, the expression "sum(1:10)" represents i=1' x.
expr <- "sum(1:10)"
evaluated_result <- eval(parse(text = expr))
cat("Result of eval(parse(text = 'sum(1:10)')):", evaluated_result,
↪  "\n")


# ---------------------------------------------------------------
# 5. Performance Timing Demonstration:
# ---------------------------------------------------------------
# Measure the execution time of the customSum function on a larger
↪  vector.
# This timing reflects the O(n) complexity of the algorithm.
large_vector <- 1:1000000   # A vector with one million elements
time_taken <- system.time({
  custom_total <- customSum(large_vector)
})
cat("Time taken for customSum on 1e6 elements:",
↪  time_taken["elapsed"], "seconds\n")
```

317

```
# ---------------------------------------------------------------
# 6. Accessing Extended Documentation Resources:
# ---------------------------------------------------------------
# Check for and load an external package (e.g., ggplot2) then access
↪  its documentation.
if (!requireNamespace("ggplot2", quietly = TRUE)) {
  install.packages("ggplot2")
}
library(ggplot2)
help(package = "ggplot2")

# End of R Code Snippet
```

Chapter 65

Data Type Coercion and Conversion

Foundational Concepts in Data Type Conversion

The architecture of a computational system is intrinsically linked to its treatment of data as discrete entities, each endowed with a specific type that rigorously defines its permissible operations and transformations. In this context, a data type is not solely a description of the physical storage format; it also encapsulates a range of semantic invariants and operational constraints. Data type coercion, therefore, is the systematic process of transforming an object from one type domain to another, ensuring that the essential properties of the data are preserved while rendering the object compatible with a different computational context. This process is critical in environments where heterogeneous data must interact within unified operations. A coherent theory of type coercion underpins the fidelity and predictability of computational outcomes, as well as the maintenance of semantic integrity throughout such transformations.

Explicit Conversion via the as.* Function Family

The as.* family of functions constitutes the cornerstone of explicit type conversion within the computational framework. Each function in this suite adheres to a deterministic mapping protocol, whereby an input value is methodically examined and transformed to meet the criteria of a designated target type. These functions initiate an evaluation of the intrinsic properties of the source object and assess its compatibility with the target representation. For instance, conversion from a floating-point numeric value to an integral form often entails a systematic rounding or truncation process that reconciles the continuous domain with its discrete counterpart. The as.* function family embodies an unambiguous and deliberate mechanism for coercion, thereby mitigating the risk of incidental or semantically ambiguous transformations. Through this explicit conversion process, the conversion rules remain consistently applied, ensuring that the integrity of both the original and the resulting data is maintained in line with the system's type paradigms.

Implicit Coercion in Heterogeneous Data Operations

In computational expressions that amalgamate operands of differing types, the environment may invoke implicit coercion to reconcile these local discrepancies. Implicit coercion operates under a well-defined hierarchy of type precedence, whereby lower-ranked types are systematically elevated to match the requisites of operations involving more dominant types. This dynamic resolution mechanism is engineered to ensure that composite operations yield coherent and predictable results. However, the implicit nature of this conversion process may introduce subtleties; the automatic transmutation of data types hinges on context-specific heuristics that may not always align with the desired precision or semantic intent. The principles underlying implicit coercion are thus embedded within the overall design of the type system, serving as both a facilitator of operational fluidity and a potential source of survivable information loss when converts from a higher-fidelity domain to a lower one.

Mechanics and Limitations of Coercion Techniques

The internal mechanics of coercion are governed by a sequence of validation protocols and transformation heuristics that collectively ensure adherence to the established rules of the type system. Initially, the coercion engine conducts a comprehensive compatibility check against the metadata and structural attributes of the source object. Upon establishing a measure of compatibility, the system then proceeds through a series of conditional transformation steps, each incrementally aligning the object with the criteria of its target type. In certain scenarios, the conversion process may yield values that cannot be represented within the confines of the target type, often resulting in special markers such as NA to signify an indeterminate conversion. Such outcomes are emblematic of the inherent limitations imposed by finite precision and the potential loss of information during transmutation. Consequently, the dual imperatives of maintaining computational consistency and preserving the semantic content of the data impose a delicate balance on coercion techniques, necessitating a nuanced understanding of both the benefits and the constraints inherent in the process.

R Code Snippet

```
# Data Type Coercion and Conversion: Comprehensive Example

# ----------------------------------------------
# Section 1: Foundational Concepts in Explicit Conversion
# ----------------------------------------------

# Example 1: Numeric to Integer Conversion (Truncation)
num_value <- 3.14159
int_value <- as.integer(num_value)
cat("Original Numeric:", num_value, "\nConverted to Integer
↪   (truncated):", int_value, "\n\n")

# Example 2: Explicit Conversion using as.* Functions
# Converting numeric to character
char_value <- as.character(num_value)
cat("Numeric to Character:", char_value, "\n")

# Converting numeric to logical (non-zero becomes TRUE)
logical_value <- as.logical(num_value)
cat("Numeric (", num_value, ") to Logical:", logical_value, "\n\n")
```

```r
# Example 3: Correct Factor to Numeric Conversion
# Create a factor from numeric-like character strings
fac <- factor(c("10", "20", "30", "40"))
# Incorrect conversion (using as.numeric directly returns underlying
↪  integer codes)
incorrect_conversion <- as.numeric(fac)
# Correct conversion (first convert factor to character)
correct_conversion <- as.numeric(as.character(fac))
cat("Factor Levels (incorrect conversion):", incorrect_conversion,
↪  "\n")
cat("Factor Levels (correct conversion):", correct_conversion,
↪  "\n\n")


# ------------------------------------------------
# Section 2: Implicit Coercion in Heterogeneous Data Operations
# ------------------------------------------------

# Implicit coercion occurs when combining different types in a
↪  vector.
vec_mixed <- c(100, "R", TRUE, 3.5)
cat("Mixed Vector with Implicit Coercion:", vec_mixed, "\n")
# Note: Here all elements are coerced to character because of the
↪  string element.


# ------------------------------------------------
# Section 3: Mechanics and Limitations of Coercion Techniques
# ------------------------------------------------

# Example of a conversion that leads to NA due to incompatible input
bad_numeric <- "abc123"
converted_bad <- as.numeric(bad_numeric)
cat("Attempted conversion of", bad_numeric, "to numeric yields:",
↪  converted_bad, "\n")
if (is.na(converted_bad)) {
  cat("Warning: Conversion failed and resulted in NA.\n\n")
}


# ------------------------------------------------
# Section 4: Custom Function for Safe Conversion
# ------------------------------------------------

# A user-defined function to safely convert input to numeric.
safeConvertToNumeric <- function(x) {
  result <- as.numeric(x)
  if (is.na(result)) {
    message("Conversion of '", x, "' failed. Returning NA.")
  } else {
    message("Successfully converted '", x, "' to numeric: ", result)
  }
  return(result)
}
```

322

```r
# Testing the safe conversion function on a variety of inputs.
inputs <- c("42", "99.99", "not_a_number", "100")
converted_results <- sapply(inputs, safeConvertToNumeric)
cat("\nSafe Conversion Test Results:\n")
print(converted_results)

# -----------------------------------------------
# Section 5: Conditional Vector Assignment using ifelse()
# -----------------------------------------------

# Using ifelse() to evaluate and handle potential coercion in a
↪   vector context.
values <- c("1", "0", "TRUE", "FALSE", "not_a_bool")
# Convert string representations to logical values based on known
↪   patterns.
logical_converted <- ifelse(values %in% c("1", "TRUE", "true"),
↪   TRUE,
                        ifelse(values %in% c("0", "FALSE", "false"),
                        ↪   FALSE, NA))
cat("\nResult of Conditional Vector Assignment using ifelse():\n")
print(logical_converted)

# End of Comprehensive R Code Example for Data Type Coercion and
↪   Conversion
```

Chapter 66

Formatted Output and Reporting

Motivations for Formatted Output and Reporting

In modern computational environments, the generation of formatted output constitutes a critical aspect of data presentation and interpretability. The systematic transformation of raw data into clearly delineated textual representations underpins the reliability of reporting mechanisms across a range of applications, from statistical analysis to complex system logging. Formatted output permits the conveyance of intricate data summaries and diagnostics with precision, often necessitating control over aspects such as field width, numerical precision, and alignment. The inherent value of such techniques is evident in the enhancement of both human readability and automated parsing of output streams.

Mechanisms of Data Presentation

The methodological foundations for producing formatted output are rooted in disciplined approaches to string construction and the systematic representation of diverse data types. Functions such as *sprintf*, *format*, and *cat* have emerged as fundamental tools within many programming languages, each contributing unique capabilities to the formatted output process. The *sprintf* function provides a template-driven formatting strategy, supporting complex specifications that govern the conversion of numerical values and textual data into consistent representations. In parallel, the *format* function emphasizes the transformation of values into aesthetically organized strings, ensuring that aspects such as significant figures and padding are rigorously maintained. Meanwhile, the *cat* function streamlines the assembly and output of multiple formatted components into a single cohesive report, preserving both structure and clarity.

Precision, Localization, and Alignment Considerations

A detailed examination of formatted output techniques reveals a multitude of parameters that determine the quality and precision of reporting. At the core of these techniques lies the capacity to manage numerical precision by stipulating the number of digits printed, either through rounding mechanisms or by enforcing fixed-width field constraints. Localization emerges as a secondary but vital aspect, wherein considerations regarding numeral formatting—such as the use of commas as thousand separators or periods as decimal delimiters—must be judiciously handled. Additionally, meticulous alignment of output, frequently achieved through left- or right-alignment directives, ensures that tabular data and columnar outputs retain a coherent structure when rendered. These factors collectively underscore the importance of a robust formatting framework that is both flexible in its specification and rigorous in its execution.

Integrative Approaches to Enhanced Reporting Clarity

The application of formatted output functions within complex systems necessitates an integrative approach that balances precision with aesthetic coherence. The orchestration of *sprintf*, *format*, and *cat* in a coordinated manner enables the construction of comprehensive reports wherein numerical data, categorical labels, and textual explanations are seamlessly interwoven. Such integration is vital in contexts wherein output is utilized for both real-time diagnostics and archival reporting. The precision afforded by *sprintf* ensures that numerical outputs adhere to strict formatting rules, while the versatility of *format* allows for the dynamic adjustment of field widths and the standardization of variable representations. In turn, the sequential concatenation performed by *cat* facilitates the construction of multi-part reports that maintain clarity even under the constraints of variable data types and fluctuating output sizes.

R Code Snippet

```
# Comprehensive R code snippet demonstrating formatted output,
↪   equations, and reporting

# Clear the workspace
rm(list = ls())

# Set seed for reproducibility
set.seed(123)

# Generate sample data for a simple linear regression model
x <- seq(1, 10, length.out = 10)
y <- 2 + 3 * x + rnorm(10, sd = 1)   # y = 2 + 3*x with added noise
data <- data.frame(x = x, y = y)

# Compute basic summary statistics for x and y
mean_x <- mean(x)
sd_x   <- sd(x)
mean_y <- mean(y)
sd_y   <- sd(y)

# Fit a linear regression model to the data
model <- lm(y ~ x, data = data)
coeffs <- coef(model)

# Create a formatted regression equation using sprintf
regression_equation <- sprintf("y = %.2f + %.2f*x", coeffs[1],
↪   coeffs[2])

# Construct a formatted summary table for the descriptive statistics
↪   using sprintf
header <- sprintf("%-10s %-15s %-15s", "Variable", "Mean", "Std
↪   Dev")
row_x  <- sprintf("%-10s %-15.2f %-15.2f", "x", mean_x, sd_x)
row_y  <- sprintf("%-10s %-15.2f %-15.2f", "y", mean_y, sd_y)

# Demonstrate the use of format() to align numbers in a vector
↪   output
numbers <- c(1234.567, 89.1234, 4567.89)
formatted_numbers <- format(numbers, width = 12, nsmall = 2)
```

```r
# Begin report output using cat() to concatenate and display
↪    formatted components
cat("----- Formatted Reporting Example -----\n\n")

# Print summary statistics with aligned columns
cat("Summary Statistics:\n")
cat(header, "\n")
cat(row_x, "\n")
cat(row_y, "\n\n")

# Display the linear regression model summary with a formatted
↪    equation
cat("Linear Regression Model Summary:\n")
cat("Regression Equation: ", regression_equation, "\n\n")
cat("Model Coefficients:\n")
cat(sprintf("%-15s : %.2f\n", "Intercept", coeffs[1]))
cat(sprintf("%-15s : %.2f\n", "Slope", coeffs[2]))
cat("\n")

# Present a vector of formatted numbers
cat("Formatted Vector Output:\n")
for(num in formatted_numbers) {
  cat(num, "\n")
}
cat("\n")

# Additional demonstration: Dynamic report generation with iterative
↪    computations
cat("Dynamic Report for Computed Values:\n")
for (i in 1:5) {
  computed_value <- i * 3.14159  # Sample computation:
  ↪    multiplication by pi
  # Format each report line with proper alignment for the iteration
  ↪    and computed value
  line_output <- sprintf("Iteration %-2d | Computed Value: %8.3f",
  ↪    i, computed_value)
  cat(line_output, "\n")
}
```

www.ingramcontent.com/pod-product-compliance
Lightning Source LLC
Chambersburg PA
CBHW070933050326
40689CB00014B/3185